IN SEARCH
OF CHRISTIANITY

NINIAN SMART

In Search
of Christianity

Published in San Francisco by
HARPER & ROW, PUBLISHERS
New York   Hagerstown   San Francisco   London

Christianity

FIRST U.S. EDITION

Library of Congress Card Number: 78-19494
International Standard Book Number: 0-06-067401-6

79 80 81 82 83   10 9 8 7 6 5 4 3 2 1

Contents

Preface

Another book on Christianity? But how many are there?

There are many excellent works of scholarship about the faith – more perhaps than can be found concerning any other religion. Indeed Christianity can pride itself on the way it has generated such a tradition of self-examination. There are many works of inspiration and expositions of Christian doctrines. And there are one or two fine general histories, notably Paul Johnson's *A History of Christianity* and Edwyn Bevan's little *Christianity*. But there is surprisingly little on Christianity as a *religion*.

In this book I am trying to approach Christianity, then, as a religion; but in doing so, as we shall see, I am trying also to break up something of modern man's image of the faith. Christianity is not a single thing, but a kaleidoscope of different lived interpretations of the meaning of faith, some good, some bad, some (it may be thought) more normative, others less so. It is too easy for us to suppose that we know what Christianity is and to dismiss the varied realities of alternative ways of expressing its essence. Indeed it is doubtful whether there is some 'essential' Christianity.

Further we often forget that one achievement of a religion is a kind of time travel: past events are re-enacted today. Christ is not just a historical figure: he is also present to the Christian today. I have indulged in some time travel myself, in order in part to break up the image of Christianity as a single historical progression. I have made my chronology often inverse, reaching back from the present into the past, in the hope that the collage of varieties and of times will give us a new picture of what is so familiar, and yet surprising and strange. Christianity is maybe the least understood of the world's religions.

There was a time when I used to go to Northern Ireland from

time to time in connection with a project on religious education I directed. We were getting Catholic and Protestant teachers to work together on teaching concerning Christianity. I met on the boat once, crossing over from England to Belfast, a cheerful if somewhat fierce Scottish paratrooper. His solution to the 'problem' there involved the expenditure of a large quantity of bullets on the Catholic population. When he discovered that I taught history of religions, he asked what the students had to do. Lying, but in a good cause, I told him that they studied Northern Ireland and the Sermon on the Mount and then had to write a piece explaining any possible connection between the two.

The point is that we have to keep a real interplay between a religion's ideal character and its realities. Too often the latter become obscured through preoccupation with the former. Frankly, a lot of Christian history can look like special pleading, and therefore dishonest. But it is not my aim in the present book particularly to present the dark side of Christianity. Rather I want to look at it through the eyes of phenomenology.

Phenomenology is a long word for two fairly simple things. One, too often neglected, is using empathy: seeing what the agent sees, or in this case seeing what the believer sees – trying to enter the thoughtworld of Christianity, but not necessarily with any endorsement (or criticism) of the standpoint. Or rather standpoints. For if we abandon any stereotypes which we may have we will find how diverse Christianity is. In a sense it will not be what we thought it was. And what is empathy? It is a kind of warm distance. For instance I have a love of Buddhism and I feel sometimes I can understand parts of it, and enter into its meanings through people. But I am not thereby a Buddhist (actually I am an Episcopalian). Distance is perhaps especially difficult for Westerners with regard to Christianity. Paradoxically, their closeness may prevent a good understanding of the religion in its diversity. I know people who, believing Christianity to be false, think it is unimportant; and others who, believing it to be true, identify it with their image of it. Both reactions, naturally enough, are short on empathy and a sense of proportion.

8

The second thing which is phenomenology is analysis and classification. Much work has been done on the examination of kinds of religious phenomena (the reason why the word phenomenology is used), and it is possible to see recurring motifs in religions. This is not to say that Christianity is not unique. Every religion has its own character, and the stamp of Christianity is both strong and unmistakable. Every person is unique, but there are plenty of traits which can be observed as common to differing persons. So then I shall in the second part of this book especially try to give some analysis of Christianity, in relation to various dimensions of the faith.

Before turning to these let me draw the reader's attention to two terms which I use in the analysis of Christianity which may not be clear – one because of its relative unfamiliarity and the other because of its technical use. The first term is *numinous*, coined by Rudolf Otto for use in his famous book *The Idea of the Holy*. It refers to both a kind of experience and that which is experienced. As the former, it is intense dread or awe (for Otto it was the central type of religious experience); and as the latter it is the tremendous, mysteriously awe-inspiring quality of that which is holy. Otto derived the term from the Latin *numen*, a spirit. From time to time I shall comment on the numinous aspects of God in the Christian experience. The other term which in its present use may not be clear is *myth*. Religions incorporate sacred stories – such as stories of creation. Since Christianity is very much involved in stories – of the Fall, of Israel's troubles and glories, of the life, death and resurrection of Jesus Christ, of the end of the world – I shall speak about Christian myth. In using the term I am not intending its ordinary or vulgar meaning, in which a myth is a false or merely fanciful story. For me, a myth may be true, profound or the opposite: in this respect I use the word neutrally. There is a further discussion of the matter in a later chapter.

So far, then, I want here to look at Christianity in a phenomenological way, and at the same time to bring out something of its variety.

To give a fresh look at the religion, whose familiarity can breed distortion, I have begun with a chain of perspectives,

9

which I form into a kind of collage. The pictures are drawn from various societies, and in the course of exploring them we come to other places and other times. Thus I have not attempted the more usual task of beginning with origins and working forwards. Still, by this method it will be possible to go back to some of the key eras of the history of Christianity. In any event, there are some good histories which carry the story forwards.

I happen also to believe that the times are propitious for a new discovery of Christianity, partly because so many people in the West have been making the mental voyage into Eastern religions and the novel ideas of a romantic counter-culture. Even if sometimes imperfectly understood, the motifs of Oriental mysticism are widely current; and religious questions have entered more into the mainstream of public consciousness. Some of the hangups about the Christian tradition have been worked out of the Western system, so much polarized about the faith. There is some feeling that there is a richness to be found in Christianity hitherto somewhat obscured by older debates. This book, then, is a contribution to this new quest for the understanding of Christianity. But it is in no sense a defence of it, or a work of theology or apologetics. It is meant to be a portrait, a geography. Naturally, I would not have undertaken the task of writing it unless I thought Christianity important, both in its effects on history and in its slant upon life.

Christianity and its offshoots constitute so vast a phenomenon that it is absurd to claim to cover the field in any detail, or even indeed in coarser outline. I have been very selective, therefore, but the selection has aimed at a good scatter. In the first part I begin with Romanian Orthodoxy, as a sample of the whole Orthodox wing of Christianity. From there I move to Italian Catholicism and its evolution, and there explore the heartland of the Catholic wing. In order to show something of the forms of the faith which anciently, after Chalcedon, existed outside the ambit of the Rome-Byzantium axis, I next visit Monophysite Ethiopia. Then it is the turn of Sweden, to illustrate something of the nature of mainstream Lutheranism and of one main tradition of Reformation Christianity. To Calvinism I come circuitously, through the Scottish background of Livingstone's missionary involvement, and through him to the emergent new independent expressions of Christianity in Africa. Before that I move to the radical Reformation, through the examples of the Mennonites, the Anabaptists in general and the Baptists. A last chapter in the first part looks at the varieties of Christianity in a conspectus, and considers some modern movements at the edge, such as Mormonism.

It is as if Christianity were a mighty river flowing through a great delta: we begin by tracing the streams as they empty into the sea, and then begin here and there to move upstream, to plot the geography of all the waters, including some of the tributaries that contribute to their volume. We seem to find one river, but even beyond the delta it changes course, divides, twists and is fed by other streams. We hope to reach its source or sources. We begin from the sea, however, which is the present time into which the waters of the delta flow. But unmistakably the streams differ, and this is one of the fascinations of Christian geography. What do the Amish of Pennsylvania have in common with a Zulu Zion? What does Sweden share with the old faith of Ethiopia? What transition is to be made between the Catholicism of Lombardy to the Baptism of Georgia or the Calvinism of the Voortrekkers? And where are the limits of the faith? What a variety Christianity presents, and one is often tempted to drop the singular and speak only of Christianities. One can, it is true, return to the source: or is it sources – again the plural forcing itself upon us? That question I partially deal with in one of the chapters of the second part, on the faces of Christ, as he glances mysteriously at us out of the pages of our early records and proclamations.

In the second part, in general, I try to present and analyse, again very selectively, the various aspects and dimensions of the religion. As to the dimensions of doctrine, myth, ethics, experience, ritual and institution, I attempt by selecting treatments of them to give a reasonably full-bodied picture of the faith. There is often a tendency to place predominant stress upon doctrines in the unfolding of Christianity. Theology is important, but must be seen in the milieu of practice – of worship, experience and conduct. I have thus, in the second part, included chapters on the following: asceticism and mysticism, which takes us both into the cloister and into the soul; worship and the numinous, in which we take note of the expressions of awe and communion with God; the faces of Christ, for the shape of Christian experience is determined by the mysterious physiognomy of the God-man glancing through the pages of the New Testament and reverberating in the impulses and ideals of men; Christianity's mythic dimension, the Bible, itself a powerful instrument of arousal and consolation, and story-teller in chief for the Christian tradition; war, peace and the ethical ambiguities of Christianity, as it is urged on by the dynamism of love and faith; and doctrines and philosophy. A concluding chapter looks at Christianity in comparison and retrospect: I 'place' Christianity to some extent among the religions.

In all this I have necessarily, I repeat, been greatly selective. There are too many streams of Christianity to chart adequately, too many eddies and waves to picture in detail. Rather we enter the faith by some streams of its delta and chart what we can. The delta is reminiscent of the Danube, and that indeed is where we begin.

I have been helped by Sarah Coakley, Birger Pearson and my wife Libushka who have read portions of this book in draft. I have also been encouraged by a number of students, both at Santa Barbara and Lancaster.

I
The Roots of Romania

In Bucharest, the warm evening of 23 August 1944 marked a momentous turn in the affairs of Romania. Michael, the young Hohenzollern king, together with some older liberals, arrested the *Conducator* or Leader, Antonescu. They also caused German troops in the city to be surrounded and took the country out of its increasingly miserable war against the Soviet Union. Romania turned on its ex-allies and fought, like the Italians, their linguistic cousins, on the winning side. But the fates of Italy and Romania were very different. For the Soviet Union virtually annexed Romania, and in the dreary aftermath of the war, a social revolution accompanied a period of exploitation and grey austerity.

Yet in 1975, I could slip into a small church near the presidential palace where Michael had had Antonescu covered by pistol-brandishing officers over three decades before, and find it alive with candles and well-dressed worshippers. In snow-covered Neamt in the foothills of the Carpathian mountains the monastery flourished, and monks and seminarians sang the marvellous liturgy, while tourists barely disguised their piety even if they were members of the Communist party. In Iasi during the city's saint's day leather-coated secret police chatted affably with a file of abbesses waiting to process in the great, packed cathedral. Afterwards the bishop preached from the steps about the need for hard work in the fields (of the collectivized farms) in order successfully to bring in the harvest. Throughout Romania there were overwhelming signs of the popularity and prosperity of the Orthodox Church, after times of trouble and persecution. It had achieved a new means of living together with an ideologically hostile regime. How does it manage this marriage with atheist politics? To understand the answer it is necessary to reach back into a deep past. But at one level the answer was supplied to me by a layman who said, in reply to my perhaps naïve enquiry about whether there was dialogue between Christians and Communists in Romania: 'Why should we have a dialogue when we see each other every day?'

The prestige of the Orthodox Church and its relative freedom under a red administration stem in part from its historic role in the expression of Romanian identity, but it is also of a piece with so much of Eastern Christian history, living over long periods in captivity. The Romanian story is itself a surprise. Indeed many visitors from Western Europe are somewhat taken aback to feel the Latin quality of life in the Eastern Balkans, virtually surrounded by Slavs. That a Romance language should have survived remains something of a mystery, which has much to do with geography. Running like a boomerang through the midst of the country are the Carpathians, going first south and then west, and enclosing the disputed lands of Transylvania, struggled over between Hungarians and Romanians and others. In 106 the Emperor Trajan annexed the whole area and made it into the fertile province of Dacia. Roman soldiers and others settled and married into the population, so that in under two centuries the Latin tongue was firmly implanted. But Rome itself had to withdraw from the colony in 271, and Goths and other peoples swept across the land; yet mysteriously, perhaps because of the shelter of the mountains, the Romanians persisted across a thousand years, about which we know nothing. All we know is that in the thirteenth century they surfaced into recorded history speaking their Roman tongue, now evolved, like the other Romance languages, into a characteristic and separate form. The Romanians were to undergo many more troubles at the hands of their neighbours and the Turks, but they showed themselves adept at sheer survival. The Church played a strong part, for it used Romanian in the liturgy, and religion gave Romanians a sense of identity in the face of Catholic and Protestant Hungarians and German-speaking settlers, and Islamic Turks. Already in Roman times the process of conversion had started, and the Romanian liturgy was a focus – still is a focus – of extraordinary piety.

14

As elsewhere in Orthodoxy, the sacred liturgy is the chief glory of the faith. Over three hours of chanting, prayers and ceremonial might prove tedious; not so, for the whole thing is what it is often claimed to be – heavenly, and the three hours go like twenty minutes. But to root the faith in such extensive re-enactment of the Christian drama of redemption means something about survival. The physical churches and the priests need somehow to continue. Some monasteries are fortified, to repel pillaging invaders. In other times the Romanians even had churches in wagons to facilitate tactical withdrawal under threat.

In addition, the Orthodox system implies not just that the liturgy should survive, but that the monasteries should too, in that bishops, vital in the ongoing priestly order, are chosen from among the monks. So turning monasteries into fortresses not only helped to defend the glorious painted churches, so beautifully preserved and restored today largely at government expense, but also was a defence of the ongoing communities of monks and nuns. But basically and in the long run some kind of accommodation with the ruling power is called for. This was possible, for instance among Transylvanian Orthodox under the Austro-Hungarian Empire (though, incidentally, a large section of Transylvanian Orthodox were Uniate, that is, they recognized papal authority while retaining their own rites and clergy: mostly they were reabsorbed under pressure in the post-war period). The modern Romanian Church has reached a kind of concordat with the government. It and other recognized communions were summoned in 1968 to a religious summit by the communist President Ceauşescu, which helped to reinforce what may be described as a system of religious establishment, though in a plural setting. Churches were free to maintain their own services and so forth, but basically their right to proselytize was denied – Orthodox should stay Orthodox; Jews Jews and so on. Baptists and other 'unlicensed' evangelical preachers therefore attract a good deal of hostility from the government and from the security police. Whereas the Bible is portable, and so evangelism can be carried on in guerrilla fashion, Orthodoxy cannot be moved so easily,

15

despite the wheeled churches. In reaching accommodation with the regime, the Orthodox follow somewhat the patterns of the Byzantine tradition and the memory of captivity in Muslim lands.

Western Europeans sometimes use the term Caesaro-Papism to describe the old Byzantine system, which in evolving the close liaison between Church and State, also gave the Emperor sacred status. Some aspects of Eastern liturgy, indeed, reflect the court rituals of the Byzantine era. At any rate a certain parallelism existed between the functions of the Emperor and the patriarch. The former, with his military and bureaucratic arms, dealt with security and order, while the patriarch and his bishops mediated the earthly passage to salvation. The long continuity of the Byzantine Empire down to its demise in 1453 gave a much greater stability to the system than could ever be possible in the West, which, of course, experienced the collapse of the Western Empire and a stronger consolidation, ultimately, of ecclesiastical power as a separate force. But a new situation had developed in parts of the East from the seventh century onwards, as a consequence of the spectacular conquests of Islam. In the new Muslim dominions Christianity had a place, but it could of course no longer exist in parallel with the secular arm. Much of Orthodoxy came to live in a kind of captivity in which the Church was the official body through which the regime dealt with the Christian population. Russia, resistant to Islam, remote from conquest out of Turkey, held on to a new role to preserve Christian independence: Moscow came to see itself as the Third Rome and ultimately the Messianic power which would renew Christendom. Alexander Solzhenitsyn still retains something of this old mesmerizing vision.

The captivity of the Church under Islam involved something of the feeling of modern Romania: it was not so much the Church's task to convert as to conserve. It proved very apt at that, for there were always pressures to conform to the dominant ideology – pressures in terms of money, opportunity and status. Even now in Romania it greatly helps to be a Party member, as in older days in Syria, Istanbul and beyond there were

16

tangible attractions in Islam. And theoretically as a Party member one is an atheist.

Some critics might think of Orthodoxy as involving a sell-out. Can this be the true faith, if it proves so pliable to authority? Those nurtured in protest and reform, and thinking back to Jesus driving the money-changers out of the Temple, might feel uneasy (but: 'Render unto Caesar . . .'). This is where one must enquire into the central values of Orthodoxy and consider how they are conserved, for perhaps the Romanians exhibit a picture of Christianity which remains faithful to the main tradition. Let us, then, scan that picture in a little more detail: from there we shall trace something of its ancestry.

First, we can look at the Romanian Church in a physical way. That the spiritual world shines through the material world is a deep sentiment in Orthodox thinking. Church buildings range from the painted buildings of Moldavia, where the churches are decorated outside as well as within, through the elegance of the reconstructed and twisty chapel at Curtea d'Arges which was once the former royal summer retreat, to the cruder but lovingly built new churches in mushroom suburbs of many a town. These new churches, built largely through the part-time labour of workers using holidays and spare hours, symbolize the new confidence of Orthodoxy which can tap wells of popular affection and respect. The paintings, sometimes sublime, sometimes naïve, face outwards partly to show that the Church teaches her message to the outside world. Yet the most sacred pictures, the ikons, are essentially for the interior: for the sanctuary and for the home. Yet the sculpture, even the sculptured crucifix, is absent.

This already tells us of one motif in Orthodoxy. There have been times, especially during the stormy period from 723 to 845, when ikons were under attack. The wonderful mosaics and paintings of the period could perhaps tend towards idolatry, and in any case the saints were transformed out of all recognition in salvation. Islam threatened Christianity, and perhaps too something of its image-breaking zeal was imitated by Christian reformers. The Old Testament's ban on graven images moreover was to be taken into solemn consideration.

17

When the battles of the Iconoclastic Controversy were over, Orthodoxy settled down to a middle point – between the austerity of those who had rejected the ikons and the full acceptance of sculpture, as happened in the Western Church. It is, incidentally, as we shall later see, one of Christianity's great ambiguities, its attitude to the visual and other arts in worship. However, in Romania, as elsewhere in Orthodoxy, the visual glories are great, though stylized, even restrained, for the ikons represent a special tradition in which heaven and earth are blended and in which the artist is not creative but, as it were, created *through*.

Music also overwhelms. A young man who applies for a place in a seminary must have a letter from his parish priest which must say at least two things – that he has a good character, and that he has a good voice. This, taken together with the ikons, indicates a certain priority – that the faith is shown forth through the action of the Eucharist, rather than that it is lengthily preached. The priority is apt in the present situation of the Church, where schooling in Christianity, save at the seminaries, is ruled out – for atheism is taught as part of the regular curriculum of the high school, in the course of the propagation of 'scientific socialism'. Typically, people learn of Christianity through the liturgy. Though sermons are an integral part of the system, they are quite secondary to the impact of the sights and sounds of the Eucharist.

Intellectually, Orthodoxy is less adventurous than Western Christianity, but in Romania the intellect nevertheless, within limits, has a role to play: thus two of the seminaries, one in Bucharest and one in the old city of Sibiu, to the north of the capital, on the inner rim of the Carpathians, have university status and grant degrees. There have been attempts to combine the Orthodox theological tradition with some modern philosophizing whose inspiration is rooted in the West. There has been the reinterpretation of ancient treasures, such as the mystical tradition of Hesychasm quietude, which continues to flourish in the monasteries. There is, indeed, a much stronger sense of the contemplative approach to God in modern Romania than might be expected in a country undergoing rapid changes. But there is a practical side to the search for the blessed vision of God's uncreated light.

For the monastery in Romania is not something isolated from the people. Many come to the monks not just for the services but also for spiritual counsel. Very often the monk on whose face shines something of the interior vision is the one who is especially sought out as having a deeper insight into ordinary, for instance marital, problems. The monastery thus becomes a kind of practical frontier. Paradoxically this is reinforced by collectivization, for though the monasteries have been deprived of their formerly huge landownings for the most part, it is only for the most part: they retain sufficient land to feed themselves and otherwise maintain themselves through modest industry, and so they are on a par with the surrounding collective farms. Also thus the Church maintains its own equipment – there is scope for the printing of Bibles and other literature, the painting of ikons, the weaving and design of vestments, the manufacture of candles.

In the building of new churches, the interface with the secular world is even more striking, for the permits and materials have to come through local officials; much of the money is raised from local people, and it is by no means extraordinary for the local Party chairman to be closely involved. There are echoes of a Balkan Don Camillo, but the atmosphere differs from the exuberance of Italy, and the new painted churches retain a very different air of mystery. And it all seems light years from Scottish Presbyterianism or the spirit of the Mennonites. But it is an authentic midpoint in Orthodox experience, between the laughing islands of Greece and the gripping skies of Novgorod. And what distinguishes Orthodoxy from the Western faiths?

Basically, Eastern Christianity drifted apart from Western Catholicism for cultural and political reasons. As the Roman Empire in its Italian incarnation disintegrated it forged a new style in its Byzantine manifestation. The rulers of Constantinople could synthesize Greek and Roman tradition with Christianity the more easily, perhaps, because the faith had taken its early shape so emphatically in the Greek-speaking milieu both of

19

Greece itself and of the Eastern Mediterranean. The continuity of Empire, moreover, gave the Church greater stability and control, and at the same time a conservative regard to the body of faith as defined by the first seven Councils of the Church. The confident traditionalism of the Orthodox lead them to think of the Pope as the first Protestant, for it was upon insertion of the so-called *Filioque* clause that the major doctrinal rift between East and West focused and that, as we shall see, had to do not only with the nature of the Trinity but just as importantly with the authority of the Pope.

Literally the phrase means 'And from the Son' and refers to the way in which the Holy Spirit proceeds (that is eternally derives) from the Father 'and from the Son'; it was inserted into the Nicene Creed at a Council of just the Western Church. This insertion in effect implied the authority of the Pope to alter a historic creed. For the Orthodox, definitions of belief had to be worked out at Councils representative of the whole Church. Still, what would such a small phrase do? Could it really be of much spiritual significance?

To answer these questions it is useful briefly to look at the whole matter of creeds. We have become so used to the idea that we even use the word 'creed' to mean a particular religious tradition. We enquire as to a man's creed, as though somehow right belief is the most important thing. Christianity has not only produced the historic *credos*, but also such hedges of correctness as the Thirty-Nine Articles of the Church of England and the Westminster Confession, a Presbyterian norm. The emphasis on formulae results not so much from a concern for truth, though that is in its own way present, as from a worry about Church order. After all, the New Israel – the Church itself – was not defined by descent and tradition; rather it was constituted by those who shared a common life and a common idea about its purpose. Community and ideology went together, and with the increase of the faith, and especially its success in permeating and conquering the Empire, unity, dangerously split by various heresies, became both more desirable and more difficult to achieve. But at any rate the Council of Nicaea in 325 and other Councils seemed capable of bringing an explicitly agreed unity in matters of doctrine, even if the issues were getting more complex and refined.

Most famously, Nicaea was a victory for St Athanasius over Arius, the Egyptian priest who was chief leader of the Arian movement. But the Arians remained a strong force, and indeed had been highly successful missionaries among the northern peoples who had broken up the Empire and had come to dominate Spain and northern Italy. When however in the late sixth century the Visigothic kingdom of Spain deserted Arianism for Catholicism, the clause 'And from the Son' was approved as part of the creed in order to emphasize the status of Christ. The creed as amended was a sign of the acceptance of the discipline of the papacy by the Visigoths, but as is often the case what is appropriate in one context causes trouble elsewhere.

The addition of the clause came to be symbolic of the rift between East and West, and there were, as we shall note in Chapter 13, some serious doctrinal matters at stake. One can indeed look upon the great ecumenical Councils beginning with Nicaea (that is, not counting that very first Council in Jerusalem when Christian policy concerning the Law and the Gentiles was clarified) as signalling a second main stage in the solidification of the tradition. One stage involved the coming to be of the main substance of the Canon of scripture – the composing, assembling and sifting the writings which came to form the New Testament. Another stage was the definition of key doctrines about Christ and the Trinity. In all this there was implicated the seminal writings too of the Greek and Latin Fathers. The mixture of the three – scripture, Councils and Fathers (especially the Greek Fathers) became the normative basis of Orthodoxy, and the superimposition upon it of Roman authority disturbed the balance, as it was perceived in the East. So the *Filioque* became a bone of contention, and a sign of dangerously innovative tendencies in the West.

The relative conservatism of Orthodoxy with regard to liturgy and doctrine is also the basis of its devolution. Thus the establishment in recent times of the Patriarchate in Romania is one more development of Churches which are autocephalous, that is, have their own head and function as separate hierarchies. This is indeed a different pattern from that evolving in Rome, which by the eleventh century was to project the powers and status of the Pope very far indeed.

Perhaps the difference in attitude is symbolized by the fact that it is possible in the Eastern monastery to pursue the 'idiorhythmic' method, according to which each monk may set his own rhythm – so that he need not necessarily go to the liturgy today or eat with the other monks. Within the limits imposed by the Abbot's general oversight there is a certain autonomy.

Here is also perchance a good place to pause a while to sum up the features of Orthodoxy as seen from the direction of Bucharest. First, the Orthodox do not have an easily portable Church or faith. The faith hinges on the liturgy and in part on the monasteries. Accommodation with the State, or else bitter resistance, are thus essential to its survival. Thus from the Church's point of view it is no great paradox that it subsists in the environment of Communism. Second, the Orthodox have been less concerned with doctrinal correctness than the Westerners, confining themselves to the early creeds and councils as sources of authority. By contrast they see the West as innovatory, and the usurpation by the Roman Pope of an authority which ought to reside in the whole body of believers. Third, in accord with its emphasis on worship, the Orthodox set great store by their ikons and their music. They thus express the way in which the divine permeates the material world. They have never gone over to the artistic revolution which the Renaissance brought to church and other painting – a revolution which came to exalt material perspectives and give glory to a world increasingly robbed of its mysteriously divine dimension. Fourthly, and this is implicit in any discussion of East and West, the historic experience of the Orthodox has been so different from that of the Roman West. Rome succumbed to alien invaders but converted them. Rome thus was a focal point in the projection of classical and Christian values into the Middle Ages. In the East, a long independence gave the Church stability, but ultimately it was conquered by those of a different faith, whom it did not convert, though it could look with joy upon its effective conquest of Russia, the huge repository of political independence for the Orthodox faith – the third Rome. Fifth, the split between East and West significantly came to turn upon a clause put in with papal permission, designed against Arianism, but more deeply involving the very different conception of authority. The fact that Orthodoxy finds itself with different churches according to region and language means that it can never be as monolithic as Rome has tried to be in the past. It also means that it has tended to be, if old-fashioned, national and vernacular, and so in Romania it has proved to be a potent vehicle for the voyage of national identity from the old Roman days to the modern era of comrades Gheorghiu-Dej and Ceauşescu.

But what does all this signify at a deeper level? In a moment I shall try to portray the essence of Orthodox spirituality. But depth is already on the surface, so let me describe two small events at the surface which indicate hidden, and un-comfortable, depths. Coming out of Romania in November 1975, I encountered complex searches at customs. I had a book with me by a well-known Romanian theologian, published three decades back. He would like it translated into English to reach a wider readership. It was titled *Jesus Christ and the Restoration of Man*. It had a rather modernistic portrait of Jesus on the cover behind the title. It was seized upon by a customs man. He took it to a higher official. After confabula-tion, they agreed not to pursue the matter. A dusty tome about Jesus being a menace? Yet, had it been Baptist, I could be a bible-smuggler, an evangelist. So Orthodoxy shows forth its captivity: it must conform to the dictates of a conservative dictatorship. That is disturbing. The other story is this, about, on the same visit, a young nun. She was attractive, skittish even. We stayed at her convent. She spoke French and had been a languages student. Why become a nun, I asked? She said, with cheerful simplicity, perhaps indeed naïvety, that she felt no awe when she passed a (Communist) palace of culture, but did when she passed a church. The divine magic of Orthodoxy, in other words, could still work. I suppose by being magic, it was no longer really captive. The Orthodox have their own special version of freedom. Doubtless that has gone deep into the spirit of the peoples it has come to permeate, the Greeks, varieties of Eastern Europeans, and perhaps above all the Russians. Many visitors from the modern West remark on the great warmth and vitality of the Russians in their private and inner lives, despite the grey conformism of the outer conditions under which they live. That already perchance tells us something of the light which burns purely in the Orthodox heart.

Also, before going on to delineate the essence of Orthodoxy let us briefly look at its varieties. The Romanian Church we have seen, beginning from missionary roots as early as the third century AD (some say even earlier, and that St Andrew preached there). Bulgaria was essentially later in its adherence to the faith: here of great importance was the work of the great missionaries Cyril and Methodius in the ninth century. Cyril gave his name (Cyrillic) to the Slavonic alphabet he devised and which with some modifications is used today among Slav nations, above all Russia. In the area now known as Yugoslavia, there is the Serbian Church, which had its own patriarchate from the fourteenth century, and survived later the troubles of Turkish rule. About half of the present Yugoslav population could be accounted Orthodox by tradition. Of greatest antiquity is the Greek Church, with its offshoots, as in Cyprus, for Greece was of course one of the early centres of conversion to Christianity through the work initiated by the Apostle Paul. With Greek independence from Turkey in the nineteenth century it has come to be organized as a separate established Church. But the most famous and powerful of the Orthodox Churches is the Russian.

The introduction of Christianity into Russia followed a pattern common in northern Europe, namely by the conversion of rulers. Thus in 955 the Grand Duchess Olga was baptized and in 988 Duke Vladimir introduced Greek missionaries from Constantinople and imposed the new faith by force. The choices had been some Western form of Christianity and, significantly, Islam. Had Russia become Muslim it would have decisively altered the balance of world history. Though in theory subservient to the Patriarch in Constantinople, the Russian Church became increasingly independent, and with the fall of the Second Rome in 1453, Moscow came to be seen as the Third Rome. It was therefore not surprising that in the late sixteenth century the see of Moscow was transformed into a patriarchate. The Patriarch was styled 'the Patriarch of all the Russias and of the new Rome'. What if that new Rome turned out ultimately to be a red one? The messianism remained.

In general one can see that Orthodoxy spread effectively northwards. But its older strongholds in the Eastern Mediterranean and in Egypt were overrun by the Muslims. Whereas large numbers of people in the Balkans stayed loyal under Muslim occupation, this was scarcely so in these areas. Thus the Patriarchs of Alexandria, Jerusalem and Antioch in Syria rule over very limited populations. However, the Cypriot Greeks have stayed faithful, on the whole, as is signalled by the fact that after independence from Britain they chose Archbishop Makarios as their President. Finally, there are scattered Orthodox churches in Finland, the Baltic States and Czechoslovakia, together with emigrant and exiled churches in Britain, Canada, the USA, Australia and elsewhere. For all its setbacks Orthodoxy has been persistent and has shown remarkable vitality, notably as we have seen in red Romania. Why? What is its heart and essence?

We can think of it as a triangle: Trinity, ikon and Easter. On the night which ushers in Easter, Bucharest is alive with candles. In the countryside women have been preparing elaborately painted eggs. Old ideas of spring and renewed fertility mingle with the Christian joy of the salvation wrought by Christ's rising from the dead. We may note that the East wing of Christianity stresses the Resurrection and the glorified Christ. The typical symbol of the Catholic West is the crucifix: Christ's atoning death is at the centre (though Christmas has become the big feast of the year). What does the Resurrection mean, for the Orthodox? Above all it means the transformation and glorification of Christ's human nature. And that in turn holds out a promise to us all – for though we are, in our human selves, mortal and liable to sin and error, we can, through solidarity with God and Christ, be transformed. We can be made divine. In other words, the Orthodox look on salvation as becoming godlike, and on Christ's work as highly positive, raising humanity to new heights. There is much less emphasis on original sin than in the West. Let us retrace briefly this web of ideas about man's fall and sin.

The Genesis story relates, of course, how Adam and Eve, prototypes of us, disobeyed God's mysterious injunction about not eating from the tree, and were driven from the garden and paradise, into a world of hardship and indeed mortality. From being incorruptible, deathless and dispassionate, men became and still become the opposite, though still capable of good. Often Christians have seen Christ as the second Adam, come to restore the situation. As a famous hymn has it:

> A second Adam to the fight
> And to the rescue came . . .

But the question of how salvation is achieved can be looked at negatively and positively. Both viewpoints are present in both East and West, but the Christian East leans more towards the positive. The negative perspective is this: that man's original sin, transmitted from generation to generation (some say by the very act of procreation, thus damning sex), must be atoned for. Man must atone, but only God can save. Thus Jesus came to the earth as the God-man, saving divinely, atoning humanly, dying for our sins upon the Cross – a cosmic gesture of humility and atonement. Through the Church we are united with Christ and so delete the terrible effects of sin.

The positive way of looking at the affair is less concerned with original sin, though it recognizes man's frailties and wicked-nesses. But man was created in the image of God for the purpose of contemplating God. He was made to see, and re-enact, the creative love which is God's nature. Christ's life was the central point at which God causes earthly transformation. The Easter message is that man has the opportunity to resume his original destiny.

The negative is Good Friday. The positive is Easter. The candles in Bucharest are eloquent testimony to people's intuitive recognition of the possibility of the divine transformation of this world. It is thus no surprise that a recurrent theme in Russian writing, especially in Dostoievsky, is the way in which the face of Christ can be seen in the faces of those whom the world treats as degraded – the prostitute, the thief, the idiot. So the first apex of the triangle, Easter, means, in brief, the possibility of the divinization of us humans.

What does the Orthodox view of the Trinity mean? The Trinity is invoked much more intensely in Orthodox liturgy than in the West. The Holy Spirit is seen, for instance, as a very alive reality – while often Western Europe has lost a sense of the word of the Spirit. The fact that Orthodoxy prizes its speculations about, and praises of, the Trinity partly accounts for the passion against the *Filioque* clause, seen as tampering with a holy mystery of central importance in the whole economy of the universe. The way the Trinity is described is a nice blend of Greek and Hebrew ideas. The Father is in a sense the source of the other two members of the Trinity, just as the personal, dynamic Yahweh of the Old Testament was seen as the central figure in the first act of the divine and human drama. Christ was the theme, of course, of the second act, with the Spirit coming fast into the events, as secret engine of the ongoing Church. (The third act is the culmination of history, the last things – not for nothing do the Orthodox, with wisdom often and with wildness sometimes, earnestly consult the Book of Revelation, neglected by most Christians these days.) But though Orthodoxy could see the drama of history through Jewish eyes, they could see too that the followers of Plato, the spiritually-minded Neoplatonists, had something important to say. If the Neoplatonists were more abstract about God, thinking of him as the *ontōs on*, for instance, or real Being, this helped as a corrective to picturing God as a man writ large; it helped too to bring together the dynamism of Semitic

27

religion and the depths of Greek culture. That mingling, incidentally, is heard also in Orthodox music, where synagogue and the musical modes of old Greece echo strongly.

Perhaps the early synthesis, the work of the still vital Greek fathers, giant ancient Cyrils and Gregories, was too powerful. Perhaps it has inhibited Orthodoxy from new developments in ideas and theology. Yet I sometimes reflect, in secondhand bookshops, as follows. The shelves are stocked in part by dead theology. Even some great men, such as Cajetan and Archbishop Temple, no longer speak to us. The price on their books is marked down, not up. But there is still a good market for Dostoievsky and Solzhenitsyn. Often the Orthodox have done their theology, through laymen, by means of the arts. But let us not here be too idealistic: the Orthodox often display a strange lack of interest in modern knowledge, and so of the important problems with which Temple and others were sincerely and ingeniously engaged.

The dynamics of the Trinity display inner love: but outer love is also part of the character of the Three-in-One God. Hence the created order, both visible and invisible. Angels, fallen and otherwise, lurk behind the fabric of our daily life. The saints shine unseen awaiting the final outcome of history. The Virgin Mary, above them all, is a sweet presence behind the fragmentary glories of the material world. And this world? As we have seen, it is created as a kind of mirror, in which the destiny of mankind is to reflect God. Since God's life is joy, men should be brought into life to experience that joy. Yet paradoxically, for various reasons, the Orthodox, especially the Russians, are well aware of suffering. Under the wide and awesome sky of the steppes, the Russians have known much misery, from the Vikings to Stalin and beyond. Yet somehow they have made evil positive. Even the suffering can be glorified, so that the creation, for all its flaws, unintended by the Trinity, is the backcloth of individual and collective spiritual dramas, portraying a Christian nobility.

These notions are summed up visibly in the apex of the triangle, the ikon. For in its static directness, its beautiful power born of devotion both by the anonymous artist (what man would dare to put his signature on a portrait of Christ?) and by the faithful who grime it with kisses and candle-smoke, it means that the divine and human interpenetrate. Orthodoxy does not feel the distance between heaven and earth. It does not slit the fish of the Christian universe. Such, in brief, is the triangular heart of Orthodoxy. That is enacted in the liturgy, so let us follow that enactment. As I have pointed out, the liturgy is the heart, too, and one reason why the faith is less easily portable than some others. It is said that delegates from the Grand Duke Vladimir of Russia attended the Eucharist at Santa Sophia (the Church of the Holy Wisdom) in Constantinople, and reported that they were uncertain as to whether they were in heaven or on earth. That is something.

In theory a Romanian church, as in the other Orthodox domains, has three sections. The initial part as you enter used to be a vestibule in which those who were not yet admitted to communion stood. Typically the division between this and the next section, where the laity congregate, has been abolished. The third section is screened off by the so-called iconostasis, or ikon-screen. It has three doors, the central one being the 'royal' door. The priest or priests operate behind the screen, punctuating their divinely mysterious activities with ritual forays into the body of the church. It may not be quite like the Last Supper, but it re-enacts both it and the saving acts of Christ. After confessions and much prayer and chanting, there is the Little Entrance, when the priest takes the Gospels in his hands and passes it to the deacon. They come through the north door into the middle of the worshippers.

This means the coming of Christ to earth. The words of the Gospels are not so much important as what they represent. They represent Christ. As the priest and deacon go back through the royal door, the choir chants an unaccompanied anthem to Christ.

After readings from the Gospels and other events, there is the Great Entrance. Incidentally, it is worth noting that the entrance is from the altar towards the congregation: it means that the laity are the stuff of the Church. The altar is a means of service. You do not enter the Holy of Holies: you enter the people from it. The Great Entrance symbolizes Christ's entrance into Jerusalem in the last days of his ministry. The priest and deacon bear the wine (and water mixed) and the bread (leavened). As yet the bread and wine are not consecrated. They are not yet the body and blood of the Lord. Again the return is through the royal door. The singing and prayers go on. Nor is the congregation conformist. People drift in and out, and people take individual opportunities to kiss the ikons. We meet the idiorhythmic style again.

So far Christ's birth and entry into Jerusalem have been powerfully enacted. The culmination is, naturally, the Lord's Supper. A great prayer is offered up. The Spirit is invoked to come down, so to say, to transform the bread and wine. Only then is the meal truly divine.

The consecration of the bread and wine precedes the final main act of the symbolic drama. The priest gives communion to some of the faithful, dipping the bread into the wine and serving it on a spoon. He issues forth from the royal door to do this. Thereafter come some prayers and a benediction, and the distribution of the blessed bread and wine – blessed but not consecrated: holy but not divine.

Thus do the Romanians and other Orthodox latch on to the saving events in faraway Palestine in those distant but awesome days. Thus does Orthodoxy bring other times and other places into the living presence of the people.

That, then, is a small sketch of one great branch of Christendom. By numbers it has been about the equal of Rome (till the times after Columbus). It has been, by numbers, more than the equal of Protestantism. It has strong meanings for the interpretation of Christ and the early faith. It is a swathe of the Christian faith much used to glory and suffering. And it keeps its own character even in the days of official atheism. Later, we shall return to it. I mentioned the monasteries. They nurture and nurtured Eastern mystical practices – much more vital to Christianity than is often thought. But now let us move to Italy, to trace the features of a rather different mode of being Christian.

2
Italian Catholicism and its Cousins

Through all its splendours, catastrophes and reforms, Roman Catholicism retains its magic, a magic evident still in modern Italy, even if the faithful are somewhat less so than they used to be. Some of its spirit can be seen from three pictures.

One picture is strong in my mind, for my wife comes from the village of Tremezzo on Lake Como in the far north of Italy, which though some distance from the Po, shows some of the character of those places on the Po of which Giovanni Guareschi wrote in his jolly, although perhaps too smug, stories of Don Camillo in action against his Communist adversary, Mayor Peppone. As often elsewhere in modern Italy, only some folk attend the whole of mass on Sunday in Tremezzo. But quite a number partially go. Between the parish church and the lake there is a little square, and the road. In the square stands a gun as a war memorial (the dead alas fought on several sides). By the road, on the edge of the lake there is a fence. On it sit men and youths during mass, smoking. Perhaps they take off and go into the church once a signal from a comrade has shown them that the priest has finished his sermon. It is a partial participation in the service. The church is still vital culturally to the community. You cannot draw a line between Communists and Catholics: they overlap considerably.

Another picture is the pilgrims going to Rome, now in charabancs, once arduously on foot and horse, looking towards that mysterious and imperial city, glorious, if dirty and quarrelsome, even in the late Middle Ages before the great structure of St Peter's was built. Near Todi in Umbria is a church built on a smaller scale in the design which the architect put up as one of the alternatives under consideration. It is roughly in the shape of a Greek Cross. The actual St Peter's is definitely Latin, and in its scale imperial. Italians are especially proud that in some sense they are still at the centre of a

31

Latin empire, albeit of the spirit.

A third picture is of monasteries. Italy was one of the great breeding places of the Orders – Benedictines, Dominicans, Capuchins, Franciscans. Italian religion is fun-loving, but underlying is a seriousness issuing in austerity.

Yet there is something strange that Catholicism should have its centre in Italy. Negatively, of course, one might say that the first centre, Jerusalem, was sacked in AD 70, so the faith needed a new capital. One can also see that with the adoption of the faith as official, through Constantine and his aftermath, it was natural for the Bishop of Rome to claim precedence. But the fact is that Rome proved a vital focus of Christianity before it conquered the Empire, and its importance was evidenced even before the Fall of Jerusalem and the dispersal of the Jerusalem Church under the presidency of James the brother of the Lord. Partly it was accident or providence – that Paul went there to appeal his case as a citizen of the Empire. But Peter went too. Both were martyred there, it seems, and St Peter's is supposed to stand over the grave of 'the Rock', to give Peter the nickname conferred on him by Jesus. The secret of this concern with Rome perhaps was this: that once Paul had opened up the faith to Gentiles, so that converts would not, for instance, need to be circumcised (an offputting prospect for adults when few converts were little babies), Christianity spread through the cities – Ephesus, Athens, Corinth and so on. It was natural therefore to look to Rome as a main recruiting ground. Also it had a modest Jewish community, and often Christians first preached in the relevant synagogue in their travels, so that there would be both Jews and Gentiles integrated into the new-born community.

At all events, the Jerusalem Church faded, while the successors of Peter, first of the disciples, came to assume great importance as bishops of Rome. It was therefore not surprising that the imperial city – the eternal city as it is often called – came to assume a symbolic meaning for Christians. As we have noted elsewhere Byzantium, re-named Constantinople, became the other Rome of the Empire, while Moscow aspired to be the Third Rome. It is interesting that often in religion places of sacred and vital significance become as it were transferable. Every river in India can become for Hindus in principle the sacred Ganges (though the real Ganges is still more sacred!). Blake wrote of building a new Jerusalem in England.

Christianity conquered the Empire, in its ambiguous way, as a result of the change of policy of the Emperor Constantine. But later the Empire disintegrated, bringing new powers from the north into play and infusing the Italian nation with new blood. Shortly we shall trace the causes of that great junction in human history, when the Christian faith turned from its earlier, more martyred and passive, destiny to a new role as the faith of a wonderful civilization. And hence a destiny in which politics were to become intertwined with spirituality, and the sword was to be more than a spiritual one. But before we come to that junction, let us consider who the Mediterranean peoples, and in particular the Italians, were.

Like most peoples they were a mixture, but perhaps more of a mixture than most. They were united, as a result of the Empire, through certain shared ideals and a language. But in Italy in imperial days, there were Celts in the north, Latins, Etruscans, Greeks and so forth, while later the invasions from the north which broke up the Empire infused Gothic and more generally Germanic elements into the population.

Thus Lombardy in the north of Italy sports many fair-haired folk. Already too in Rome there had been an influx of people from all over the known world. To the west, Spain had people of Iberian and Basque stock, and Romans. Across the Alps in France, and in Britain, there were other mixtures. They remained somewhat different from those who faced downwards to the Mediterranean Sea, the basin and fastest channel of transport across the heartlands of the Empire, at least during the navigation season. But to the East the spell of the Greek language created a somewhat different culture. The Latin-speakers and the Greek-speakers never fully fused their cultures – one reason, as we have seen, for the drifting apart of the Eastern and Western Churches, and already a cause of concern at the Council of Nicaea called by Constantine in 325. Also,

33

the foundation of Constantinople as an Eastern capital of the Empire foreshadowed the creation of two Empires, both claiming descent from the true Roman heritage.

One vital ingredient in the less brilliant Western culture was law. Rome knew how to regulate its domains. The Church was to be profoundly affected by that. Canon law was evolved, a Church law parallel to secular law. It was an irony that the Church, not accepting the most part of Jewish law, came to soak itself in Roman law. But of course Christianity came to absorb much else besides from Roman civilization, and indeed to ensure the transmission of such elements in the chaotic centuries after the collapse of the Empire. How then did it make the transition from persecution to officialdom?

To understand the earlier situation of Christians, liable to sporadic and brutal persecution, it is necessary to glance at religion as it prevailed around them, in the early Roman Empire. It was woven together from many strands. Partly it was State religion, used in official ceremonies, and recently extended to include the cult of the Emperor as divine – a means of cementing the loyalty of citizens to the centre. Partly it retained elements from agricultural religion, dating from Rome's early days, in which the earth and the world about us are perceived as containing spirits, sometimes dangerous, called in Latin *numina*. But it was religion hospitable too to Greek ideas, ranging from myths to philosophies such as Stoicism. Further, Rome had in its midst a number of mystery religions, such as the cult of Mithra. These mystery religions were sacramental in character: by undergoing initiation and attending ceremonies, typically reserved only for the initiates, a person would be changed and gain assurance of immortality or other spiritual benefits. Now Christianity looked very much like one of these cults. It had a God who died and rose again, like Dionysus. It had initiation, through baptism after a period of instruction when a person was known as a catechumen and could not yet attend the full ceremonies. As in Mithraism its followers partook of bread and wine as having sacred significance. And the faithful were assured of grace and immortality. Why then were the Christians persecuted when the other groups

34

were not? Why did the Roman mob often riotously call for their blood – 'Christians to the lions'?

The answer lies in an element not so far mentioned in Roman conceptions of the relation of the gods to men – the idea of the peace of the gods, the *pax deorum*. According to this idea, the welfare of the Empire and of its people, its internal peace and stability, required a respectful attitude to the gods. Some intellectuals might be sceptical about the gods, but would still acknowledge them at an official level. The fault of the Christians was that they both failed to recognize the divinity of the Emperor and failed to acknowledge the gods in general. They were dubbed 'atheists', meaning that they denied the gods. So when things went badly, like when a grain fleet was mauled by bad seas, the Roman mob would cry for the persecution of Christians, and often Jews too.

The worst outbreak of persecution was unleashed in the first years of the fourth century, under Diocletian. Its motivation is obscure. But, happily, a calmer period was not long in coming. In 312 Constantine used Christian magic against his opponent Maxentius at the Battle of the Milvian Bridge, not far from Rome. His adversary was reputed to be using pagan magical methods, and Constantine became convinced, as a result of a vision, that Christian magic would prevail. So his army was led into battle behind a standard consisting of a gold-coated spear with a cross bar, from which there hung a wreath of gold and jewels containing Chi and Rho, the two Greek letters for Christ – a sign already long in use among Christians. And the power of Christ's magic proved to be the greater. In the following years Constantine was more and more favourable to the Christian cause. A *pax Christi* came to replace the *pax deorum*.

Yet very rarely does a religion totally displace another. There are elements of the older Roman religion in modern Italy, notably in the countryside. To take a few examples round the region I know best – Lake Como. There is a mountain sanctuary associated with a cave where once mysteriously the statue of a black Madonna was found. There is a church where votive offerings of pictures are made, depicting cures

35

and escapes from storms on the lake, road disasters and the like. There is a spring associated with the Madonna where bathing your eyes will cure them or preserve them. Bus drivers have medallions on the dashboard to keep them safe. But now the old *numina* are not invoked, but rather the saints, and above all the Madonna.

The Italian affection for the Madonna is not unique in Catholicism, of course, but it is intense. What are the roots of this attitude? There are several. First, there is, fairly obviously, the importance of Mary in the Gospels, so already she was portrayed in the catacombs. In the early Middle Ages her cult became especially developed in Italy, with the introduction of the invocation *Ave Maria* and of the Angelus bell calling the faithful to repeat the *Ave*. The increased devotion to Mary was symbolized by the definition of two dogmas, one in 1854, another in 1950. The first was that of the immaculate conception of Mary – namely that she was born without taint of original sin. As according to Church doctrine Jesus was sinless, this could be accounted for by the sinlessness of his mother (and of course the Spirit). The second dogma was that of the Bodily Assumption of the Virgin Mary, that is that she was taken up to heaven in the same manner as was her son. This had long been a popular belief in Italy and elsewhere.

Again, the old Empire had been accustomed to mother goddesses, like Isis, who figures so movingly in the Latin novel *The Golden Ass*. Often such deities have their origin in fertility cults, for the analogy between procreation and sowing seeds in mother earth was not lost on the ancients. The male god very often was in the sky, the female on or even below the earth. There was thus a deeply felt need to have some female element at the heart of religion. And though Mary was never treated as divine, she was next to it – the object not of worship but of the deepest reverence. She was given in the East the title of *Theotokos* – one who bears God.

For the Italian the virginity of Mary reflects their ambiguity towards women. The mother is very much idealized in Italy, and the pictures of Mary and Jesus, Mother and Child, are constant reminders of the glory of child-bearing and child-raising. There is scarcely a people in the world more devoted to children. Yet the Italian prides himself as lover, and is unscrupulous in seduction and, on trams, bottom-pinching and other ploys. Yet the seduced woman is not really respected. So the cult of the Virgin fits in with, and moulds, the Italian psychology.

For many Protestants, however, the cult of Mary is seen as idolatrous and unjustified by the Bible. The second dogma mentioned above, the bodily assumption of the Virgin Mary, was seen, therefore, as almost a deliberate move to keep Roman Catholicism apart from many other Christians at a time when there was increasing interest in Christian unity.

Another figure that commands, of course, reverence and respect is the Pope. The papacy has long been controversial: the Pope was seen by the Eastern Church as the first Protestant, because he could presume the authority to add to doctrine, and so fail to acknowledge the idea that ultimately all dogmas should be a matter of consensus of the whole Church. The papacy strengthened its position after the disintegration of the Empire, though in the rich and glorious period of the Renaissance it was weakened by schism and corruption. The Borgias were the culmination of such degradation of the moral life of the papacy, seeing the office as mainly to do with power politics.

The Reformation forced reforms on Catholicism, of course, and though some of the stronger Protestants vilified the Pope and Rome as the Scarlet Woman, the office gradually increased in respect. But it was always a matter of partisanship and often affection among the population of Italy, especially of Rome itself. The picture of the white-clad figure of the Pope on the balcony in face of a quarter of a million people at Easter in 1977 is a sign of the continuing magic of the office. Italians were especially enthusiastic about John XXIII, mainly because he was a man of the people – 'one of us'. I remember taking an old relative on a trip, really a pilgrimage, to Sotto il Monte near Bergamo in North Italy where John was born. We looked over his house, and he marvelled that the family used the old oil lamps, like sauce boats with a floating wick, reminding him of his peasant youth. A feature too, paradoxically, which appeals to Italians is the ideal of simplicity of life surrounded by great pomp and circumstance: the Pope has his splendid Swiss Guard, the stately litter on which he is sometimes carried in procession, his palaces at the Vatican and in Castel Gandolfo, the magnificence of St Peter's, the offices and gardens of Vatican City. He has his own state, his own ambassadors, his own representation on international bodies. It is all reminiscent, indeed part of, the baroque art and architecture which animated the eyes of the Counter-Reformation: flamboyant. Roman Catholicism has retained a degree of flamboyance suited to the Italian character. Religion should impress.

Of course, the Pope's state has been greatly shrunken. The papacy went through a difficult time, partly of its own making, during the events of the nineteenth century known as the Risorgimento. This period saw the creation of a unified Italy through the skill and heroism of such figures as Cavour and Garibaldi.

It must be recalled that in most of the period since the disintegration of the Empire, Italy was divided up into different states and principalities. Parts of it in more modern times were under foreign rule. Let us look at a map, for instance, of 1815. Beginning in the south: Sicily and about a third of Italy (like a boot on the Italian leg) belonged to the Kingdom of the Two Sicilies, a combination of the older kingdom of Naples and that of Sicily. It had long been under a Spanish dynasty, the Bourbons. Then there was a band across Italy running nearly up to Venice – the Papal States. To the west was the separate principality of Tuscany (under Napoleon the Kingdom of Etruria). One or two further smaller States intervened before we get to the north-west, part of the Kingdom of Sardinia, and basis for the Kingdom of Piedmont, later to play such a vital role in the Risorgimento.

Finally Lombardy and the Venetian region were under the Hapsburg Empire of Austro-Hungary. The aim of the Italian nationalists was to unify Italy, but among other forces working against was the papacy, defending its States and status, like a bone in the gullet of Italian unity. Some of the nationalists too were deeply affected by liberal ideals largely derived from Britain, and the papacy was not yet ready for such freedoms, which might seem to threaten religious authority. A certain anti-clericalism played a role. Thus the great hero, Garibaldi, was anti-clerical. The papacy played its cards badly.

Garibaldi in 1860 had conducted his flamboyant, almost miraculous, campaign in which, with one thousand men, he landed in Sicily and rapidly overran both Sicily and southern and central Italy. By 1861 all of Italy save Venice and Rome (plus some surrounding countryside) was part of the unified Italy. That Rome held out was partly due to a French garrison, there since 1849, it being in the French interest to resist the unification of Italy. In 1862 Garibaldi made an attempt to attack the city, but was stopped by the government. What proved decisive was the outbreak of the Franco-Prussian War in 1870, leading to withdrawal of French support from Rome. The papal territories were invaded. Rome was to be the new capital. The Pope, Pius IX, was bottled up in his palaces. Pius's successor modified the hard line. The position of the papacy had been that the existence of the Papal States was a guarantee of the independence of the papacy from government coercion. Leo took the same theoretical line, but asked for less than the old dominions. He also was clear in saying that he did not want to reopen the issue of Italian unity. But for fifty years or more the popes remained shut up in the Vatican, not even pronouncing the blessing from the balcony in St Peter's Square. Ironically it was Mussolini and the Fascists, who had a strong streak of anti-clericalism, who arranged the Concordat which settled the present pattern of the papal situation and brought the Pope once more out on the balcony, reconciled to the new aspirations of the Italian people.

By the treaty, the Pope's temporal jurisdiction was restored by the creation of the Vatican as a mini-state, covering 109 acres. Church marriages were recognized as conferring civil status (that is there was no need for a couple to go through a civil ceremony as well, as obtains in France and elsewhere). In principle Roman Catholic ideas on marriage, abortion and so on became State policy, and Catholic instruction was incorporated into the curricula of secondary schools. The clergy were given privileges, though the State had some say in their appointment. The Church thus came in from the Italian cold. Meanwhile the seeds of Christian Democracy, which was to be the main party in Italy after World War II and had a warm relationship with the papacy, were being sown, even if the members of the movement, such as Alcide del Gasperi (1881–1954) – destined to be Italy's impressive post-war premier – were for a time imprisoned, part of a recurrent conflict between Fascists and Catholics which continued even despite the Concordat.

Meanwhile the intellectual life of the Church had been undergoing various changes and challenges. Leo XIII had issued in 1879 his famous encyclical or general letter to the faithful known as *Aeterni Patris* ('Of the Eternal Father'), after the first two words in it; it urged the serious study of the philosophy and theology of St Thomas Aquinas, and was a main factor in the revival of what came to be called Neo-Thomism. However, the Church continued to be hostile to other intellectual trends – loosely known as Modernism, in which Catholics tried to update the faith in the context of modern knowledge and social changes. Let us examine these two aspects of Catholic response to the turbulence of the nineteenth century. But to do so we need to retrace our steps to the time of Aquinas (1225–74).

Thomas Aquinas produced one of the great systems of thought in Christian history. Born near Monte Cassino in southern Italy of a noble family, he was educated among the Benedictines of Monte Cassino, but in his late adolescence he was attracted to the Order of Preachers, the Dominicans. His family opposed this, and forcibly restrained him for a year from leaving to join the Order. But as he was a determined person, he escaped and made his way to Paris – Paris then being the great university of the Western world. From there for a time he migrated to Cologne to study. His nickname was 'the dumb ox' because he was quiet and big. But on his return to Paris he soon made a name for himself as a great teacher and thinker. His life was, within the framework of Church piety, one unusually dedicated to the intellectual task of creating a new system of thought in which Aristotle and Catholicism were brought together in a vital and powerful synthesis. So strong were his ideas, that they came, after some early opposition, to be the foundation of late medieval scholastic philosophy, and as we have seen underwent a revival in the late nineteenth century. It is hard to boil down the teachings of so voluminous and subtle a writer to a few sentences. All that can be given is a glimpse.

Much of his system depended on his idea that man's reason can know something about God even if for fuller knowledge we need revelation as contained in the words of the scriptures. In particular, by the use of reason men can come to realize, independently of faith, that God exists, through various arguments known as the 'five ways' which Aquinas elaborated. For instance, everything in the world has a cause, and that cause has a cause and so on. In order to explain the world one needs to assume a First Cause, itself not caused. That is God. Now if reason and revelation go together, religion is both natural and supernatural. It is relevant to the world about us. Further, Aquinas used the categories of the philosopher Aristotle, whose ideas later formed the basis of much medieval science. So in a sense Aquinas brought science and religion together. It was for a revival of such a framework of reconciliation that Leo XIII called, even if both philosophy and science had adopted a very different shape from Aristotle by the late nineteenth century. Still, Leo's promulgation led to reforms and a deepening of seminary education for priests, both in Italy and in other Catholic parts of Europe and the Americas.

Modernism was another matter. The intellectual, social and political changes of the nineteenth century could hardly fail to affect members of the Catholic Church. Attempts were made to digest the new findings of historical probings of the New and Old Testament (see p. 233); questions of a revival of Catholicism within the new Italian political milieu arose; Catholicism needed to adapt to the new industrial Europe being created in France, Germany, Italy and other countries with substantial

Catholic populations. But the Church cracked down on such tendencies for reform. To those living secluded in the Vatican too much of the old tradition might be lost. There remained heavy deposits of the Middle Ages in the Vatican's attitudes. And the Roman pontiff retained the vital power of excommunication, which itself depended on the fact that it was distressing to the faithful – when faith declines, of course, excommunication loses its sting. Also very often, as in Catholic faculties in German universities, conformity was a condition of holding a teaching post, so men could lose their jobs for what was deemed to be heretical or schismatic in character.

Of those who were condemned by the papacy in Italy none is perhaps as attractive as the great Catholic novelist Antonio Fogazzaro (1842–1911), author of the novel *Il Santo* (*The Saint*). It gives a feel for the Italy of the period. Incidentally, though Fogazzaro had his book placed on the Vatican's index of banned books, he did not, like some other people in the modernist movement, leave the Church but submitted.

Fogazzaro's dreams of reform from within were partially fulfilled in the twentieth century by two major developments – the coming into existence of a powerful lay Catholic party, the Christian Democrats; and by the calling of the Council known as Vatican II (1962–65). The Christian Democrats were part of a wider European movement, expressing liberal ideals and moderate social democracy. Their coming to power in Italy was the result of the climactic events of World War II. Mussolini's fleet of beautiful warships was largely destroyed at Matapan and Taranto by the British; and his armies collapsed in East Africa and Libya. Finally, he became thoroughly dependent on the Germans, who were however driven up Italy to beyond Naples – at which point a new Italian government under Badoglio was formed, destined to fight alongside the Allies. This gave added impetus to the partisan movement in central Italy and the north. Out of it emerged a strong and respected Communist Party, while the Christian Democrats were grouping for the opportunity they would have in post-Fascist Italy. Thus were set the patterns of post-war politics. In the early years the party expressed new hope and often a true dedication to Catholic values – though later, after the death of de Gasperi, it slowly slid into a quagmire of faction and inefficiency. Still, it gave a new meaning to lay participation in a Church still highly dominated by priests and hierarchy.

Vatican II was a surprise. Cardinal Roncalli, when he became Pope, was thought to be an aged stopgap. He was indeed aged, but vigorous, and a visionary. Robustly he set in train what he believed the Holy Spirit was infusing into the Church – a breath of change, of updating, of *Aggiornamento*. Many of the institutions and practices of the Church, deriving from the Council of Trent (1545–63), were modified. Let us pause to consider the structure of Trent's reforms and affirmations.

The Council of Trent was called to define and renew the Catholic faith over against Protestantism. Thus it treated the Latin Bible, the Vulgate, as the authoritative text. Vatican II was to modify that view, and to change the liturgy so that it should be in the relevant vernacular languages in the various countries of the world. Trent affirmed the doctrine of the transubstantiation of the bread and wine into the body and blood of Christ. The bread and wine retained the qualities and the look of bread and wine, but the real substance within them was changed. This became a factor in the cult of the elements, for example the display of the bread, the Host, in an elaborate and ornamented object called the monstrance. The doctrine reinforced the position of the clergy, in that the priest (and only a priest) could perform the mass. The Council as well as reforming and cleaning up the hierarchy and the diocesan structure, also affirmed the supremacy of the Pope over all patriarchs and bishops. New patterns in training the clergy were set. A new catechism was devised and Trent ushered in a renewal of the spiritual use of the sacraments. With the revitalization of the Church went fresh church building and decoration. The appearance of Catholicism became intertwined by the new religious art of the Baroque period. For all the intervening changes, Catholicism up to Vatican II bore the stamp of Trent. Now a new upheaval was at hand, initiated by a shrewd, holy and peasant Pope, John XXIII.

Why was an *aggiornamento* necessary? Several factors combined. One was that Catholicism existed in Western Europe and America and in some countries elsewhere in the context of an open society. What effect is there in banning a book when it has become freely available? How could discipline about birth control be enforced? New ideas and practices necessarily were filtering into the life of the laity. Second, the world had changed much since Vatican I, nearly a hundred years earlier. Third, the movement towards Christian unity was having some influence upon Catholics. Fourth, there were signs of decline in practice and alienation from the Church among more and more Catholics. The Church needed new vigour, credibility and spiritual appeal.

Vatican II brought about a modernization of the Catholic doctrinal stances. This included many of the aspirations of the nineteenth-century Modernists whom the Church had tried to discipline. To some degree the monastic orders were opened up more to the world. The social aspect of Catholicism was reaffirmed. But of all the changes, the most far-reaching was the use of the vernacular languages in the mass. It has led to a paradox – here perhaps I can revert to our village of Tremezzo. The paradox has to do with lay participation.

It was Good Friday, 1976. As was the custom, there was a procession from the church up behind it through a small park, originally the grounds of a villa, given to the church. Above some tennis courts there is a belvedere, to which you ascend by two or three flights of steps. The priest had put much thought into the affair, having had lights slung from trees to mark the way, as well as recorded music playing from loudspeakers here and there. Some carried candles. There were prayers from the belvedere, and the procession wound its way back to the church. Inside, after the priest had finished there was a strange demonstration. Maybe thirty of the older folk, mainly women, sat in their seats and demanded to sing the older Latin hymns they were accustomed to on Good Friday. For them the new Italian way had actually deprived them of meaningful participation. And it was puzzling that in any case it was still a kind of order from the priest that the laity should participate in the newer mode. Was this much freedom? So the modernization of the Church in Italy has caused some strain, and as elsewhere the erosion of magic and authority seems to have led to a decline in observances. Yet the heady new freedoms of post-Vatican II (a wit is supposed to have remarked at a fashionable party, 'No one gets married these days, except of course a few priests') has undoubtedly infused vitality into what previously had become a rigid and somewhat defensive system.

The history of religions tends to show that religions need an interface between the higher spiritual domain and men's ordinary concerns – as in much of Mahayana Buddhism, where the problem is recognized clearly. That interface is magic. For secular man in the modern world, the structure of science often corresponds to the spiritual domain, and technologies supplying goods are the magic. The reforms of Vatican II have not supplied a new magic for the old, and this remains a problem for the modern Italian Catholic, even if Christian democracy presided over the famous economic miracle.

It is now time, briefly, to look at the cousins of Italian Catholicism. The most important in terms of human history and influence have been the Churches of Spain and Portugal, for it was these countries that transmitted the faith to Central and South America, and to segments of Africa and some areas of the East, notably the Philippines, which is the only pre-dominantly Catholic country in Asia. 1492, the year of Columbus' historic voyage to the West, had a double significance. It also marked the fall of Granada, the last Muslim dominion in Spain. From the seventh century, Spain had been partially – early on nearly wholly – under Muslim rule. Because of Islamic teaching about tolerating Jews and Christians, they lived in reasonable conditions under Islam, though many Christians converted. During the course of the reconquest, pressures in the opposite direction were created, and in the fifteenth century more or less forcible conversion, with the alternative of migration out of Spain, was imposed on Jews and Muslims. Queen Isabella was strong in this direction, and she had, to help her, the famous Torquemada (1420–98),

45

Inquisitor General – pious, austere, fanatical, learned, being (as he saw it) cruel to be kind. The stake, heavy fines, exile – these were the choices. Many Jews converted, being known as *Marranos*, as also indeed did many Moors or *Moriscos*. Spanish Catholicism acquired a rather fanatical stamp, yet it also produced in this, its golden age, spirituality in the lives of famous mystics such as St Theresa of Avila (1515–82) and St John of the Cross (1542–91), together with zeal and energy through the Orders, notably the Jesuits founded by St Ignatius Loyola (1491–1556). The new vigour would find extraordinary outlets in the New World. Yet the history of the faith in Spain, including the Spanish Civil War in the twentieth century, noted for ferocious anti-clericalism in many areas, makes Spanish Catholicism harder, rather more austere, than its cousin in Italy. But in the New World, the Church played a part in protecting the Indians from the often destructive treatment which they received at the hands of the Conquistadors. It was, however, a paternalistic operation, as in the Jesuit control and conversion of Indians, clustered in model villages, in Paraguay; and the famous Californian missions run by the Franciscans. Yet also in the New World new mixtures were created: the old gods of Mexico reappeared disguised as Catholic saints.

French Catholicism had a rather different flavour and a more ambiguous destiny. First, France had been rather profoundly affected by the Reformation, even if the monarchy remained Catholic. But it was overthrown in the Revolution, and marked anti-clericalism prevailed. Soon the Industrial Revolution brought about deep changes in social structure, and so there was a progressive de-Christianization of France in the nineteenth and twentieth centuries – very different from the real situation in Italy. The intellectual and spiritual life of the French Church is considerable, but its numbers (effectively) small.

Outside France the chief concentration of French-speaking Catholicism is in Quebec, where the religion maintains something of the tradition of before the Revolution.

Of other branches of Catholicism, suffice it to mention three more – the Irish, American and Polish Churches, which illustrate three differences in mood as compared with Italy. Ireland's long adherence to the faith gives the religion strength, but in the last four centuries the life of the Church has been much bound up with the struggle against the British. The Irish priest, often ill-educated, was close to the people. Perhaps because of a certain cheerful disorganization in the life of the Irishman, the Church retained a much tighter, tougher grip than one would find in Italy. Customarily too the Irishman has married very late, for economic reasons, and a strong discipline in sexual mores has been imposed.

The Catholic country with the highest church attendance is Poland, land of John Paul II. The faith there resembles some of the properties of Orthodoxy in Romania, for it functions both as religion and as expression of national identity, over against the depredations of Protestant Prussia on the one side and the Orthodox Russians on the other. This dual role carries on even under Communism.

Irish, Italian and Polish Catholicism became the most vital ingredients in the American Church, during and after the period of mass immigration. The task of retaining the allegiance of these immigrants and at the same time helping with the process of integration required great energies, and the establishment of a network of Catholic education, hospitals and new socially oriented orders. Thus the American Church has been highly activist, and not much noted, until the latter half of the twentieth century, for deep scholarship, nor for contemplative depth, but rather for its organizational skill. Moreover some of the more traditional attributes of Catholicism have been underplayed – street processions, wayside shrines and the like were inappropriate on the whole in a plural society, where the Church had to live with both Protestants and Jews.

What, then, is the essence of Catholicism? Unlike Protestantism it has not got fragmented seriously, despite occasional breakaways and defections. It has proved itself tough in survival. Its heart is Rome, but not just the imperial city, for it combines there memories of Peter and Paul and the fish painted in the catacombs on the one hand with the traditions of Roman law on the other. That Rome bears both the stamp

47

of the Middle Ages and that of the Baroque period of the Counter-Reformation. It still retains a certain style of piety, and a strength born of the interplay between hierarchy and burgeoning monastic orders. Above all Catholic Christianity has combined doctrinal correctness with a centrally sacramental system. It has rarely been a religion simply of inner experience or enthusiasm. Though strong in the devotional spirit within the framework of the sacraments, it has not encouraged individualistic experience.

But it undoubtedly has problems in the Western world, increasingly plural in character. Vatican II was one method of trying to adapt, though it meant importing much of the Protestant ethos.

3

The Coptic Connection

The deposing of the Emperor Haile Selassie, Lion of Judah, and the domination of the country by the Marxist military regime of Mengistu somewhat bloodily in the second half of the 1970s marked the end of a Christian empire. It marked too a new period of turbulence, as Ethiopia crumbled at its Muslim edges.

That Christian empire is the symbol of a number of things. It was a continuously (until Mussolini) independent African region, and focus of many aspirations both in black Africa and in the Caribbean. It was also importantly perhaps the most Semitic of Christianities that developed – reminiscent of Old Testament times with its dancing and sistra, its minstrelsy and psalms, its circumcision, its arks and its memories of Solomon. Coptic Ethiopia, partly bonded to Coptic Egypt, represents a swathe of Eastern Christianity which drifted away both from Orthodoxy and from the Catholic West because of Chalcedon and related difficulties arising from the decisions of that Council. It also has a romantic train of legends swirling through the minds both of Ethiopians and outsiders – of how the Empire harked back to the fabulous Queen of Sheba, and how in later times it was ruled by the virtuous and powerful Prester John, hammer of Islam. Even Haile Selassie was a legend in his own lifetime, for his sturdy and noble defence of Abyssinia against the Italians, who were too late in their colonial adventures to be respectable among older imperialists, and for being Ras Tafari, focus of hope for Africans. The Ethiopians are also proud exponents of the supposed heresy of Monophysitism and so by a paradox are also spiritual cousins to those who followed Nestorius – Nestorius who in his zeal went too far the other way in defining Christ's inner constitution and so too was rated heretical. To such consequences of the Council of Chalcedon later

49

we shall need to return, but meanwhile let us look briefly at the physiognomy of Ethiopia.

Its civilization has been anchored in the highlands, which run about a thousand miles from north to south, beginning close to the Red Sea and going down to near the border of what is now Kenya. Towards the southern end of this massif there is a long tumbling spur thrusting towards the arid regions of the Horn of Africa. So the shape is like the profile of a high boot with the toe pointed right. The area above and round the toe is relatively dry and flat, and is constituted in modern times by Eritrea, Djibouti and Somalia. Between Somalia and the ancient walled city of Harar, on the toe, lies the Ogaden, contemporary and traditional scene of fighting between Islamic Somalis and Christian Ethiopians. Indeed for a thousand years or more Ethiopia has come to exist in an Islamic sea, for to the west and north the sandy Sudan lies between it and its Egyptian contacts. But though sometimes overrun and devastated by excursions from its neighbours, Ethiopia has mainly maintained its independence as a sprawling cultural empire.

The story of the Queen of Sheba points to a vital feature of its early culture, for it was deeply affected by Semitic religion across the Red Sea. The Sabaean culture in the Yemen, hydraulic in character, was advanced, and seems to have produced a population surplus which spilled across the waters into Eritrea and Ethiopia. In the plateaux they found reasonable opportunities to plant an exile civilization, Sabaean in character. The newcomers and the indigenous people of Aksum, Tigre and Amhara – relatively fertile regions running in an elevated chain from north to south – became merged, and form the basis of modern Ethiopian populations, though the situation was further confused by the conquest and assimilation of various pagan and occasionally Islamic tribal groups. So Ethiopia, though eventually based on the Amhara group, is a mosaic of languages and peoples. There is, however, a strong Semitic infusion, which accounts for many traits of Ethiopian Christianity. The mosaic makes Ethiopia more an empire than a nation, held together traditionally by the ideology of a Christian monarchy going back to Solomon and Sheba. The existence in modern Ethiopia of large Islamic populations in Eritrea and in the Ogaden is a potent source of breakaway movements and of the bitter warfare in these regions. It is open to question whether a new Marxist ideology can easily replace the older Christian one in a way which will successfully fuse the diverse tendencies in the old empire.

The mountainous upper regions are windy and rocky, with few trees, precipitous monasteries and hermitages, and surprising flowering plants. The heart of the culture tends to rest on plateaux and valleys a little lower down, a region of towns and villages, vines and crops. The low country has its rainy season and colour, but mainly it is dry and prickly, subject in the shimmering heat to brush and grass fires. And through the region runs that rift valley which further north cradles the Dead Sea and many scenes of Jewish and Christian history.

The scriptures were translated into the ancient language of Ge'ez in which also other written works were composed, and which was a vehicle of Christian civilization. It has a Sabaean base but contains an infusion of Greek, Syriac and Hebrew elements. Though alive in liturgy it is in everyday use dead, where local languages count, and also Amharic, the imperial tongue.

The Semitic side of the religion is evident in a number of ways. First, there is the ideological point to which I have referred: the tracing of the royal lineage back to the Jewish and Sabaean monarchies. It is believed that the offspring of Solomon and Sheba, Menelik, became emperor. And more than that: he supposedly was, after being brought up in Ethiopia, anointed by his father in Jerusalem – and anointed as ruler of an empire from the Nile right down to Shoa in the southern part of the highlands and across to eastern India. He was then sent back with twenty young Israelites as Levite priests, and managed too to take the Ark of the Covenant to his kingdom, via Egypt and the Red Sea. Thereafter the empire was ruled according to the laws and religion of Israel.

The effect of the myth is to produce a nice parallelism – between pre-Christian and Christian Ethiopia on the one

51

hand, and the Old and New Testaments on the other. Moreover, the anointing of Menelik incorporates the idea that half the world is assigned to the Israelite monarchy, the other half to Menelik and his descendants, as though the bifurcation of the Covenant through the transfer of the Ark must mean the bifurcation of the holy kingdom. The myth has its ritual use, not surprisingly, for the Ethiopian Emperor, Lion of Judah, is hailed as 'King of Zion, son of David and Solomon' at his elaborate, but now defunct coronation ceremony.

All this gives Ethiopia a special role in Christian history. It represents an Eastern, Semitic variant on the Romano-Greek imperial faith. It is the most powerful version left of Christianity of the circumcision. It is in its own way an alternative to Pauline, Gentile Christianity. A strong affinity is felt for the culture of Israel. The use of sacred dances with drums, sistra and other instruments is consciously reminiscent of the sacred minstrelsy of the Davidic period. It is no coincidence that strong emphasis is laid upon the Psalms. Moreover, Christian Ethiopia keeps the sabbath on Saturday, like early Christians, and also celebrates Sunday, and so maintains both the Jewish tradition and the memory of the Resurrection. The use too of ceremonial arks, replicas or reflections of the one Ark which Sheba's son brought back from Jerusalem is a further feature to recall Israel: indeed many visitors are powerfully reminded of ancient biblical times when they visit Ethiopia.

Perhaps most importantly of all the Semitic features, circumcision on males is practised as part of Ethiopian religion. The custom fits in, as it happens, with those of some East African tribes as well, to the south. It binds the Ethiopian kind of Christianity back to the Law.

But naturally much of Ethiopian Christianity cannot be traced back directly to the Semitic past – for instance the characteristic sacred music evolved in the medieval period is a creative synthesis out of various elements. Also the Greek and Egyptian elements absorbed into the system were vital too. To them, and the vicissitudes of the Council of Chalcedon I shall return, but in the meantime let us glance at the contacts between Ethiopia and the West, and in particular the Portuguese incursion, for it tells us something important about the contrast between the ethos of Rome and the spirit of Aksum, the ancient and sacred capital of the Empire.

The rounding of the Cape of Good Hope gave the Portuguese the key to the Indian Ocean and so the Red Sea. As early as 1499 Vasco da Gama bombarded Mogadishu, which was then an Arabian trading post, and is now capital of Somalia. By 1520 the first ambassador to Ethiopia had landed, harbinger of an ambitious plan. This was to enlist the aid of Prester John or his successor in the launching of an expedition against Mecca. It was part of a latterday crusade, for Islam lay, a formidable barrier, athwart the land routes from Europe to farther Asia, and it was for this reason that the great voyages round Africa had been made, to open up a new way. Now there might be the opportunity to strike right at the heart of Islam. Had the plan come off, who can calculate its consequences? It would have been a shattering spiritual blow to millions of Muslims to have had to prostrate themselves so frequently in the direction of a sacked Mecca.

Contact with Portugal proved, for the Ethiopians, a somewhat ambiguous matter. Not long after the first embassy the Empire was badly defeated and ravaged by a holy war out of Somali country, under a charismatic and ferocious Imam. The highlands were widely and terribly plundered, and the finest shrines of Christianity were devastated. The Emperor was forced to call upon the Portuguese for aid, and they sent Don Christofe da Gama and a few hundred volunteers, together with cannons and muskets. Though the Don, initially successful, was captured, tortured, killed and quartered, the new Emperor Claudius was able to defeat the Imam after a bitter campaign. The surviving Portuguese stayed on and took Ethiopian wives, though they retained their Catholic faith, and this prepared the way for events which took place some sixty years later.

Part of the deal whereby the Portuguese sent in their force was that in due course Latin Christianity would be introduced into the country. Jesuit fathers accordingly set up houses at Adowa and near Lake Tana. They began using Amharic for commentaries and other theological works, and for articulate preaching, thus replacing the mumbo-jumbo that Ge'ez had in effect become. They were also energetic in architecture and the arts, important in the period after the tragic devastation wrought by the Imam's forces. In 1608 a new and powerful monarch came to the throne, called Susenyos. Though he expanded, reformed and consolidated the Empire, he greatly shocked many of his subjects by converting, in 1621, to the Catholic faith.

The Jesuits had based much of their work on the Portuguese families, and these in turn had influenced other noble families. Thus there was already a nucleus of converts at court when Susenyos proclaimed his faith. Under a Latin patriarch, Ethiopian religion was to be transformed. However, the pace was too brusque and fast. Already the observance of the Sabbath (Saturday) had been abolished, to fall into line with Latin custom. All Ethiopians were to be re-baptized (though since annual baptism was a local custom, the demand was not perceived as too radical: but it does tell us a lot about Jesuit attitudes to Ethiopia's ancient faith, which had in many respects travelled a shorter distance from early Christianity than had the Pope). The arks were to be removed from the shrines, Ge'ez was to be replaced by Latin and various saints were to be banished from the calendar. All this the Emperor tried to impose by force, and wielding cruel punishments. However decadent the Ethiopian religious hierarchy may have been in an age which had seen so much misery and disruption, the new order was unacceptable to a large part of the people, and the net result was revolt and civil war. Though Susenyos won after bloody fighting, his son appealed to him, pleading that the dead were his countrymen and former co-religionists. The price of the new faith was too high; and Susenyos, proclaiming that his subjects could return to their altars and former liturgy, abdicated.

Briefly, these events had two sides. The inner feeling of so many Ethiopians that their Church, with its Ge'ez, its priests, scribes, painted shrines, festivals, confessionals, meteoric

54

monks and holy men, bishops, magical rites, ancient foundation, saints and the protection of St George and the Virgin,
was essentially *theirs*. It was part of the fabric both of local
existence and of the federal Empire; and it was something
which they had fought for against the cruel depredations of
the Islam in recent memory, some two or three generations
back. Second, on the other side the Portuguese had their
ideology, but it was a very different one. The papacy had
awarded them the East, in effect, and before that Africa. The
Jesuits stood for a universal Church, and for a kind of transnational conformity. So nations, whether they were thinking
of the English or the Ethiopians, which diverged from the main
tradition should be brought into the single structure. There was
no Roman Empire, but still a spiritual one, and for that as
soldiers of Christ the Jesuits fought. And the uniate solution
scarcely appealed to them in the Ethiopian context, that is
the solution whereby a branch of Eastern Christianity could
retain its own liturgy and customs but acknowledge the
supremacy of the Roman Pope. This had the merit of creating
unity in diversity.

Thus the events up to 1642 showed a profound clash of
ideologies. For all the dynamism of the Jesuits, which left its
imprint in Ethiopian literature, architecture and art, the new
uniformity which they tried to impose was an alien one. And
the experiment created an anti-Western backlash. The
Jesuits, like other missionaries and politicians before and since,
were not aware enough of the attractions of religious and
ideological pluralism. The irony is that they were failing to
see something to which the leaders at the crucial Council of
Chalcedon were also blind, and which lay at the root of the
Coptic rebellion, and so at the roots of Ethiopian Christianity.

It will be recalled that the first great ecumenical Council
after Constantine's revolutionary change of attitude towards
Christianity had been called because a new faith for the
Empire should avoid factional division. A similar motive
later lay behind Chalcedon, in 451. But here the issue focussed
not so directly upon Christ's status in relation to the Father,
but rather upon his constitution: did he have two natures,

one divine and one human, or one?

The question had a liturgical and spiritual significance, as well as a political background. It had, for example, become common in Eastern piety to refer to the Virgin as *Theotokos*, God-bearer (that is, mother of God). But Christ and the Father are one, and Mary is not mother of the Father. Surely it is only in respect of Christ's *human* nature that she is the mother. Yet if we say he has two natures. one divine, the other human, is this not splitting him in two? The whole issue was fraught with peril: if alternatively you say that Christ had a human body, but the Logos as soul, then it made his humanity a sham – he was not really like us, yet the Church had from early times insisted that he was.

The problems can be seen by the fate of Nestorius, who had become Patriarch of Constantinople, but who was dislodged as a result of the Council of Ephesus. One of his chaplains had in a sermon preached against the Theotokos title. Since the title had been in use for some time, and expressed a strong strand of growing devotion towards the Virgin Mary, the attack scandalized many, but despite this Nestorius, fervent in his desire to root out possible heresies, began a series of sermons arguing against the Theotokos, chiefly because he considered that it involved an implicit return to Arianism. Actually, many who used the title interpreted it as doing the opposite, insisting on Christ's fully divine nature. However, Nestorius' opponents considered that he taught two natures in a way which split up Christ, turning him in effect into two Persons, one divine and the other human. This was not really the case – Nestorius' intentions were quite orthodox, and he was highly concerned to avoid underplaying Christ's humanity, but the way he expressed his position gave a handle to his enemies, who succeeded in having him condemned, after much turbulence and chicanery, at the Council of Ephesus in 431. The Emperor Theodosius sent him back to his monastery near Antioch, and later he was exiled.

Much of the opposition to Nestorius emanated from Egypt and in particular from Cyril, Patriarch of Alexandria. There were political aspects of the struggle, which involved a tug of war between Constantinople, Rome, Antioch and Alexandra. Roughly, Ephesus was a consequence of the combination of Rome and Alexandria against the delegates from Antioch, who supported Nestorius. Likewise the Council of Chalcedon, called to finalize the matter of Christ's natures, involved a political struggle, which was resolved somewhat ambiguously. From one point of view Rome came off best, in that the doctrines propounded by Pope Leo in the so-called *Tome of Leo* were accepted and embodied in a creed – the Nicene-Constantinopolitan Creed, sometimes confusingly referred to as the Nicene Creed. From another point of view Rome's authority was not fully acknowledged as she might have wished, in that the Emperor affirmed the equal status of Rome and Constantinople. Antioch's position was perhaps weakened by the elevation of Jerusalem to be the seat of a Patriarch, and as we shall see Chalcedon proved to be less a cause of unity than a signal for further division.

Part of the definition arrived at at Chalcedon was as follows:

> Like us in all respects, apart from sin; as regards his Godhead, begotten of the Father before the ages, but yet as regards his manhood begotten, for us men and our salvation, of Mary the Virgin, the God-bearer; one and the same Christ, Son, Lord, Only-begotten, recognized in two natures, without confusion, without change, without division, without separation; the distinction of natures being in no way annulled by the union, but rather the characteristics of each nature being preserved and coming together to form one person and subsistence, not as parted or separated into two persons, but one and the same Son and Only-begotten God the Word, Lord Jesus Christ; even as the prophets from earliest times spoke of him, and our Lord Jesus Christ himself taught us, and the creed of the Fathers has handed down to us.

Briefly: there are two natures fused into one. On the whole, but only on the whole, the Chalcedonian formulae brought stability. Part of the trouble was how to bring definitions to bear upon a paradoxical myth.

But it was not long before some Eastern Churches began to

break away. The unity achieved through the Council was partially illusory. The Eastern Churches in Syria, Egypt, Armenia and elsewhere were destined to break away, adopting either Monophysitism, i.e. the doctrine of one nature, or Nestorianism. Thus the Persian Church, partly to show its independence of a foreign power (the Roman Empire) became Nestorian, and proved to be powerfully dedicated to mission – spreading the Nestorian faith as far as China and influencing the faith too of the St Thomas Christians in south India, which had early roots and a Syriac liturgy. If now Nestorianism only comprises a little over 100,000 members scattered in Syria, Iraq, Persia and elsewhere, this gives an inadequate conception of its past glories; for it was, of course, much affected by the great wave of Islam which swept over the area and dimmed, but did not quench, its light. In the move towards Monophysitism in Syria, Armenia and Egypt, a kind of nationalism was involved, together with a tendency in devotion and liturgy to stress greatly the divine character of Christ and the sacred status of the Theotokos. The nationalism, if we can call it such, arose from the fact that in Egypt and elsewhere in the Middle East, the cultures had a strong Semitic or other non-Hellenistic base. It was not long before armed monks in Jerusalem had rejected Chalcedon, and they had to be put down bloodily. Soon Egypt turned against it also, and 'One Nature' became in effect a national and partisan slogan. Despite various attempts to reconcile the parties, Chalcedon was the main occasion of the establishment of a separate Coptic Church in Egypt. Here was a culturally separate branch of Orthodoxy, not acknowledging the results of an ecumenical Council. Chalcedon did not, then, bring unity, but defined the first great juncture in the history of the Christian Church. In any event Rome and Constantinople were beginning to drift apart. What would emerge into a later age was a three-fold Christianity – Latin, Greek and Eastern, largely Semitic, of which Ethiopian Christianity with its close traditional ties to Egypt formed a part.

The seventh century perceived the formation and colossal expansion of Islam, the inauguration of a quite new civilization in the Middle East and beyond. It was a civilization not wholly favourable to, though not altogether disastrous for, Christianity. Syrian and Palestinian Christians, for instance, might be restrained by the new rule, but they had after all through it escaped the often imperious religious and fiscal demands of the Byzantines. The revolt over Chalcedon prepared the way for a measure of co-operation with the conquering faith which had arrived so unexpectedly out of the deserts and cities of Arabia. Yet Islam was bound to be a great magnet which largely drew to itself the Christian populations of the Middle East. Only minorities clung to the various churches.

Thus two events befell the Semitic style of Christianity – the Fall of Jerusalem in 70, which seriously weakened a development of the Christian faith which would have momentously affected our total understanding of the tradition; and then the outburst of Islam, which submerged so much of Semitic Christianity and left only three major anti-Chalcedonian Churches outside its embrace – the Armenian, the Ethiopian and the Egyptian.

If Alexandria was one of the main foci of this style of Christianity, it also through its learning, wealth and monastic traditions was bound to have an influence upon Ethiopia to the far south-east, in those three centuries before the Islamic conquest, and more quietly still thereafter. Egypt was the main conduit through which the faith flowed into the mountain Empire. Thus the Patriarch or Abuna as head of the Ethiopian Church was almost invariably an Egyptian as often were the bishops. Thus even if in many respects the customs and dynamics of Ethiopia differed from those of Coptic Egypt, there remained an ecclesiastical and spiritual bond between the two regions. This gave Ethiopia an extra line of ancestry in addition to those going back to Solomon to which we have already referred.

There had been a powerful pre-Christian civilization based on the northern region and the imperial city of Aksum. The new faith did not begin to permeate Ethiopia until the mid part of the fourth century, at least in any substantial way. Already Judaic influences were strong, but there was too a mixed indigenous complex of cults, of the Arwe or Serpent. Thus as ancient texts indicate, the people were partly under Mosaic law and in part they worshipped the Serpent. No wonder St George is patron saint of Ethiopia – his slaying of the Serpent-dragon is a mythic representation of the conquest of the older cult by Christianity (just as St Patrick's banishment of the snakes from Ireland reflects a similar cultic victory). Other elements flowed in from pre-Islamic Arabian religion: for instance, the triad of Venus, the Sun and the Moon as embodying divinities. Incidentally the Sun was feminine (in most cultures it is male) and this substructure of devotion to the Sun may be reflected in the later high reverence towards Mary the Mother of God, who rates no less than thirty-three festivals in the Ethiopian calendar.

The conversion of Ethiopia is said to have stemmed from the work of two brothers called Frumentius and Edesius from Tigre, who worked in Aksum. The former was consecrated bishop by St Athanasius in Alexandria, and this was the beginning of the formal link between Ethiopia and Egypt. The arrangement, however, was ended after the return of Hailé Selassie to his Empire in 1941, after the Italian domination had been broken by the British Army. He signed a new agreement to indigenize the office, in that though the See of Saint Mark in Alexandria would participate in the election, the person elected would have to be an Ethiopian monk.

The fact that as elsewhere in the Orthodox-related segment of Christendom a bishop had to be a monk, though a priest could be married, means that monasticism has traditionally been an integral presupposition of Ethiopian Christianity. Indeed, the basic framework of monasticism in the country derives from the two great figures of Egyptian asceticism, St Anthony and St Pachomius. It was indeed out of Egypt that the mingled ideals of hermit and monk radiated. In Ethiopia, geography, providing soaring cliffs and wild sites for recluses to occupy, conspired with the austerities of Anthony to shape the monastic spirit of Ethiopian Christianity – as witness for instance the great rocky cliff-perching monastic village of Debra-Damo in the old imperial Tigre region, which is only accessible like some similar locations in Greece by rope. In principle, however inhospitable the milieu, monks are supposed to make their own living by labouring, not by begging. The same applies to married priests. The condition is not too difficult to fulfil for traditionally the churches and monastic foundations are landholders, sometimes on a grand scale. As for true hermits (as distinguished from those who belong to a group focussed on a particular monastery), some can survive on wild plants.

The Egyptian connection also involved the maintenance of monks at several communities in Egypt, and above all at the monastery of St Anthony near the Gulf of Suez. There a number of important Coptic works were translated into Ge'ez. But over a long period the most important foundation has been that at Debra Libanos, which is north of the modern capital of Addis Ababa. The prior of this prestigious foundation was, unlike the Abuna, an Ethiopian and was in effect the chief administrator of the Church, and confessor to and close adviser of the Emperor. Here again perchance we see an ancient passion for a triadic structure, in which Emperor, Abuna and Ichege traditionally saw jointly to the temporal and spiritual concerns of Ethiopia.

The Emperor wielded the greatest power, but subject somewhat to the other two. The importance of the Ichege lay in the weight of the Church itself as a massive landholder within the feudal structure, and in the advisory capacity he wielded close to the Emperor. The importance of the Abuna lay in his being a living symbol of the ideology, both Christian and imperial, which cemented the loose and plural empire together. The fact that the Abuna was Egyptian until quite recently therefore was not altogether so worrisome for Ethiopians as might have been expected, and indeed reinforced the sense of Christian gravity, since it expressed an ancient link to the sources of the faith. Thus an integrated system existed at the top, and the Jesuit attempt to give the Abuna a Catholic cast represented a profound disturbance of the existing pattern. For that expressed Ethiopian reverence for sacred emperor, patriarchal priest and supreme monk.

The very virtues of the system (operating, however, in a context of bursts of warfare and mountainous poverty), stretching from feudal times into the modern epoch, made it hard or impossible for Ethiopian Christianity to do two things which other forms sometimes achieve. Though, firstly, it can in a sense be a light, in its own strange way, to the Gentiles – it is an example of the Christian faith to non-Ethiopians – it can scarcely be a missionary type of Christianity, so deeply are its institutions embedded in a particular history and area. The price of success in fitting one culture is failure to fit others, and, of course, Coptic Christianity is not alone in this condition. Indeed, the various remnants of Eastern Christianity outside Orthodoxy are in effect similarly disposed.

Second, the feudal success of the Church presents a host of problems of adaptation through modern social change and (more recently) revolution. True, the Ethiopian Church opened up a new higher seminary in Addis Ababa and has moved in other ways to do something about the education of at least the clerical elite. In becoming involved in the work of the World Council of Churches it has felt an ecumenical breeze blowing through it. But inevitably there has grown a gap between the conservative ideals of the Church and the aspirations of younger folk touched by the forces of modern education, technology and social thinking. The ideals of the Mengistu regime are bloodily far removed from those of the old imperial tradition. Haile Selassie's paternal moves towards modernization themselves accelerated his own demise: even the Lion of Judah could not learn new tricks. The ideals of the old religion were perhaps seen in its liturgical complexities and holy dancing, but this dimension of faith also contained a strength and weakness which helps us to understand further its modern crisis.

If priests and monks represent two poises of sacredness, respectively concerned with ritual and other-worldliness, there was a third class of persons closely employed both in the cult and beyond it in that penumbra of religion often called magic. These people are known as *debterras*. Their primary art is to sing, and they must study over a long period not merely the complexities of traditional religious music, but also the sacred language of Ge'ez. Though their knowledge is archaic, they have traditionally formed the learned class and so have been employed often in administration. Also, they often get involved in the lore which controls the magic of life and in the spells and formulae which can ward off evil and disease and can out-face the spirits which threaten existence. In some ways they hark back to the demonology which pervades the New Testament, but they operate more particularly at the interface with Ethiopian magic.

But primarily they are cantors, for much of Ethiopian Christianity is danced out and sung. The cycle of the year, the calendar of feasts and liturgical celebrations are elaborate; the instruments and chants are challenging to master; and so the expertise of the *debterra* has a practical dimension which touches the daily life of ordinary people, and because it is mysterious it brings them prestige. By comparison the priests have little knowledge – most often their vocation comes with parentage, and they learn the liturgy by imitating their fathers. Music and learning, then, traditionally belong to the cantor class. But they also deal, as we have seen, in magic, at the boundary between the numinous power of the Christian religion and the old conceptions of an agricultural society. Judaic, Christian and pre-Christian elements blend together in Ethiopian religion, headily. Yet the magic is after all an aspect of pre-modern medicine and technology. In most cultures, ordinary folk expect the religion or ideology to deliver goods here and now, as well as if possible in the beyond. But the crisis is acute, in such a religion, with a revolution in knowledge. This is where modern Ethiopia is riven between its old ideals and the up-to-date magic of scientific medicine, technology and Marxism.

In its fusion of Jewish, Christian and African motifs, the Ethiopian tradition has shown, right into modern times, a variant on the high imperial theme once expressed differently in Byzantium. In doing so it created a world, rooted in the Fathers, independent through the Monophysite teaching, Eastern in spirit, a Church of the circumcision, capable of change yet intensely conservative. Its mythology is rich. The roots in the religion of Solomon, the use of Old and New Testaments, the emphasis on the place of Mary in the drama of salvation, the story of St George and the myriad other saints, the memory of the desert ascetics – all these elements were welded into a symbolism rich in ritual enactment. They can be seen too in the distinctive art which Ethiopia created: the mature, bearded Saviour is there, the Virgin, the Disciples and the Evangelists, clad in traditional long robes; holy saints on chargers battling with dragons and the supernatural evils of the world; armed and winged archangels attending the Virgin and the Child, their feathers forming a canopy over them, the threesome of greybeards, the Trinity, like clones in their features – elderly triplets signifying thus the identity of the Three-in-One – and all with calm, quizzical features, through which the divine dimension looks through the visible on to the created world. And the rooting of the faith in the very land of Ethiopia is perceived in the monolithic rock-hewn churches, in which the square and the cruciform impose new shapes upon the serendipities of nature.

The distance from Tigre to the shores of India is great – India where the St Thomas Christians implanted an ancient Eastern Christianity; but the distance to America is much greater – America in which the plain white wooden churches of New England provide a very different presentation of the traditions of the faith.

4

The Transformations of Sweden

The Western Church was proud of its antiquity, persistence and authority; but pride comes before a fall. Western Christianity in the sixteenth century broke apart, and the first fissure in the cracking edifice was caused by Martin Luther, one of the few people to have given his name to a whole way of life. Rome from beyond the Alps heard the creakings in the German Church, but she was not to know that she would lose much of northern Europe. Lutheranism conquered Scandinavia as well as great tracts of Germany, and in Sweden it expressed itself in a classical form. In contemplating Sweden we perceive a major form of Protestantism.

Protestantism? Does it always protest? I remember staying with a pastor in the village of Hammarö near Karlstad in central Sweden, in his delightful vicarage by a lake, his garden frequented in the early morning by occasional deer from the woods coming to munch the dropped apples of his orchard. He was a good man, prospering modestly in his good vocation, salaried by the State. He took me to his church, and in an annexed building showed me the library of files he had to keep of marriages, births and deaths. Partly he preached and saw to his flock, but partly too he was a bureaucrat. The roots of this particular relationship between Church and State go back to Luther. Is the bond too cosy? It is not for us here to judge, beyond seeing that the Reformation led, in its principal early direction, towards the conception of national Churches.

For my pastor the files had a human significance beyond their contents: the fact of registering a birth or whatever brought people inevitably to him – people who for the most part rarely worshipped in his church. For despite its impressive history, the Swedish church is ill-attended. It is an oddity, however, that though in Sweden itself there is little formal observance of the national faith, the Swedes who migrated to America, which they did in great numbers in the nineteenth century, Sweden then being desperately poor and over-populated, have tended to practise their religion far more. The New World, in its strangeness, gave them a new sense of roots, and new opportunity eroded alienation.

What then is the ancestry of my friend the pastor at Hammarö?

Already we have seen that Christianity, hemmed in from the south by the curling arms of Islam, looked more intensely northwards in its missionary gaze. Of all northerners of the period the most formidable were the legendary Scandinavians. Wherever there were seas and rivers the Vikings sent their long ships – to England, Ireland, Normandy, throughout the Baltic, deep into what became Russia, down the Volga and through the Black Sea to the gates of Byzantium and the Mediterranean. Iceland was soon to be colonized and the icy rim of Greenland, and the ships went even as far as Newfoundland. The Scandinavians were sustained by their own brand of Germanic religion – their gods live on, indeed, in the names of the English days of the week: sun and moon, Wotan and Thor. But their conquests brought them contact with a Christianity of renewed prestige – its heart in Rome, still a magical name with which to conjure, and showing both piety and scholarship it was 'modern' compared with northern forms of paganism. It had a cosmology, a system of salvation, a pattern of social order to commend. It could be attractive as a new ideological framework for rulers to use in reshaping and consolidating society. For all that it was slow in permeating Scandinavia, and it was not till the end of the eleventh century that it had taken a near total grip upon the people of the northlands. Eventually three provinces of the Church were established, one based on Lund, a city in southern Sweden (though it was Danish till the mid part of the seventeenth century), and stretching over Denmark; another at the ancient sacred spot of Uppsala not far from modern Stockholm, stretching over most of Sweden and Christian parts of Finland; and the third at Trondheim on the coast of Norway, which looked not just to Norway itself but also to Iceland, Greenland, the Faroes, the Orkneys, the Shetland Islands, Dublin and the Isle of Man.

Though there had been missionaries, marriages with Christian women and occasional conversions, the main force behind the Christianization of Scandinavia was the decision of their rulers to adopt the potent new faith. Some of the old religion was woven into the new. Roughly speaking, then, Scandinavian Christianity has always been official, and the same principle was evident in Reformation times.

Luther broke with Rome, though he did not intend to, as a result of a spiritual struggle within himself and its expression through a new found theology at variance with the spirit of some aspects of Roman religion; but he could scarcely have foreseen that for many rulers and others in the Germany of his day the new doctrines could be a convenient vehicle for casting off transalpine authority. The sixteenth century was a time of the forming of nation states: royal muscles were being flexed and popular sentiment harnessed. So Lutheranism was bound very early on to acquire a political significance. In Central Europe the results proved tragic, for the new instability of relations brought warfare, ultimately the bitter Thirty Years' War. Early on there were the hostilities and persecutions which led up to the Peace of Augsburg (1555) which established the principle later to be dubbed by the Latin tag *cuius regio eius religio* (literally 'of whom the region, of him the religion'): for every principality its own religion. One of the interesting provisions of this treaty was that minority groups should be free to emigrate, their right to sell property and so on unimpeded (would our own twentieth century not benefit by this arrangement?). Europe was thus carved up along religious lines.

By the end of the sixteenth century, Europe was divided up as follows: north Germany down to the fringes of Bavaria was largely Protestant, as were Scandinavia, East Prussia, Estonia and Latvia. In these countries the religion was Lutheranism, though there were here and there, as in Sweden, some admixtures of Calvinism. England had gone over to Reform, though in its own manner; Scotland to Calvinism, as also areas of Switzerland and the Low Countries. In Eastern Europe the situation was mixed, but, save in Bohemia, Catholicism was dominant. In France Catholicism remained the majority faith, but lived in tension with Protestantism. Partly because of the strenuous work of the Counter-Reformation, southern Europe stayed Catholic, as did Ireland, looking not only to its ancient Christian heritage but to its dislike of England. The right to emigrate was well implanted in the European imagination, and when the New World opened up, minority emigrants became a potent force in the political and religious liberty and pluralism which animated America.

The human trigger of the changes that brought about these new dispensations of Christianity was Martin Luther. As Roland Bainton, famous historian of the Reformation, remarked significantly, Luther was a German. German nationalism had yet to be born, but he was one of its parents. His strong sense of the German tongue and of the German ethos were expressed magnificently and formatively in his hymns, writings and translations of the scriptures. The invention of the printing press was a condition of the amazing spread of his ideas and of his earthy German independence of spirit. Yet he was a loyal son of the Church. He had deep criticisms of the traffic in indulgences, and unhappy memories of the unseemly side of holy Rome when he visited it; but he was an Augustinian monk and university teacher of theology. He had not precisely intended his spiritual crisis and its solution to bring about so great and thunderous a roll of events. To understand, though, the new form of Christianity which he helped to forge, we need to look to his spiritual problem and his understanding of scripture.

Luther was a man in the grip of the numinous; he was overwhelmed with awe. His God was a late medieval giant. He was committed to God through his monkish profession, and yet God was frightening: condemning the damned to hell, judging men, ruling the universe. The Son was no Jesus meek and mild, but bound up too in the rightful vengeance which was the prerogative of the Lord; while the Spirit sanctified and permeated a Church liable to burn the unbeliever and the heretic. He felt in an acute form the sense of alienation from God which many remedied through interceding with the Virgin and the saints.

One of the things which came to his help in his increasing despair, which he felt however faithfully he carried out his obligations as an Augustinian monk, in an order noted for its austerity and learning, was the pondering of the psalm which Jesus is reported as having quoted from the cross: 'My God, my God, why have you forsaken me?' If even Jesus could feel abandoned, then Luther's own sense of helplessness did not escape a remedy. He came to see that salvation is not through works, through the meticulous and even desperate attempt to obey the rules in order to get into God's good graces, but rather by faith alone.

Though some have not shrunk from the inference that if that is so everything in the way of conduct is permissible, Luther intended no such moral orgy inference. His new found freedom was of a different order, and it flowed both from the logic of religion and the logic of the scriptures.

Even if we begin with the awful numinous majesty of God, we can see light for the sinner. For God in his uniqueness is uniquely holy. If any one is to gain salvation, that is to partake of holiness, that result must flow from God, not from man. Given too that in the Christian faith it is God's loving action in becoming man and suffering on behalf of mankind that is the central act of the drama of redemption, it is doubly logical that man is saved not by any action of his own, but through the loving action of God. All that a person can do is turn to God in faith. This is at the heart of the Pauline message – and it is perhaps no coincidence that in certain ways Luther echoes Paul's own career and psychology. Man cannot justify himself, then, and only by faith can he be justified. A practical consequence of this perception of the situation was Luther's attack upon indulgences. The debate which he initiated when he posted ninety-five propositions for debate at the cathedral door in Wittenberg were fairly strong, but their consequences could hardly be predicted.

Indulgences were in their own way a logical deduction

from the general doctrine of the Church. If it were true that the Popes were successors of St Peter, and if to him had been entrusted the keys of the kingdom, the Church could, under the Pope, grant remission from purgatory, that lengthy penitential state which sinners not in a state of mortal sin would undergo before paradise. Now it is true that the sale of indulgences gave the Church's dispensation a venal air, especially when the system was under strain in order to pay for the great new basilica in Rome, to replace the old St Peter's. Part of the trouble was that the Church's mediation between man and God was, through the sale of indulgences, made mechanical and commercial, even if there were a certain outer logic on its side. But this was not Luther's sole objection: much more deeply, the system offended against true theology as he saw it and as he interpreted it in the New Testament.

Luther's theological objections to indulgences were subversive, for they cut at the doctrinal foundations of the Church of Rome. They in fact cut at the root of the whole theory of the Church as mediator between God and man. If salvation was by faith alone, then ultimately all the good works of Christendom were of no avail – pilgrimages, confessionals and acts of penitence, fasting, celibacy and so forth. Paradoxically the very numinousness of God in the end exalted the individual: if in his abasement he could do nothing, he was the only one who could have faith. Out of what was a subsidiary issue, to be debated in Wittenberg in 1517, the general assault on the Roman system flowed. When he was challenged, Luther fought back sturdily, like an ox, and in the development of his revolutionary ideas he went far beyond his own personal crisis.

One major consequence of his position and of the Reformation was the collapse, in Protestant lands, of the monastic system. Though Luther himself and some other Reformers were much influenced by mysticism in the sense that they looked to inner experience as vital to the understanding of the faith, the general effect was a decline in the contemplative life. There was thus a shift in the characteristic style of Protestant spirituality.

Another effect of Luther's ideas was that a new arrangement had to be worked out regarding the relations between Church and State. Generally, each nation or principality could define its religious sphere, independently of Rome. With the growth of nationalism, to which as we have seen Luther markedly contributed, it was natural for the Church to fall under the domination of the political arm, and Luther's teaching that Church and State had very different aims could issue in a passive acceptance of political regimes. This has often led Lutheran churchmen into dilemmas, as during the Nazi period.

Third, Luther made Christian ideas accessible to the people. The vernacular, rather than Latin, ruled. This meant a move towards a democracy of knowledge which was to have profound effects on the Western world. But in the meantime the Bible not only had wide distribution through the printing presses; it became a kind of portable sacrament and oracle, and for many a printed Pope. Perhaps the presses and the currents of humanism present in Luther's day would have released a mass-produced vernacular Bible on the world in any case – already it was happening, for instance through William Tyndale. But the Reformation made the spread of religious ideas more swift and volatile, and emphasized the fact that the word of God did not have to be mediated by priests, but was directly accessible to the individual.

Revolutionary as Luther was in some ways, he was for all that rather conservative in others. The Lutheran Churches, as they came to be called, tended to retain bishops – in Sweden, for instance, where the doctrine of Apostolic Succession was also retained – that is that there is a chain of consecration of bishops going right back to the early Church and the Apostles, thus guaranteeing the validity of the ministry. The Eucharist was changed into the vernacular, it is true; but its general shape was kept; and in a Swedish Lutheran Church, with its statues, candles, crucifixes, the atmosphere on the surface is not so distant from that in a Roman Catholic church. But there is, in the Eucharist, and in the disposition of the church, an inner difference between Lutheranism and traditional Catholicism.

71

Rome, infused with high medieval philosophical achievement and a love of legal definition inherited from the old Empire, still a potent myth and memory, considered that the bread and wine were, in the mass, changed in substance: though the appearance and the material qualities remained the same, in essence they changed into Christ's body and blood. There was a sort of hardness and literalism about the doctrine. It followed that if the elements were not consumed at the mass they had to be preserved reverently, say for the sick or the next mass. As we have noted, it was a short step to using the elements more or less independently of the mass: elaborate containers for them were fashioned, and their holy properties tapped in various ways by the faithful. The whole approach expressed an important aspect of Roman Catholic religious life: a sort of concretion of the numinous. But it was an approach swept aside by Luther as redolent of magic. For him, rather, the Eucharist implies that Christ is really present to the faithful, but not through a change of the substance of the bread and wine.

Yet a strange paradox afflicted the successors of Luther in Scandinavia and elsewhere. Though Lutheranism in many ways was a humane reinterpretation of Christianity, with its emphasis on individual conscience, and while it was one of the ancestors of modern democratic ideas, yet it also was establishmentarian. It was a State religion imposed upon the people – at least in the sense that in Sweden and elsewhere it was not possible for a citizen to belong to any other form of Christianity, such as Roman Catholicism and Calvinism (even if some Calvinist ideas were incorporated into Church thinking as also was the case in England). Only foreigners were allowed to practise Catholicism, etc. The paradox then is that while salvation is seen very much as an affair of the individual's faith, Church order is dictated collectively.

The fact that Lutheranism spread often from above, for reasons of state and national independence, and that its support was more evident among the educated, lies behind the decay of formal religion among the lower classes. In its magicality, Catholicism had subsumed elements from pre-Christian religion in a way which made sense to the peasants and the poor. The decline was accelerated by the Industrial Revolution.

That came late to Sweden, in the latter half of the nineteenth century. The population had been growing, putting much pressure on the land, eased in part, though, by migration to the United States, where a new rural landscape was available in the Midwest. Partly too it was eased by migration to the cities and the new settlements which grew up along the railroad tracks. The old parish system could hardly cope: town parishes could become overwhelmingly crowded. The vernacular language of the Reformation had hardened into an archaic and often unintelligible lingo, alien to the Swedish worker. Furthermore, the ordinary man was alienated by the bourgeois ethos of the churches. Going to service on Sunday meant dressing up: in poverty-stricken Sweden, how could the ordinary man do this properly? No suit, no faith!

Politics did not help the Church either. Marxist ideas seeped into the growing workers' movements, though the main drive of the Scandinavian labour movement was Social Democratic, humanistic and libertarian in aim, but for all that embroiled in stormy and bitter conflicts with the employers. Often the clergy sided with the latter and with the landowners, and so the Church was frequently the target of strong and bitter criticism. Demands were launched for the sundering of the bond between Church and State. With the voices for disestablishment were mingled those calling for the widening of religious instruction in schools, to make it non-denominational, and for the nationalization of much Church property. Anticlericalism flourished, then, in the labour movement. As a reaction the clergy were often driven into a stance against the new socialism; and Lutheranism was in effect paying for its old advantages in the new social context. Moreover, the very success of social democracy in the period after World War I conflicted with the Church's interest, for the new welfare state being created seemed to take away the rationale of the old parish system, which had traditionally ministered to the needs of the poor and sick. Hence it comes about that the pastor can turn out to be, like the pastor of Hammarö, a respected

73

member of the community ministering to a minority in church and to the majority by the final rump of social work, the registering of births, deaths and marriages. The Church therefore was, throughout the Industrial Revolution, going through a crisis of identity. Yet it can also be said that in some measure the humanism of the Social Democratic movement owed something to the Protestant heritage: it was, so to say, an unruly offspring, one of whose parents was the Church.

With variations, a rather similar profile can be drawn of the other Scandinavian Churches. Yet Iceland is to some degree an exception, and the history of its conversion is both well attested and of deep interest. Before I tell the story, let us reflect briefly about this amazing island, half-way from Scandinavia to the American continent, of which the old Icelanders had merely heard rumours. Iceland is a mountainous, volcanic, virtually treeless, winter-dark, cold and glittering country, seamed with fjords, attractive therefore to the Norsemen who settled there in the ninth century. Before it had been empty of humans save the occasional Celtic hermit.

The story of such Irish ascetics is surprising in its own right. Their name, *papar*, is found numerously in Icelandic place names, attesting to their amazing wanderlust ever outwards from human settlement in the pursuit of solitude. The legend that St Brendan sailed in a coracle to America might just have been possible. The intrepid holy men went at least as far as Iceland, and were forerunners of those who later settled the island, chiefly Norse who had intermingled with the Irish and Scots. So one could speak of a trace of Christianity already on the Icelandic coast, and some influence already in the mixed culture from which they came. Celtic Christianity was indeed in the centuries from St Ninian onwards (from the fourth century) a flourishing faith. But it by no means followed that the conversion of Iceland was easy: rather, it occurred as a result of a traumatic episode in the story of that rugged country.

The Icelanders were divided. Their old culture involved sacrifices, the repetition of heroic myths, a virile and tough attitude to life. It seemed incompatible with Christianity, dimly understood by many and adhered to by a few. Yet the

74

island retained bonds with Norway and northern Europe, and in Norway towards the end of the tenth century the king, Olaf Tryggvason (Olaf, son of Tryggva), was eager to propagate the faith. He was rough in his piety, and it seems that during the year 996 on a visit to Iceland he and his retainers burnt idols and demolished temples. The inhabitants were scarcely amused, and the Allthing or assembly dealing with law issued orders against such sacrilege. Still, the debate as to whether Iceland should have one religion or two continued. Imagine the place: the population was widely dispersed under different chiefs, and though there was a highly developed law it incorporated some of the older religious ideas and practices in its fabric. If the island had two allegiances, this boded trouble, and in a harsh environment disputation was not conducive to survival. A decision had to be made, and so it was in principle at a meeting of the Allthing held in the fateful and significant year 1000, at the start of a new Christian millennium.

Two chiefs who had been to Norway were on the side of Christianity, and others argued against: the storms of debate could have issued in violence, but it was decided to leave the decision to an arbitrator – a non-Christian lawgiver. He went into the hut erected for the meeting and lay there all day and all night, wrapped in a cloak and a trance, culling sacred dreams doubtless for insight. His verdict was sage: Christianity should reign but certain aspects of the older religious tradition should continue, if necessary in secret. Iceland thus became officially Christian, though not for another fifty years or so was the first Icelandic bishop ordained. Yet though the first conversion was by agreement, the second, to the Reformation, was not really so, for by the sixteenth century Iceland was under Danish rule, and the new state religion was imposed upon the Icelanders by King Christian III. It is true that through the labours of various people and above all of Gudbrandur Thorlaksson (1541–1627), a great reformer and father of the Icelandic Bible, the new faith became acceptable. But its imposition from above may be a reason why ultimately Icelanders were to be sparse in their observance: as is the case in much of Scandinavian Lutheranism.

It is interesting that by contrast American Lutheranism, including its Scandinavian – chiefly Swedish – variety, has flourished so significantly. This was partly because of the conditions of the new land, as we shall see in the next chapter. It was partly due to revivalism, giving the faith a more evangelical character. Not surprisingly, one branch, the Missouri synod, has taken a conservatively biblical turn.

If the challenge of modernity and industrialism has been one challenge to Lutheranism in the last two centuries, another has been the need to reconcile its evangelical vision derived from the revolutionary ideas of Luther to the conservatism of its institutions. At an intellectual level, it was remarkably successful, since Lutheran biblical and theological scholarship was at the leading edge of Protestant and Christian thought in the nineteenth and twentieth centuries. Another problem, intertwined somewhat with intellectual questions, as it happens, was more intriguing and terrible: how to deal with the Nazi menace. A black period, this, pierced by but a few shafts of light.

To see it in perspective, let us retrace our steps to the updating of Christianity to which Lutheranism so signally contributed in the period after the Enlightenment, which was to have such widespread political and other effects. In the nineteenth century scholars turned increasingly to the study of history, partly under the inspiration of the mighty Hegel. It was inevitable that scientific methods of sifting documents should be applied to the scriptures too. The results turned out to be, for many, alarming. Would a dispassionate modern historian accept at face value the story of Jesus' first miracle? Was Moses a historical figure, and if so whence did he derive his religious ideas? How much of what is woven into the Gospels has the character of propaganda? These and other questions stirred a sharp reaction (which we shall see again in other chapters): fundamentalism in the sense of a reaffirmation of the literal inerrancy of scriptures. But the new learning, especially florid in Lutheran Tübingen, was too vital and persuasive a force just to go away. How could men divide themselves into two compartments, one belonging to the ancient and prescientific world, and the other to the burgeoning scientific and industrial world of modern times?

Out of the theological ferment was born, mainly in Germany, what came to be known as Liberal Theology. Its chief architects were two wide-ranging scholars, Adolf von Harnack (1851–1930) and Ernst Troeltsch (1865–1923). Part of the solution of the problem of scriptures was to see in them something of an evolution of man's consciousness; and in general history could be perceived as an extension of the upward thrust of the evolutionary process as described by Darwin. Christianity could be considered the central strand in man's progress towards the establishment of the kingdom. Such optimism and liberalism were a blend of faith and the motifs of secular thinking. This outlook, admirable in many ways, was, however, easily able to strike a compromise with fashionable politics, and, as it turned out, to express support for the Kaiser's war.

If that war, in all its long ghastliness, shattered optimism, it led some Christians to find inspiration in the revolt against liberalism in belief instigated by Karl Barth in his dramatic commentary on *Romans*, which heralded, in 1917, the stance of a minority of Christians in Germany who were to stand out against Nazism and the Nazi reorganization of the Church. But times were confused and threatening. There were the Bolsheviks to consider too. The Nazis capitalized on the fear of Communist atheism among many Christians, and the puritan streak in Hitler appealed to many adherents both of Catholicism and Lutheranism. Many pastors were shepherded into the German Church, which was the vehicle for the Nazification of Christianity. Two flaws in Luther's own message were now to be seen in their full dangerousness – his doctrine of Church and State and his anti-Semitism. But some stood out against the times, and formed the Confessing Church. Notable among its martyrs was Dietrich Bonhoeffer, a pastor and theologian who was involved in the bomb plot that failed to kill the dictator in Rastenburg, East Prussia, in 1944. Bonhoeffer's development of the idea of a secular Christianity fully involved in the affairs of the world was to make a marked impression on post-war Christian thinking.

Lutheranism, as we have indicated, became one strong element in the plural experience of America, and in the conditions of the New World it took on some of the colour of pietism, which itself was partly a reaction to the events of the Thirty Years' War. Consider: that struggle had laid waste swathes of Germany, and it ranked with later world wars as a source of misery: if not so widespread it was five times longer. Admittedly for a time the exploits of the great Swedish commander Gustavus Adolphus, grandson of Gustavus Vasa, who had imposed Lutheranism on Sweden, looked like tilting the war in favour of the Protestant powers, but despite his capture of Prague and devastating victory at the battle of Lützen the stalemate was not broken, for he lost his life there. After another sixteen years of strife in Central Europe the exhausted combatants signed the Peace of Westphalia in October 1648. In recovering from the suffering Europe took some new turns. One of them was pietism, which entered strongly into the fabric of American Lutheranism (and more generally that of evangelical Christianity).

Its roots lay in Protestant mysticism, notably the life and thoughts of the shoemaker Jakob Boehme (1575–1624) – whom we shall meet again in Chapter 8. Another major figure was John Arndt (1555–1621) whose *True Christianity* developed the more experiential and interior aspects of the thought of Luther. But the chief architect of pietism was Philip Jacob Spener (1635–1705).

Like Boehme he saw the faith primarily in terms of experience: it is what happens in a person's soul which counts, not what he subscribes to in public. The war itself was fought, after all, over the issue of outer conformism to rival state Churches, and yet such a struggle missed the essence of the faith. The wounds and the bereavements were really not suffered on behalf of Christianity. The achievements, arguably, of the reformed wing of Christianity were not too inspiring, in any case: the liturgy was often too formal and the sermons boring. Spener's inward turn could thus be a challenge to official Lutheranism, though he worked within its structures.

78

The name of the movement derived from the Latin designation of the groups Spener formed in his own house and in the houses of other Christians in the Frankfurt parish where he ministered. Such devotional meetings were to foster prayer, reflection and the application of the faith to ordinary life. The groups were called *collegia pietatis*. Despite its Christian intention this practice of house-meetings, reminiscent of early Christianity, met resistance. Were these associations little Churches within the Church? Like some others in the history of Protestantism, Spener encouraged a moderate, this-worldly asceticism – his followers should abstain from such frivolities as cards and the theatre, and be moderate in matters of dress, food and drink. He seemed to be encouraging a Reform beyond the Reform. It may well be of course that it is characteristic of Protestantism and perhaps Christianity as a whole that it represents a kind of continuing 'cultural revolution' in the affairs of the spirit.

His pietism was a forerunner of that type of Christianity often referred to as Moravianism, in which an influential figure was Count Nikolaus von Zinzendorf (1700–60), who turned over his estate to form a commune of pious Christians. The word 'Moravian' was used of those who followed the lead of the Moravian pre-Reformer John Hus (1369–1415). A notable figure in Prague, where he was Rector of the University, one of the finest in Europe, Hus was rather radical in his preaching – arguing that if a priest or Pope were in a state of mortal sin he was no longer Pope or priest. This revolutionary view, cutting at the authority of the Church as a sacred entity independently of its individual members, did not commend him to the schismatic Pope John XXIII, who had him turned over to the secular arm and burned at the stake. Incidentally, the twentieth century John XXIII took his name partly to set the record of succession straight, and so perchance to make some amends to the memory of Hus. The earlier John had been appointed by the Council of Pisa, not regarded as representative of the whole Church.

The Moravians came to be groups of pious Christians who typically worked within the framework of the national Churches, not as a breakaway sect. They were keen on mission and sent out preachers to the New World. Their influence was important too on John Wesley, whose rather similar movement, Methodism, was, however, obliged for various reasons to break away from the Church of England.

Pietist and Moravian ideas helped to revitalize the Swedish Church in the later part of the eighteenth century and prepared the way for revival movements in the mid nineteenth century. Among the Scandinavian Churches there was born the strong idea of the home mission, in which there could be a revival of moral and devotional life, and an emphasis on bringing Christianity back into the family. Yet such revivalism was only partially successful, as we have indicated, in an age of increased estrangement from the official, rather bourgeois character of the Church. But it did have its effect in the wider reaches of America, where the old social assumptions of Scandinavia did not hold, and where in any case a new society called forth a type of Christianity emphasizing moral reform and a warm sense of salvation.

Intellectual life in Scandinavia remained vital, and perhaps, in the perspective of Christianity, the two most significant figures of modern times were the philosopher Søren Kierkegaard and the churchman and theologian Nathan Söderblom. Kierkegaard (1813–55) is now recognized as the Danish writer with the greatest influence outside his own country. That in one way does no credit to Lutheranism in Denmark, since he was a fierce, contemptuous critic of established Christianity as he experienced it. In his own day, however, not too much attention was paid to his highly charged voluminous writings. But in the twentieth century, from the between the wars period, he came to form a vital strand in Christian thinking. He has been seen as a forerunner of modern Existentialism and of a philosophy which sees human feelings and decisions as necessary components of our apprehension of reality – so there is a sense in which truth is subjectivity. Such a stance, worked out in Kierkegaard's case through a wealth of psychological and autobiographical detail, was congenial to interpreters of Christianity – partly because it helped to draw a distinction between faith, which has to do with subjectivity, and science, which has to do with objectivity; and partly because its emphasis on the centrality of personal existence harmonized with the central teaching of the New Testament. Kierkegaard's passionate approach to philosophy spilled over virulently in his assault on the Established Church of his day: he accused bishops and pastors of being half-Christian, since their other half was being bureaucrats. Likewise he was violent and ironic in his attacks on Hegelianism, the dominant philosophy of the day. It was too optimistic and too intellectual, and thereby shrunk Christianity into a system of ideas, rather than the experience of the living gap between the Creator and creatures and its overcoming in Christ. It tried to resolve paradoxes – following the general rationalist instinct – instead of seeing that Christianity rests centrally on a contradiction. Between the grace of God and our moral responsibility there is a collision (between Pelagius and Augustine, one might say). Between Christ as God and the Jesus of history there lies the contradiction between the eternal and the temporal. Yet what cannot be conceived by man can be brought about mysteriously by God. So philosophies or theologies which try to iron out these contradictions in effect rob Christian faith of its centre and its mystery. But the individual needs to decide: he cannot solve his problems by taking thought.

This emphasis on faith found a rich embodiment in Kierkegaard's writings: his literary output was, as we have noted, vast, but it is full of wit, psychological insights and scintillating examples, despite or perhaps because of the author's depressive attitudes and eccentricities. He displayed a portrait of individualism unleashed by Reform and by a new reading of the New Testament; but it was deeply incompatible with the official Christianity of northern Europe. His brutal attacks on the Church were written off, and he was perceived as a neurotic crank, while the fact that he wrote in Danish meant that he was not afforded a wider European readership for quite a long time. Moreover, he died young.

If he became influential after World War I onwards it was due to two main factors. The first was that optimistic, evolutionary Christianity, compounded out of Darwinism, Hegelianism and the social Gospel, took a heavy beating from the terrible guns of World War I. Men had fought the worst war in history, or so it seemed to most people in Europe. The heroic optimism of the young who went gaily into battle on the Western front, oblivious of the fatal dominance of the machine-gun and the destiny of wet and bloody trenches, came to be replaced by a new graveness. A darker perception of human problems was perceived as more realistic: the alienation of man from man and man from God could thus return to the centre of the Christian stage. The second factor was that existentialism lent itself as a framework for interpreting what lies behind the mythological style of the New Testament. Kierkegaard was thus the forerunner of a new Christian personalism. (There remains a question as to whether the existentialist turn in Protestant Christian theology in the thirties through the sixties of this century did not in fact draw too strong a line between religion and science, between the personal and the objective: could this turn out to be a new intellectual ghetto in which Christianity is shut away from the bustling progress of the great city of knowledge?)

If Kierkegaard was a product of Lutheranism by way of reaction, this could hardly be said of the other great figure whom I have selected as a representative of the intellectual life of the Scandinavian Churches. A cheerful activist, he was very different from the dark emotional Dane. Nathan Söderblom (1866–1931) was to become Archbishop of Uppsala, once an ancient pagan religious centre, now seat of one of the three old sees and site of a venerable university. He was a fine scholar and vigorous reformer, who was involved in social questions: he spoke out against the war in 1914, and was the leading spirit in a new movement called Life and Work designed to relate the Christian gospel and social issues. Moreover, he was a main engine behind the construction of the Ecumenical Movement, which has brought together, ultimately through the World Council of Churches, founded seven years after Söderblom's death, a large spectrum of Christian Churches and denominations – from Eastern Orthodox to Pentecostalists. The Swedish

Church, with its moderate tradition of the Magisterial Reformation and its incarnation in a neutral country, was well placed, as was the Church of England for differing reasons, to play a bridge role in the Movement.

And in continuance of the powerful Lutheran and in particular Swedish tradition of scholarship, he took a keen interest in the relationship between the Christian faith and the religions of the wider world, which he summed up in an important book, *The Living God*, given as lectures in Edinburgh in 1931, not very long before his death. He was mindful of the Swedish mission field, for Sweden had been active in the East and in Africa. Such neutral countries as Sweden and Switzerland were in some respects in a better missionary position than those which were identified with colonial and imperial rule. One of Söderblom's main contentions is that Christianity stands at a kind of midpoint among religions: thus Buddhism with its mystical emphasis stresses self-help – it is through human efforts that salvation is achieved; on the other hand Indian devotionalism as found in the *Bhagavad-Gita* and elsewhere emphasizes that only through God will they find salvation; Christianity sees a fusion of divine and human efficacy through Christ. Though, naturally enough given his commitment, he saw Christianity as a culmination of man's religions, he gave religions a positive evaluation, unlike some Protestant theologians of the period who saw them as products of sinful man.

Söderblom had not the genius of Kierkegaard, but precisely for that reason he could act as a summation of important forces in Lutheranism. His warm concern for Christian co-operation and for mission work was part product of the pietist strand. His ability to view other religions with empathy owed much to the strong liberal tradition in modern Lutheranism. Indeed his devotion to scholarship echoed a vital feature of nineteenth- and twentieth-century Lutheran Christianity – one of its strongest features. His commitment to relate the faith to social problems was in part stimulated by a reaction against the conservatism of earlier state Lutheranism, and owed much to the thought of Albrecht Ritschl (1822–89). The latter had been critical of pietism as being too individualistic, and he interpreted Christianity as being a strongly concerned with the Kingdom of God on earth, that is with man's social and corporate existence. Thus Söderblom brought together in his own person some of the varying elements which vivified the Lutheran movement.

These elements were also evident in the Lutheranism which Sweden and other countries exported to the United States. The pietist background blended with American revivalism; while the social Gospel has always had a strong appeal in the New World, for the task of Christians could be seen as integral to the creation of a new nation, in which even the poor are to be given hope and dignity. There was, however, also a reaction to liberal Christianity, which centred on a colony of German Lutheranism founded near St Louis, Missouri, under the dynamic leadership of Ferdinand Wilhelm Walther (1811–87): the Missouri Synod has stood for a conservative interpretation of the Bible. We shall see more of this vigorous phenomenon in our exploration of the modern offspring of the Radical Reformation.

What, in retrospect, have been the achievements of Lutheranism? It has, negatively, shattered the old conception of Christendom, and replaced it with varieties of national consciousness. It was a major factor in the development and self-differentiation of modern nations. Second, it has (relatedly) brought religion to the people, at least at the doctrinal, mythical and ethical levels, by releasing the Bible and the teachings of the Church from the older confines of the Latin tongue. What it lost in magicality of ritual it has gained in the power of the scriptures. Third, it greatly humanized the condition of the clergy, though it also shattered monasticism and thereby the older tradition of contemplative mysticism. Fourth, the stimulus of the Reform paradoxically led to a strengthened and newly vigorous Catholicism, even if its territorial spread was greatly diminished. Fifth, it was able, within the framework of the State Church, to nurture such revivals as pietism and such movements as Christian socialism. Fifth it was to the fore in the modernization of Christian thought and biblical scholarship.

Especially in the universities of Germany and Sweden there has been a powerful tradition of critical reconstruction of belief. On the other hand, such liberal thinking may have contributed to the widening of the gulf between the educated bourgeoisie and the increasingly disoriented country folk swept up in the industrial revolution, even if the latter, in emigrating, could build a new society much influenced by older Christian values in the Middle West of the United States and elsewhere. There remains, though, a nostalgia for magicality in Lutheran Europe, expressed in the trees, cakes and candles of Christmas, echoing from even beyond the Catholic past.

As one strolls beside the glittering lake edging up to the garden of the pastor's house near Karlstad, one cannot help thinking of Kierkegaard. Nor will the Nazis quite be banished from my mind. The criticisms of Lutheranism are entangled in its national connections: as are its strengths, for one cannot miss either the gentle goodness and learning of many pastors, and the affection which remains for a national Church which has helped to form the Swedish soul: grave, formal, unhypocritical, median in reform.

5

Baptism and the Radical Reformation

In the gently rolling and prosperous farming country around Intercourse, Pennsylvania, the sight of patriarchal Amish in their horse-drawn buggies would not bring to mind anything radical. Conservatism in some respects could hardly go further – not using buttons, telephones, radios, television, musical instruments, sewing machines and so forth, the Amish are a technological throwback. Nor perhaps would one associate these folk with a contemporary symbol of the American spirit, a Baptist President. Yet both Carter and the Amish have roots in the radical Reformation, and the whole Anabaptist movement. And indeed the society which they both inhabit owes a very great deal to those ideas at the 'left' of the Reformation which brought on those who held them so much persecution. In this matter, the question of baptism turned out to be crucial. But first let us see how the radicals anticipated the modern world, in certain respects at least.

A prime principle of the Anabaptists was the separation of Church and State. The Reformation of Luther – what came to be called the Magisterial Reformation – led, as we have seen, to the establishment of national Churches. The famous principle of *cuius regio eius religio* was a charter for dividing Christendom, but dividing it according to the system of establishment. But the Christian revolutionaries wanted to take Luther's insight, and, more importantly, the New Testament teaching as they perceived it, to its logical conclusion. If a man is saved by faith then that faith is of course an inner matter which cannot be externally imposed by the State. It is a matter of individual calling and choice. And the sacrament of baptism should be an adult affair, where the person baptized can genuinely affirm his conscious commitment to Christ. Thus though in some respects other beliefs of the radicals than those about baptism were more important, or as important, the question of baptism became decisive. It was also highly symbolic: the first radical to be put to death by a Protestant regime was Felix Manz, drowned in the Limmat River at Zurich in 1527. Drowning was a not uncommon punishment in subsequent persecutions, prized for its cruel irony.

The radicals in so directly returning, as they thought, to the New Testament, also, in resisting or at least criticizing the authority of the Church, tended in the direction of congregationalism. This was a main element in generating a sense of egalitarian democracy which entered into the bloodstream of modern Western democracy, partly through the influence of the Puritans.

A number of Anabaptist groups practised communism, partly after the example of the early Church and partly because of expectancy about the Second Coming. This ideal of sharing goods in common was a forerunner both of modern secular socialism and of the religious communes.

Whatever may have happened to modern Mennonites such as the Amish, the Anabaptist drive was towards evangelization. This commission to preach the true faith was laid upon believers, and because of the essential individualism of the teaching, such missionary activity took on an evangelical style; and in this the Anabaptist movement anticipated some of the great modern revivals.

But though there are anticipations of modernity in the movement, it attracted considerable scorn and oppression in its early history, and it was mainly by its influence on certain types of Christianity such as Baptism that it has been actually formative of today's Christianity. Still, the Mennonites continue as a relatively small, but vital testimony to some of the major impulses of the radical Reformation. So I shall here trace briefly the history of the Mennonite connection, and see something of the ways it has been one element in the complex moulding of the Free Churches.

Menno Simons, whose name has attached itself to a whole movement, was a Friesian, born in 1496, and son of a farmer called Simon (strictly Menno's name therefore is Simonszoon or Simonz for short – 'son of Simon'). He was ordained a priest in Utrecht in 1524. Though he may, according to his own account, have wasted time in rather frivolous (though not particularly sinful) occupations, he was serious in his reflections about his faith, and though he remained a priest till 1536, there were various things which disturbed his tranquillity. Thus he was influenced somewhat by sacramentarianism, a viewpoint which was quite strong in the Low Countries. It had, for instance, been well expressed by a Dutch lawyer, Cornelius Hoen, about a decade before Menno's ordination. For Hoen the Lord's Supper is a meal with a meaning – namely Christ's promise to be present with his followers. But he rejected the transubstantiation teaching orthodox to Catholics. Hoen likened the meal to a wedding: a wedding in which the bridegroom Christ gives a ring to the bride, the Church. The ring stands for the bread (and wine). The bride in taking the ring forsakes all others to cling to the bridegroom. But the bread and wine are no more Christ's body and blood *actually* than is the ring the bridegroom.

From such ideas flowed the whole notion of the Eucharist as a commemorative act – a notion which was to be profoundly important in the radical Reformation. Indeed, by putting the weight of the sacrament on faith and relationship men such as Hoen were mirroring the essential Anabaptist view of the sacrament of baptism, for it was the faith of the believer who thus entered the community of believers which was essential. And misgivings about baptism also moved Menno. In 1531 the doctrines of the Anabaptists came to his attention for the first time and in a dramatic manner. In a nearby town (Menno was at this time priest near his native Witmarsum), an Anabaptist apostle, Sicke Freerks, was summarily beheaded for having had himself re-baptized. This caused Menno to search the scriptures regarding infant baptism, about which he could find nothing. But he did not as yet break with the Church, and when he did it came in a strangely ironical fashion.

To see how, we need to retrace our steps to the extraordinary and tragic events which had been occurring in the city of Münster. Indeed we must go back further to the fierce persecutions which the Anabaptists underwent after the Peasants' War. Though for the most part peaceful, they were not altogether immune to the psychic backlash against their oppressors which their sufferings could stimulate. Already talk of the Second Coming, of the impending thousand-year reign of Christ and the like were in the air. The Reformation and the troubles of the times had imparted a new dynamic to Christian eschatology. It was not altogether too difficult to believe that the persecutions were the period of woes foretold in the New Testament preceding the return of Christ, when he might lead the faithful, by now embarked upon a violent day of reckoning against the lords and institutions who bore heavily upon them. This rather paranoid hope was not typical of Anabaptism, which was predominantly pacifist; but it was fed by the prophecy of a certain Hans Hut that Christ would return at Whitsun in 1528 (Hut was executed in 1527). Admittedly he was proved wrong, but there were other prophets. Plague, inflation and other ills were prevalent in north-west Germany, and in the city of Münster turbulence finally brought about the domination of the government in the first instance by Jan Matthys and then by Jan Bockelson, usually known as John of Leyden. Münster was the New Jerusalem. John eventually proclaimed himself as the new King David, and a strange, partly communistic, partly aristocratic regime was created amid terror, religious fervour and the exigencies of the siege of the city by the bishop. Amid great suffering the movement was crushed. All this naturally increased the general suspicion of Anabaptists. Near Menno's home some three hundred militant Anabaptists had taken over a monastery in sympathy with the Münster uprising. Their uprising too was crushed.

Menno had had relations with some of those involved. His interest in the radical interpretation of the scriptures had led him into a dialogue with Anabaptism. However he had argued forcibly against the aggression and violence of the militants. Now they were broken, like sheep without a shepherd. It was scarcely a propitious time for him to become an Anabaptist. But he did, in January 1536. With the help of peaceful Anabaptists he began a period of preparation before taking over the leadership of Dutch Anabaptism. So great was the respect in which he was held that the term Mennonite came to apply to his followers. His later travels as far as Danzig and beyond indicate how the Low Country Anabaptists were able, with such skills as the drainage of land, to spread into areas where they could escape the worst persecution and even gain some protection from local authorities. It was at his print-shop between Lübeck and Hamburg that Menno died in 1561.

What were the principles which moved Menno and his followers – and more broadly governed the outlook of the widespread Anabaptist movement? Some vital answers were given by the radicals to questions which had revolutionary meaning. Thus first of all there was appeal to the authority of the Bible. But was this new? Was it not Luther's procedure to use the Bible alone as the fount of Christian truth? Yes; but Luther and Zwingli nevertheless accepted some practical limitation on this – thus Zwingli could wait for a year and a half for the City Council of Zürich to move on the interpretation of the mass. The radicals opposed the Bible to all other authority, and this momentously implied that the believers themselves could have full freedom of interpretation. This principle collided with the concept of a national or established Church over which the State had some measure of control.

Another way of looking at the Lutheran position was this – that since the Church was in effect coterminous with the political community, the correct governance of the Church was a matter of general political concern. But whether a person is a citizen of Zürich (say), is a matter of birth and a fact over which he has no control: but faith involves choice. Hence the Spirit does not work manifestly in the political community as a whole but where the brethren are gathered. So first: the Bible alone has authority; and second: correct interpretation is a matter of collective listening to the Spirit.

The Anabaptist position on the Bible was logical, but sub-versive. Even more revolutionary in a certain sense was the way they thought about following Christ. This was taken very literally. And this was a greater change than might at first appear. Consider how many folk in those times looked upon Christ.

First, Christ was visible in Church and painting and statue as mysterious, shot through with the other world, divine saviour, Son of God. Christ too was apprehended through the mass, and even if the Reform had brought startling changes they were recent, and did not simply overturn older piety, even where Reform was successful. Further, the Christ of Luther was still very much the Redeemer seen through the prism of the Resurrection, the writings of St Paul and the old habits of awe. The radicals, though, looked on the man Jesus as well as the Saviour Christ, in a fresh way. They were to follow Christ, and if this meant giving up the sword, as Jesus had done, so be it. A new, humanistic, but at the same time intense, imitation of Christ was the new ethic. In adopting it the Anabaptists washed away a whole number of arguments stated in terms of existing society. If a man was called upon to do this or that because of his station in life and its duties, as interpreted and laid down by the Church and the authorities of late feudalism, then the Anabaptist could oppose to such a call the much louder cry of the pages of the New Testament. This could lead to a deep separation between the conduct expected of the brethren and that of the world: this was a factor in leading Anabaptism towards holy separatism, of which one form is that of the Amish. Thus the early Anabaptist confession of faith, which is known as the Schleitheim Confession, says baldly that all creatures are in only two classes, good and bad, identified respectively with Christ and Belial. The marks of Belial are as follows: popish and reforming churches, services and meetings, pubs and bars, oaths (that is those made before conversion), arms and armour. These prohibitions are like those later adopted by the Quakers, another issue of the radical Reformation.

Of course, for the Anabaptists the imitation of Christ seriously and literally held the prospect of dying like him, painfully. Not since the days of Roman persecution was the ideal of martyrdom so strong as among the brethren. Beheading was a kindly death; next was drowning; then there was burning at the stake – if you were lucky the executioner might put a bag of gunpowder round your neck to cut the misery short, or strangle you. Otherwise the burning went the full terrifying course of dying consciousness. It was, then, dangerous to be an Anabaptist, and a true brother, out of love for his fellow men, would not resist. Indeed their ethic here was one of harmlessness and love, rather than pacifism as understood today. At any rate they repudiated the violence with which both the Catholic Church and its Protestant successors imposed uniformity.

The difference of conduct between the Anabaptist and others was reinforced by the 'ban'. This was the shunning of brothers or sisters who had sinned and not repented, and was based on a passage in Matthew (18: 15–18):

> If your brother sins against you, go and tell him his fault, between you and him alone. If he listens to you, you have gained your brother. But if he does not, take one or two others along, that every word may be confirmed by the testimony of two or three witnesses. If he still refuses to listen to them, tell it to the congregation; and if he does not listen even to the congregation, let him be to you as a Gentile or a tax collector.

This mechanism for keeping the purity of the faith was clearly open to a tyrannical interpretation, and the system of banning was a potent source of splits among the Mennonites and related groups during the period from 1550 to 1650, when the Anabaptists were partially emerging out of a period of persecution to one of reluctant toleration.

Though the Anabaptist movement was relatively strong in the triangle from Holland to Switzerland to Bohemia, it was the littoral of the Baltic which provided them with much needed space for emigration. Those from the Low Countries understood drainage, and the Anabaptist ethos made members into good farmers. They were thus at differing times in demand to open up lands, especially in Poland and East Prussia. This situation led, as we shall see, to the extension of the movement into Russia. But also their exclusion from a number of occupations and their inner-worldly asceticism pushed them towards trading and business. They could not enter the army, the teaching profession (for the most part), or government service. Especially in Holland in the seventeenth and eighteenth centuries they achieved considerable prosperity.

Their success posed a problem, as in East Prussia, whither a number had migrated in the early eighteenth century at the invitation of Frederick I, in order to repopulate areas devastated by plague. For eventually their prosperity came up against a serious restriction. Since they did not pay taxes, expansion of their considerable landholdings was vetoed, and with increase in population a class of landless brethren was formed, who needed outlets for migration. One such outlet was Russia. Catherine II encouraged German settlements on the lower Volga; partly because of imperial Russia's drive south against the Turks, Mennonites were enabled in the late eighteenth and early nineteenth centuries to set up colonies, with exemption from military service and, by and large, self-government within the wider structure of the Empire. But this had the effect of increasing further the inward-looking character of their piety – they now constituted an ethnic-speaking minority, and clinging to the German language became, in effect, an article of faith. This was not ultimately to stand them in good stead during World War II, nor indeed during the period of collectivization in the late 1920s. But already there had been pressures in Tsarist times, especially after legislation in 1874 requiring universal military service. A substantial portion of the Mennonites in Russia migrated to the New World, which had already received a number of small waves of immigration, the most important of which was that in Pennsylvania, of Swiss background. (However, numerically the later waves of migration from Russia and Eastern Europe were greater than the original settlements out of Switzerland and Western Europe.) The net consequence of such transitions to the Americas has been that the Mennonite heritage is more firmly implanted in North and South America than in Europe, where the total scattered population numbered some 60,000 in 1964.

The Mennonite groups have on the whole formed communities which have their own very particular ethos. They have often proved highly conservative, both religiously and socially, even though what they conserve was originally revolutionary. Was it the destiny of the great Anabaptist movement that it should express itself in the particular traditions of an alternately persecuted and peacefully prosperous group with roots in Holland, Germany and German-speaking Switzerland?

Here it is useful to see some of the alternatives which sprang out of the radical Reformation. The Baptists, for example, who have part of their ancestry too in Anabaptists, and with whom at various junctures the Mennonites have been in interaction. Indeed the Baptists, admittedly (as befits Protestants) divided somewhat in belief and organization, number nearly 25 million in the United States, so there are some three hundred Baptists for every Mennonite. And here we may pause for a moment to consider the place of America in Christian, and in particular Protestant, history. For the forces that drove the Amish to Lancaster County in Pennsylvania were also forces which released the most powerful impulses within Protestantism. Leaving aside Africa, which shows another new phase of Christian experience, one can say this: Protestantism, born in northern Europe, grew to its greatest vigour in North America, above all in the United States. Let us analyse some of the factors in this phenomenon.

First, both Catholics and the Magisterial wing of the Reformation were by and large intent on putting down the radicals. The New World offered opportunities of freedom and experiment for such groups as the Quakers, the Unitarians and in due course the Baptists. Second, as was indicated by such events as the Peasants' War, the tragic affair of Münster and the continuing appeal of millennialism, the upheaval effected by the Reformation and its aftermath was partially destructive. The older fabric of society was torn, and the new doctrines, imposed through national Churches or city councils, did not necessarily retain the appeal of the older form of Christianity, corrupt in many respects as it might be perceived to be. In brief, the alienation of a large segment of the masses was something which preceded rather than followed the Industrial Revolution. But the forging of a new nation, committed to a theory of toleration, presented quite a new

94

field for Christianity, and one to which the radical side of the Protestant religion was well suited. It was well suited to this by its twin stress on individualism and community. If individualism, then faith; if faith, then evangelical revival. And Baptism, like Anabaptism before it, stood symbolically for individual commitment; but though it might suffer persecution, both in Old and in New England, it was not sectarian.

A third factor about the New World was that it was New. Or more precisely, it was thought to be. Even now it is common to hear that the United States is a young nation, but it is not young, counting the years, as compared with Zambia or Singapore. But it still possesses a sense of a new start, and this sense fits in with the millennialism of the radical Reformation, weakened doubtless by the eighteenth and nineteenth centuries, but still there as a theme in biblical Christianity.

Altogether America could provide a milieu in which evangelism could thrive. And what did that evangelism amount to? Primarily it had to do with preached words and caught feelings. Here we meet a very different spirit from that which centrally animated Orthodox and Catholic sacramentalism. Indeed it is a feature of the Christian experience which is little paralleled in other religions. The preacher is not like a guru: the distance from Billy Graham to Ramakrishna is very considerable. The preacher is only partially if at all a priest in function. He may by chance be charismatic, but he is not a sacred specialist as such. He has some of the feel of a prophet. The preacher is not, however, a mystic, in the sense of being a contemplative. The gulf between Sankey and a Buddhist monk is considerable. What then is the preacher, in the context of Protestant revivalism? In defining him, we also show how Protestantism was peculiarly suited to the American scene.

Let us hark back a moment to the liturgical expression of Christianity in the mass, which can be thought of as the central focus of religion in the Catholic tradition out of which the radicals came. Here we have as it were different layers of reality. Christ is one layer; and another is represented by the bread and wine in which he is present. The priest co-operates

95

with God in bringing this presence to the people. One can look at the Bible as taking the place of the bread and wine, for the preacher co-operates with the Spirit in bringing the presence of Christ in the Word of God to the people. The Bible is one layer; God in Christ the layer behind it. But the way of co-operation is very different, for the preacher's words become a kind of extension of the Bible. The power of the words of the Bible is somehow amplified through the rhetoric of the preacher. Since the evangelical style looks upon the aim of preaching to stir the hearers to repentance for sin and acceptance of salvation, preaching typically is passionate, and thus the preacher has analogy to the prophet, for to express the truth of what he preaches he must have experienced the divine being – he must have had a call. But his charter is the Bible, which partly moulds the emotions found in the proclamations of the preacher, and gives them a special flavour – fierce sometimes in denunciation, intoxicated with the thought of forgiveness, full of a wonderingly satisfied certainty, combative, loud in ethical injunction, rhythmic in praise, quite a performance – an intense mixture of a social situation, a charter Bible, of echoes of tradition, of a particular personality.

The evangelist was well fitted to the American scene. His faith was highly portable – the equipment needed was a single book, and this was important in a society that, especially in the nineteenth century, was to be intensely mobile. And not only was the frontier moving, as gradually order crept westward over and into regions of chaos, but society too could easily succumb to disorder. Both the outer and the inner worlds had to be conquered and settled, and the strong puritanism of evangelical Christianity was an expression of the need for well-defined, upright behaviour.

Thus the separation of Church and State, so much insisted upon by the great early Baptist, Roger Williams (who in 1639 established the first Baptist Church in America at Providence in Rhode Island), was real but also deceptive. Deceptive, because the Baptists like other Protestant movements created so much of the fabric of the developing nation. Protestantism could thus be an establishment from below.

And the Gospel often became the glue of a community, the glue indeed of a large part of the nation.

Because of their concern with conversion – with the importance of being 'twice born' – and the biblical character of their preaching, the Baptists can stand too as an example of a phenomenon which does not have an exact counterpart in other religions, namely the sense of the scriptures as a living force. Sometimes it seems that they are almost an independent power. This is brought out by John Bunyan in his *Grace Abounding*, where he writes such lines as 'that Scripture did seize upon my Soul' and 'This Scripture did trample upon all my desires' and 'I came to the sixth of the *Hebrews* . . . trembling for fear it should strike me'.[1]

Various influences flowed into and out of the Baptist movement. In England there was some contact in early days with the Mennonites, but the movement had its larger roots in congregationalism and puritanism. Thus it was open to Calvinist influence. The so-called Particular Baptists were fairly rigid in their belief in predestination, holding that Christ died only for the chosen. Though this branch formed the mainstream of British Baptism which survived into the eighteenth century, it was somewhat defensive and inward-looking; but it gained an infusion of new life from the growing evangelical forces in society. It was symptomatic of new life that the last decade of the century saw the formation of the English Baptist Missionary Society, of which the greatest member was William Carey (1761–1834), a shoemaker. When the young Carey was trying, in 1791, to persuade the other members of the Nottinghamshire Baptist Association of the importance of foreign missions, one of the elders present shouted at him to sit down: 'If the Lord wants to convert the heathen he'll do it without your help – or mine!' It was in fact a cross between Baptist principles and the evangelical revival which gave the Baptists the very considerable dynamism which they displayed in America during the eighteenth and nineteenth centuries. It also was this mixture which lay behind the vigour of the

[1] Quoted by Owen C. Watkins in his *The Puritan Experience: studies in spiritual autobiography* (New York, 1972), pp. 109–10.

foreign missions from the time of Carey onwards.

The faith of the Baptists at this point can be summed up as involving the acceptance of the Bible as supreme authority (but the Baptists were not given to imposing credal statements); of the need for Believer's Baptism; of the equality of Christians and the independence of the local church (people would be equal within a congregation, but congregations might not be equal, as segregation among the Baptists of the American South showed); and the separation of Church and State. The democratic and secular principles became deeply part of American society. The question of baptism itself was less vital in the tolerant ambience of American society. It was beneath the question of the scriptures that a time bomb was ticking. The Enlightenment and its Hegelian aftermath might mean little to pious folk in Tennessee, but ideas being fashioned in Europe were beginning to burrow into the fabric of revelation. Perhaps nowhere more clearly and bitterly were battles fought than in America and among the Baptists in particular.

As it happened, much of the controversy about the Bible fastened upon Darwinism. In fact several differing strands of enquiry were entwined in the thread of theological liberalism which some saw as a threat to evangelism. One thread indeed had to do with Darwin, but it itself was composed of diverse strands. One was the simple collision between evolutionary theory and the literal reading of the Genesis story. Deeper down was the trauma occasioned by the thought of kinship with the monkey (sexual and other flavours attached themselves unconsciously to this thought and its rejection). Again, evolution suggested gradualism rather than special creation – it undermined the special drama of God's creation of man. Also, though not altogether logically, Darwinism as a theory of physical and, in a limited sense, mental evolution could easily extend into an optimism about human cultural process in society. The late nineteenth century gave birth to a number of theories of progress, and this affected Protestantism both in its liberal or modernist interpretation and in its more conservative guise. Within the ambit of the latter, America in particular, from much earlier in the century, had bred a cluster of millennial movements. Perhaps it was unsurprising that the promise and threat implicit in such a vast new social and economic venture should have made millennialism attractive. Times were pregnant with meaning: could it be that Christ's second coming would be long delayed? The New York farmer and Adventist William Miller gathered up to a hundred thousand followers who believed his prediction that the great event would occur in 1843. Such precise eschatology has a long history, of course, of disappointments to its credit. But a vaguer style of prophecy had a future, but one which had a relatively optimistic form and a relatively pessimistic one. Such were the premillennialists and the postmillennialists respectively. For the former Christ comes amid turmoil before the millennium, to rout the increasingly powerful forces of evil; for the latter the world will have come to a state where the millennium is prepared, and needs no vast climactic struggle to rid itself of the demonic, for progress will have made the world fit for Christ's return as king. It was especially among the pessimists that the issues of biblical inerrancy would arise most forcibly. For evolutionism could be fitted into a liberal, progressive Christianity in which the new forces of scriptural criticism and historical evaluation could be accommodated. But among the pessimists, the whole flavour of liberalism seemed wrong, and so an extra dimension was added to the Darwinian controversy.

Another aspect of the developing struggle was that this new divide among Christians no longer took place along strictly denominational boundaries. In England, for instance, the early nineteenth century saw the rise of the Evangelical party. In the United States, the Presbyterians and Northern Baptists were both very much divided. And in the period since World War II virtually every variety of Protestantism has a wing which is biblically conservative or else is dominated by that ideology. However, a new question is posed for those of such an evangelical wing of Protestantism by the question of whether or not to belong to or support the Ecumenical Movement. For both by its outreach towards Eastern Orthodoxy and the Roman Catholics, and more particularly by its inclusion of a strong liberal ethos, the Movement is suspect to those conservatives who consider that at heart modern Christianity really is a different religion: it is one of the many non-Christian religions. This was a view expressed clearly, for instance, by perhaps the most scholarly of the American fundamentalists of the early twentieth century, the heyday of the movement, J. Gresham Machen (1881–1937).

He argued that Christianity involved belief in a transcendent God (but on the whole liberals accepted this, though they played down God's supernatural interventions in history, etc.); the corruption of humanity by its own sinfulness (here liberal optimism differed in emphasis, though it had been shaken by the terrors and blood of World War I); the infallibility of the scriptures as source of authority in matters of faith and salvation (but of course liberal scholarship had undermined at least the piecemeal authority of the Bible, so the proof text no longer could hold sway); salvation through vicarious atonement by Jesus on behalf of man; pessimism about human institutions as well as about individual human nature; and the belief in the Church as a brotherhood of those who are redeemed and who await the bodily second coming of Jesus. With regard to the last three articles, though the liberal might hold the first, the second was less attractive and the third too literalistic.

As it happened there also ran through Machen's teaching a strong strain of Calvinism – indeed he saw true Christianity as going through a line to modern conservatism via Augustine and Calvin. The insistence on a particular doctrine of the Atonement is one way in which true conversion is to be distinguished from false. Such Calvinism is also prominent in a number of the conservative wings of Protestant denominations.

Something of the temper of the modern fundamentalist can be seen in the life and teachings of John Roach Straton, who was minister of Calvary Baptist Church in New York from 1919–29, a period which saw the culmination of the struggle between the fundamentalist and modernist movements, and was also roughly the period of that great victory of conservative Christianity in America, namely Prohibition. He was sometimes seen by his contemporaries as the successor to the politician

William Jennings Bryan as leader of the fundamentalist movement. By a strange conjunction, he died, of a stroke, on the very day of the great stock market crash, 29 October 1929. A fervent preacher, a strong orator, of Scottish descent, he was both spectacular and dour. His opposition to the liberal position was powerful, and he would refer to liberal preachers as animated question-marks 'trying to heal the awful cancer of human sin with soothing syrup; they are sprinkling cologne waters upon the putrid iniquities of a rebellious race'.[2]

However, in his earlier days as a preacher Straton had subscribed to a form of the social gospel then being preached by the great Walter Rauschenbusch, the 'prophet of Rochester', and liberal Baptist. But the events of the war and other factors led to a pessimistic denunciation of the moral evils of the times. Like others, he fought strongly for the Eighteenth Amendment. But perhaps his most celebrated encounter, in a career studded with sensation and public controversy, was his series of debates with a prominent Unitarian of the day, Charles Francis Potter. The disputation brought into the open some of the main doctrinal issues between the conservatives and liberals.

Potter happened to be present at a big meeting in 1923 held under the auspices of the Baptist Bible Union at Straton's church and addressed by the fiery J. Frank Norris, who was indicted but acquitted on a murder charge four years later in Texas (he had in fact shot to death a friend of the Roman Catholic mayor of Fort Worth whom Norris had violently castigated – but it was a matter of self-defence, the jury decided). Norris sneered at the possibility of any revival of faith led by liberals, and remarked as an instance that King's Chapel in Boston (a well known Unitarian centre) had an endowment of twenty million dollars but a membership of only seventeen. It was untrue and Potter demanded a public apology from Norris and Straton. When this did not materialize, Potter challenged Straton to a public debate on the fundamentals of Christianity, and battle was joined. The first encounter was

[2] Quoted by C. Allyn Russell in *Voices of American Fundamentalism, seven biographical studies* (Philadelphia, 1976), p. 51.

at Straton's church, the rest in Carnegie Hall – for it was decided that the debate should in fact be a series of debates. They were carried by radio and widely reported.

The first turned on the infallibility of scripture. Straton expressed very forcibly the view that the scriptures assert their own infallibility and that without it moral and other judgements would relapse into chaos. But the three judges came out with a majority in favour of the negative. The second encounter was about the proposition 'That the earth and man came by evolution'. Here it was insufficient for Potter to defend evolutionary theory (though theory, Straton averred, cannot be science – thus profoundly misunderstanding the way science operates). The question also included by implication the whole question of whether by whatever means God had created the earth and man. The judges were unanimous for Straton's side. The third encounter was intended as a tie-breaker, but a dispute occurred over the verdict, so a fourth debate was arranged. In the third session the issue was the Virgin Birth, where the judges favoured Potter (who denied that there was biblical proof of the teaching which in any case he considered to be materialistic and an insult to marriage); and in the fourth, Christ's divinity. Here Potter, naturally, took a Unitarian position, and lost the debate. Straton argued that not only does the Bible set forth Christ as divine, but the testimony of Jesus' own words show that he was either a fool or a knave if his claims were false. Not only this, but Jesus' effect over two thousand years and his effect in particular on his, Straton's, own life, showed his redemptive power, which can only come from God. One more encounter would be needed to break the tie, but it never took place.

The conservative strand in Straton's thought also showed in his opposition to liquor, dancing, boxing, the theatre and other signs of current depravity. The frivolous twenties were not to his taste, and indeed he spoke for many, if a minority, of the American public. He also spoke for a movement within the Baptist Church which remains still vigorous, though it is significant that after World War II the most prominent conservative preacher took an altogether milder line in relation both to scientific questions and to the Ecumenical Movement. It is interesting that though Billy Graham was regarded by the redoubtable preacher of First Baptist Church Minneapolis, William B. Riley, as his successor, and was appointed head of the training schools which Riley had created and led, his position was much more flexible than that of an earlier generation.

One may look upon fundamentalism as one rather clear-cut response to the set of challenges presented to modern Protestantism. The nineteenth-century discovery of historical methods of probing the Bible, the rapid increase in scientific knowledge and the large social changes of the period were bound to provoke a need for certainty in religion which in its own manner fundamentalism has continued to provide.

But in order to see it in perspective, it should be viewed alongside other features of the modern Baptist tradition, which can be symbolized by the figures of Walter Rauschenbusch (1861–1918), greatest proponent of the Social Gospel, expressed most clearly in his book, *Christianity and the Social Crisis*, published in 1907; Martin Luther King (1929–68), whose concern for the social advancement of black people was blended with a Gandhian interpretation of the New Testament; and Billy Graham (b.1918), who represents the more ecumenical strand of Baptist preaching, and who has proved an adaptable successor to earlier mass evangelists such as Billy Sunday.

Of all the many offshoots of the radical Reformation it is perhaps the Baptists who express most clearly the force of a strong biblicism, sometimes veering in a fundamentalist direction, sometimes in a liberal direction. This loyalty to an infallible scriptural basis has given the Baptists a key place in biblical evangelism, for instance in Iron Curtain countries such as Romania (so much so that virtually all radical Protestant groups are referred to as Baptists). It also makes the Baptist preacher into the prototype of modern evangelism. The predominant role of the preacher in the religion has helped to encourage the cult of the evangelist, gearing a usually conservative message to the contemporary technology of communication. There is then a big gap between the rural old-fashioned Amish and the modernity and brashness of the television preacher. Consider where the latter kind of Christianity has come to (I quote from the *Los Angeles Times*, 11 March 1978):

> Christian broadcasters are engaged in a great space race for those big 'transmitters in the sky'. The transmitters are large communications satellites suspended high above the earth. They make possible instant audio and visual communication to virtually anywhere in the world. Taking an early lead in the race to get the gospel message across through this medium is the largest Christian Broadcasting Network in Virginia Beach, Va. CBN has acquired the use of the RCA Satcom II satellite and has ordered sixty earth satellite stations for delivery in the top sixty US markets, at a cost of $12 million.

Once the idea of an official Church has been rejected, as in the radical Reformation, there exists the problem of how to identify true believers who make up the Church as gathered in a congregation to worship and to hear the Word. One solution is to impose a very rigorous behavioural test, and this in effect is the direction leading to sectarianism. The Amish, with their system of banning those who transgress against the tradition, are one extreme example. Another solution is to make the test one of feeling, or inner conversion. This fits with the Christian weight placed upon grace and on Christ's saving power. It is a criterion which can be used in an evangelically outward-looking manner and in a denomination ambitious for expansion; but it imposes an obligation to preach in a popular, and indeed frequently a simple, style. The Satcom II which beams the Gospel preaching is the logical extension of the camps and rallies of an earlier age – though it becomes even more individualistic, for the viewer sitting in his room does not experience the mass fellowship of the uplifting rally. But television is suited to the theory of biblical religion and the call to be born again. By contrast how can sacramental religion really work through the media? Can the bread and wine be beamed and bounced from a satellite right down into the very mouths of the faithful?

In their differing ways, the Amish buggy and the electronics of the modern evangelist can be derived from the intuitions of the Anabaptists. They could not have dreamed of these consequences, nor that the plainer religion of small-town Baptism should give an air of prosperous moderation and twice-born earnestness to the White House.

6

Africa and Beyond

As everyone knows, Stanley greeted the famous missionary-explorer whom he had set out to find in the middle of Africa with the words 'Dr Livingstone, I presume'. But what was the true meaning of the event, in early November 1871, at Ujiji on Lake Tanganyika? It of course heralded the opening up of Central Africa and its mapping – Stanley became bitten with the bug of exploration: the trek to find Livingstone had been a journalistic coup sponsored by the *New York Herald*; but later Stanley was to take up exploration for its own sake, accomplishing a magnificent and hazardous journey down the length of the immense curving Congo River. But in finding Livingstone he was discovering, and in part making, a legend. He was in fact coming into contact with a person whose views were in many ways both unexpected and prophetic, and whose character was flinty, occasionally devious and above all tenacious in a rather paranoid manner – a man not quite built in the image which Stanley had formed. That character had been moulded in Scotland during the Industrial Revolution.

Livingstone's childhood was harshly dominated by three things. One was his work in the mill in Blantyre, in western Scotland – a grinding and poverty-stricken job, from early morning till evening. Another was his determination to learn, whether by going to the company school from eight till ten in the evening, after work, or by reading books in every spare moment. Third, and partly because of the fervour and discipline of his austere and even fanatical father, there was religion. The religion in question was State Calvinism – Scottish Presbyterianism as formed in the centuries since John Knox. As it happened, Livingstone was, up to a point, destined to revolt against it. But Calvinism still was a formative influence, for it posed the questions which exercised Livingstone as a youth and young man.

It is interesting that though Calvinist ideas were quite powerful in Cromwell's England they were absorbed and somewhat tamed within the fabric of Anglicanism, but in Scotland they were to form the matrix of the State religion. Ireland clung to Catholicism. It was as though the three nations, fated to be bound together, wanted to express their characters differently through diversity of religion. The fourth, Wales, was to follow suit by evolving its own form of Nonconformism.

Indeed the conversion of Scotland to Calvinism was much bound up with the problems of national independence. Though in the mid part of the sixteenth century, when the preacher John Knox focussed a rebellion against Mary of Guise (who was mother of Mary Queen of Scots), the question revolved around the French connection, England proved the major item on the agenda. Scottish patriots were concerned that Mary was betrothed to the heir to the French throne and that there was a genuine danger that Scotland could become a dependency of France. Ironically, France, a useful ally against the power of England, was now itself the threat. The rebellion did not altogether prosper, but with English help Scotland's independence was assured and French administrators and troops were banned from Scotland. Knox, appealing to patriotism and new middle-class sentiment, was a major force in these encounters, and he brought with him the teachings of Calvin's Geneva. These, entrenched but also challenged in Livingstone's early years, formed a mould for Scottish institutions and feelings.

The system for which Knox worked so vigorously and which reflected Geneva involved a variant on the idea of the State Church. It was an extension of the Geneva experiment: there Calvin had created a theocracy in a city, and now Knox was trying out the system on a whole kingdom. Since the Reformation hoped to restore biblical, and in particular New Testament, faith, church organization should not go beyond what was described in the scriptures. Thus bishops in their Catholic form were abolished, though Knox appointed superintendents (*episkopos* in the New Testament means literally overseer or superintendent) with administrative tasks together with that of nominating suitable candidates for the ministry.

Otherwise the Church was governed by local presbyteries, synods and, at the apex, the General Assembly. The presbyters were both elders and pastors, and the term was the basis of the name of the new system of religion. Because of the powers of the Assembly and because of legislation to ban non-Presbyterian practices, above all the Catholic mass and the old Church festivals, the system took a close grip on Scottish life. By the time of Livingstone, however, it was attracting much criticism, as we shall see. Under-pinning the new regime was the theology of Calvin, only a little modified in the preaching of Knox, who for a time had had charge of the English congregation in the city of Geneva.

John Calvin (1509–64) underwent, it seems, a conversion experience at the age of twenty-five. A small, precise, brilliant man, he bent his analytical powers (he had been trained in the law) to interpreting scripture, and in 1536 published the first edition of his famous *Christianae religionis institutio* (*Institutes of the Christian Religion*). The most characteristic of his teachings concerned election, that is God's choosing of the faithful and predestination. As he wrote '. . . all are not created in equal condition: rather, eternal life is fore-ordained for some, eternal damnation for others. Therefore, as any man has been created to one or other of these ends we speak of him as predestined to life or to death'. This was it seemed a logical consequence of the idea found in St Paul and elsewhere that salvation is due not to the merits of men but solely to the action of God. Multiply this idea by God's fore-knowledge and absolute dominion over his creation and predestination inexorably appears to follow.

Though Calvin was unaware of this, the emphasis upon grace is found too in other religions (and something like predestinationism is to be seen in Islam). The followers of such religious leaders and philosophical theologians as Rāmānuja and Madhva (eleventh and thirteenth centuries respectively) in India were, as theists and proponents of intense devotionalism towards God (known as *bhakti*), inclined to hold that any holiness acquired by man must come from God. It follows that liberation or salvation flows from God alone, and is unaffected by men's actions. From Calvin's point of view, Paul's statement that we are chosen 'before the creation of the world' significantly underlines God's sovereign freedom in choosing us. As for the reasons for a particular choice – these are inscrutable, but the choice does of course bear fruit in repentance, righteousness and so on. But these good works are not in any way causes of salvation. At best they are signs or symptoms. And given that those who are not chosen are not saved but damned, then the predestination is double: both to heaven and hell, to salvation and damnation.

This doctrine applied to Israel, to individuals within Israel, i.e. to those who were steadfast in the faith, and to those who belong to the new Israel, the Church. In all this Calvin was close to St Augustine. But the dilemmas of power caused strain within the teachings. Theoretically it is not for us to pry too closely into God's mysteries, why he chooses one rather than another and who he chooses. The true Church, composed of the saints, the elect, is invisible, for after all, as a Reformer, Calvin had to reject the pretensions of a Pope who claimed very visibly to wield the keys of the Kingdom: no human being can control election. But Calvin's vision of Reform led him to create a very visible Church in the shape of the theocratic community in Geneva. After initial set-backs leading to his banishment from the city, his work there reached its apogee in the years following his recall thither in 1541, more or less on his own terms. He devised there a system of Church-city relations which was to serve as a model for Knox and for others of the Reformed persuasion.

Following the New Testament, he based church government on the orders of pastors, teachers, deacons and elders. The pastors or ministers led the congregations both in worship and in the exegesis of the scriptures. The worship indeed centred on the preaching of the Word. Thus in Calvin's church in Geneva the old Catholic arrangement, in which the people face east and the altar, is replaced by another, in which the seats face inwards towards the pulpit half-way up the church. Thus is concretely symbolized the shift in focus and the crucial nature of preaching. Although the sacraments of baptism and the Lord's Supper were retained (the latter administered by the pastor and elders), the sermon held precedence in the actual life of Presbyterianism. Singing was confined to the Psalms.

The teachers were to see to Christian education – this was a vital ingredient of Calvin's system, both in Geneva and in Scotland. The deacons saw to arrangements for the poor and sick. The elders, chosen from the organs of city government, were symbols of strong lay and civic participation in the life and policy of the Church. The *consistoire*, or consistory, made up of elders and ministers, dictated policy in Geneva and had the power of excommunication. This power was considered by Calvin a vital method of ensuring that the Church retained its own independence – or to put it better, its own power in such a way that it should not be subservient to, but rather coequal with, the civil authority. However, Calvin encountered opposition which threatened to topple his rule: the influx of foreign reformers created a certain xenophobia among native citizens, while the rigours of a rather puritan regime were not to the taste of many of the citizenry.

For all his innovations, which Calvin saw as restorations of the spirit of early Christianity, Calvin was conservative on the interpretation of such doctrines as the Trinity, where he followed the councils of the Church and even defended the *Filioque* clause which had been a bone of contention between East and West. When Servetus, a Spaniard who attacked the Trinity doctrine, came to Geneva (for obscure reasons, since he was a strong critic of Calvin's *Institutes*) he was arrested, tried and burned at the stake. Calvin favoured the death penalty though not, as it happened, burning. The background of this was largely political, and the condemnation was useful to Calvin in his struggle to retain power against growing opposition. But it symbolized grimly the determination to lay down a new disciplined orthodoxy.

But Calvin could bewitch. His *Institutes*, constantly revised and extended, were logical, articulate, a new *Summa*. His defences of the new Protestant faith were powerful and sincere. His religion bore outward fruits of sobriety and good conduct, which could appeal not just to those concerned with spiritual matters, but also to the newly growing merchant class. Geneva became a pilgrimage centre for religious revolutionaries, and from it radiated influences which took Calvinism to the Netherlands, England (through English Puritanism), Germany and, as we have seen, Scotland.

But in Livingstone's day the Presbyterian system was close on three centuries old, and strains were evident in Scottish religion during Livingstone's youth. For one thing, the country was going through the Industrial Revolution. Western Scotland with its abundant coal and damp climate favoured the development of the textile industry, in which Livingstone worked. The new wealth increased the power of the bourgeoisie at the expense of the landowners, and this was a factor in undermining the system of patronage (and so was an influence on the choice of ministers) which had grown up since the time of John Knox. The changed times also stirred up a vigorous evangelical movement, fuelled partly by the values of the new middle class and partly by reaction against social upheaval. Agitation against what were seen as abuses of the system overflowed into attacks upon the close links between Kirk and State.

After all, the fact had to be faced that the Reformers, and Calvin in particular, had been selective in their use of the biblical evidence. Did the early Church really resemble the Kirk system? Calvin might go back to the orders which he discerned in the New Testament, but their function was transformed by the very fact that they were part of a national and official fabric of regulating religion. Dissent culminated in the Great Disruption of 1843, when about a third of the ministers withdrew from the Church of Scotland and were formed into the Free Church of Scotland, governed on more democratic and congregational principles and animated by the spirit of the Evangelical revival of which, in Scotland, the theologian and preacher Thomas Chalmers (1780–1847) was the most eminent ornament and leader. One of the calls, incidentally, which the movement sounded loudest, was the call to mission overseas. Christianity was moving into a new expansionary phase.

During this ferment David Livingstone had been influenced by some of the new ideas flooding into Scotland. Already he had moved away from strict predestinationism, and his more rigid father also in 1832 was persuaded to listen to a young Canadian preacher visiting an independent church in Hamilton, near Blantyre. The preacher attacked both the established Kirk and Calvinist theology mainly from the point of view of a liberal evangelicalism which emphasized the openness of salvation: the saving work of Christ was available to all who were able to open their hearts to the Holy Spirit.

Such a theology was already influential in American Presbyterianism, where the revived Christianity of the Great Awakening called in question the restrictive tendency of Calvinism: predestinationism was after all not a good ideology for the mission field, and though not intended as a kind of fatalism could easily be thought to have this effect. As a result of his father's shift towards this new emphasis and in the light of his own dissatisfaction with official Presbyterianism, Livingstone acquired a liberal theology and a commitment to independence – that is to the principle of congregational freedom from external controls, save those dictated by God.

Thus it was that after his prolonged struggles to achieve a medical education Livingstone applied to work overseas through the London Missionary Society, which was sympathetic to the congregational idea and accepted candidates from various Protestant denominations – Presbyterians, Baptists, Methodists and so on. Thus it was that in 1840 he was ordained a Congregational minister in Finsbury, London, and at the end of the year set sail for his chosen field of endeavour, Southern Africa. He was, religiously, a dour, independent-minded Presbyterian animated by a liberal theology and an evangelical resolve.

His twelve years in the mills as child and young man, his consuming thirst for education, his conscientious drive which brought him a medical education in Glasgow, his rather uncouth manner, his feeling of being chosen by God for great work, his tendency to paranoia, his staggering toughness in adversity, his fierce desire to make his mark in the mission field, his growing love of the African – these traits added up to a character which could not easily get on with fellow whites. He was, among his peers, something of a loner. But not among Africans, in whose company he was eminently happy, partly because he could boss them around, but substantially because of a remarkable sympathy and a nice unwillingness to adopt a judgemental attitude towards them.

Livingstone is thought of as a great missionary. He was and he wasn't. He wasn't, in that he only converted one African, and *he* lapsed. When he first arrived at the settlement in Bechuanaland (now Botswana) where Robert Moffat, another Scot, had worked for twenty years, he was disappointed and scornful of the fact that the number of baptized converts was only three hundred and fifty people. Little did he realize how well, in effect, Moffat, one of whose daughters, Mary, he later married, had laboured. When Livingstone set off northwards to establish new mission posts, he performed prodigies of travel across the Kalahari and beyond; but he was prized more for his secular skills by the Africans among whom he lived than for his spiritual message, which to them was strange and even ludicrous, though they respected, somewhat amusedly, his zeal. More than strange, however, it was threatening.

Thus two customs were attacked confidently by most missionaries – initiation rites, which were looked on as magical and barbarous; and polygamy, which missionaries looked upon as a kind of adultery. Moreover the cattle dowry among some peoples was perceived by white outsiders as bride buying, and not in accord with the dignity of women, as understood in Victorian Britain. There were complex problems of translation: what were the Spirit, sin, atonement, Trinity, love and so on in the relevant languages? They could be breath, dirt, coupling, threesome, sex. Intuitively, after much searching and worry, Livingstone came to believe that Christian preaching was unlikely to succeed in Africa, because it was disruptive of tribal cultures, about which Livingstone incidentally found much to admire. Partly he was no doubt rationalizing his own lack of success: but even so, if one such as he, heroic and sympathetic to the African, could fail, would not others too?

Increasingly, after his fruitless work in the years 1844–53, Livingstone was convinced that unless the tribal cultures were broken up Christianity would not take on. Clearsightedly he perceived that the main Christianization of Africa would come after, not before, colonial rule. And about such conquests and adventures as this implied the government in London was extremely chary.

Livingstone's perception of the inevitable conflict between Christianity and African tradition (to his mind a mixture of the likeable and the deplorable) both rationalized his situation and drove him on through those painful, tough, disease-ridden, optimistic explorations – right over to the west coast and back again to the mouth of the Zambezi in the east. It was an unprecedented feat. With hardly any financial support, but with the help of an African chief, he accomplished a journey of thousands of miles of swamp, savannah, rapids, forests, broad rivers, hills, scrubland, deserts. Not only did Livingstone's perception rationalize his overt lack of success as a missionary, but it justified his new consuming passion – exploration. He was opening up to European eyes the interior of the great continent some called dark. He was an explorer for Christ, but only the future could justify his fanatical drive to go on into Africa, and to bring others with him.

Livingstone's fondness for Africans led him to be remarkably objective in some ways – ascribing the ills and evils he encountered often to lack of good conditions of life. His long-term vision of an Africa opened up to Western penetration was not in one sense colonialist, but it was paternalistic. Thus he believed that Western-style commerce and education should not be used for the exploitation of the Africans, but rather that it should create conditions in which a new African prosperity could be stimulated. Hence in seeking for good sites from which new mission stations might operate, as for example in the area around Lake Nyasa, he was looking for areas where good land, other resources and freedom from malaria and the dreaded tsetse fly, fatal to cattle, would enable resettled Africans to become sturdily independent. It would also help to deal with the temptation to sell surplus members of the tribe – for Arab traders were active in the buying of slaves throughout east and central Africa: and abolition of slavery was a major strand in missionary sentiment both at home and in the field.

It is true that the settlement which he projected in the Shire Highlands north of the Zambezi River proved to be a disastrous failure in 1862, mainly due to his over-optimism. He failed to take seriously reports of the difficult nature of rapids on the Zambezi, which he wrongly thought to be navigable farther upstream than it is. A number of missionaries including the Anglican Bishop Mackenzie perished. A survivor, James Stewart, who had come out during the ill-omened Zambezi expedition with Mary Livingstone, now an alcoholic and destined to die soon along the great river, at one time was wholly disillusioned with the great man, and in disgust threw a copy of Livingstone's best seller, *Missionary Travels*, into the river. But after the latter's death in 1873, Stewart was reconverted to his vision and helped to found a missionary settlement called Livingstonia in the Highlands, under the aegis of the Free Church. Meanwhile the established Kirk founded a mission at Blantyre, named after David's birthplace, also in Nyasaland (now Malawi). Further, the Livingstonia Central Africa Company was formed to promote commerce in the area. So it was only a few years after his death that Livingstone's dreams achieved concreteness. Although in his lifetime he had failed to persuade a reluctant government to extend itself in Africa, his death foreshadowed a new epoch of colonization. The missionary and commercial settlements lay athwart the Arab slave trade, and Livingstone's books and lectures had aroused feeling about slavery. It was thus not unnatural, but ultimately fatal, for Arab mercenaries to attack the missions and traders. Pressure on the government led to the establishment of a protectorate in 1891.

War in Uganda, complicated by rivalry there between French and British missionaries, staffed by the White Fathers and the (Anglican) Church Missionary Society respectively, broke out in 1892; and in 1894 the country was annexed, as was Kenya a year later, in order to give access to Uganda from the coast. If one adds that Stanley's expeditions, which had seen the opening up of relations with the King of Buganda and the exploration of the Lualaba and Congo Rivers, were the prelude to Belgian penetration of Central Africa under the guidance of Leopold II, then a Livingstone-inspired colonial and mission belt stretched from the mouth of the Congo in the west to the Kenyan coast in the east. Admittedly the process of conquest was partly accidental, but the ideology of a Christian-based colonialism was powerfully attractive. The way was open for the entrenchment of the Christian Gospel in East Africa. But the area was also to prove to be one of the seed beds of new Africanized forms of Christianity, which have given a new dimension to the African spirit.

The latter part of the nineteenth century was also important in the fluctuations of Christianity to the south, where Boer and British and black Africans existed in a growingly complex interaction. Again, the Scottish connection was to play a significant part.

In the seventeenth century the Dutch East India Company needed a staging post to the East Indies. *De Kaap*, namely the Cape of Good Hope, was first settled by an expedition which was commanded by Jan van Riebeck in 1652. Only gradually did the colony spread outwards to the north and east and into the veld But by the late eighteenth century the whites had occupied substantial lands as far as the region of the Kei River. The early settlers who pioneered the land away from the Cape were the Boers, and they became increasingly independent of Dutch authority, some of them even going so far, in 1795, as to set up independent republics in outlying areas. But the complications of the war against Napoleon brought in the British, who occupied the Cape. In the depression following the wars, a large number of British settlers arrived, especially in Natal. Discontent with British government, legislation freeing the slaves, the dream of true independence, a sense of destiny and worry about the depredations of the robust Xhosas people – all these were factors in stirring the Boers and launching the Great Trek, which gave a myth and a sense of unity to the Afrikaners. The movement began, in essence, in August 1838, when the first large contingent left Cape Colony on its way north towards the Orange River and the Transvaal. In two decades the extent of white settlement in southern Africa was doubled, and a new ideology, drawing on biblical imagery, was born.

The Trekkers took with them, for the most part, a strong sense of God's providence, but they took little in the way of Church connection. The official Church of the Cape, the Dutch Reformed Church, was not keen on the Trek, just as secular officials too were opposed to it. The Trekkers were in any case suspicious of it: for one thing it was too close to the government, which, being British, was foreign and neglectful of the Boers' interests. For another thing it made no distinction in its worship between whites and blacks, while the Boers were essentially committed to white independence, purity and superiority. And the official Church failed to supply a single *predikant*, that is 'preacher' or pastor, to go with the Trekkers and to look after their spiritual welfare.

But the Trekkers were supplied with Bibles and a sense of the presence of the Lord. As they moved slowly onwards, the great wagons and the distant outriders would form a landbound fleet in the sea of the veld, and they felt in their own way free of the entanglements of government and the harassment of the Kaffirs. One thing they had left behind was a system, encouraged by missionary attitudes, that treated the black man as free and possibly equal. For them, there was a stricter, narrower interpretation of Christianity – and one which owed much to the Old Testament, both because they re-lived the nomadism of Abraham and later Moses, leading his people to the Promised Land, and because it supplied to them an ideology affirming the separateness and inferiority of the blacks.

On the eve of the great battle of Blood River, when the Zulus were decisively defeated, the Boers compacted with God to build a great house to him and to keep the day as one of thanksgiving in perpetuity. At the divine service, the preacher began by singing Psalm 38, verses 12–16; and the reading was from the beginning of the Book of Judges, which includes the following exchange: 'Who shall go up first for us against the

Canaanites, to fight against them? The Lord said, Judah shall go up; behold, I have given the land into his hand.'

The Afrikaans varieties of the Dutch-style religion, infused somewhat with influence from Scotland, since in the days of British rule in the first part of the nineteenth century evangelical Presbyterian ministers formed a bridge between the two white cultures, came to have an even stronger ideological significance after the conflict between Boers and British culminating in the Boer War at the end of Victoria's reign. The annual celebration of Dingaan's defeat at the great Voortrekker memorial served as a symbol of a proud, defensive people. Through such solidarity, the Reformed Churches on the whole became also committed to *apartheid* and the theory of separate development and the practice of white superiority. So in South Africa it tended to be other Churches, notably the Anglican, that registered increasing protest against the system which was created by the marriage between Trekker heroism, and the demands of a growing white industrialism. Calvinism, which had done much for education and human dignity in Holland and Scotland, here was bent in the direction of a sense of exclusiveness and caste arrangements.

It so happened that separateness encouraged not only the growth of a non-white Reformed connection, but also independent Churches amid the blacks. Indeed it is calculated that of some six thousand new Christian or semi-Christian religious movements in the whole area south of the Sahara, about three thousand are in South Africa. This of course is not just due to separateness, but that has been a vital factor (others include the unnaturally migratory aspect of labour in South Africa even in relatively settled existence as in the townships: lengthy commuting and rootlessness combine to give a feeling of impermanence).

A well-known and remarkable movement among the Zulus, who had to digest their traumatic defeats, at Blood River and elsewhere, after the proud military past under Chaka with his dynamic *impis*, and who had too to come to terms with their displacement from much of their land, was that led by the prophet Isaiah Shembe. He came from somewhere in the Orange

Free State and as a young man worked on Afrikaner farms, mainly with the horses and cattle. He had a striking spiritual experience on a mountain, which he was told to climb by a supernatural voice. It instructed him once up there to go into a cave. Inside he fell asleep and had a vivid dream, the main import of which was that he should purify his sexual life: he had, at the time, four wives. The Spirit who told him this he identified with Jehovah. Later experiences struck him with similar awe. Even though he had parted from his wives as instructed, he fell ill. Rejecting traditional medicine, he was cured, according to his own testimony, through faith in Jehovah. He became an itinerant teacher, and went about healing and casting out demons. This, incidentally, is an important motif in much of the new African independent Christianity – and is reinforced by their reading the New Testament, where of course Jesus as healer is a powerful theme (though much neglected, as Africans might see it, in 'official' Christianity).

After being baptized by a prominent independent Baptist pastor and working with him for some years, Shembe set up his own Church of the Nazarites in 1911. It had its first centre, and still the scene of a great annual festival, at Ekuphakameni, which can be literally translated 'the Elated Place', some miles from Durban. There he had another divine message bidding him go to a mountain, which was to become the scene of a great January festival. The Nazarite year swings round these two epicentres of July in Ekuphakameni and January in Inhlangakazi. This latter shrine is where on his first visit Shembe was by himself for twelve days, and threatened (according to his own account) by fierce folk who wanted to kill him, and by lions and leopards who claimed to be sent by God. But steadfastly Shembe waited on, for Jesus. At a certain point he was surrounded by rattling skeletons of the dead and he fell down terrified. One of the skeletons who had been a great White preacher assured him he was not going to die, but would be given power by God. Two angels came and fed him with bread and wine. Thereafter Shembe indeed felt new power. In 1913 he first took his followers to the holy mountain for two weeks, and they put up huts there – which transformed the occasion into a kind of feast of Tabernacles. The echoes both from Old and New Testament are, of course, vibrant in the whole experience of Shembe.

It is hard, perhaps, to determine the question of how orthodox or otherwise Shembe's Zionism was, considered as a Christian movement. Of its Africanness there can be no doubt; and one of the prophet's great achievements was to fashion a whole new cult focussing on an actualized Zion which could express the aspirations of the Zulus and, more broadly, the African peoples. Indeed, though the question of orthodoxy has some practical significance with regard to relations between the Nazarites and other groups, including official Christian churches, it is sometimes an oblique question about the prophet himself. Some of his followers seem to think him divine. He himself not surprisingly discovered parallels between his own life and that of Jesus. The fact is that his prophetic experience, his inspired leadership, healing powers, new message for Africans, identification with the Zulu people and kingly lineage – all these made him occupy a special place in history as perceived by his followers. His holy city recreated Jerusalem and also Paradise on African soil. The feelings about it are expressed in the prophet's hymns, commenting on which Bengt Sundkler writes:

> All the great power-lines of Scripture meet at Ekuphakameni: from Eden, and Sinai and Bethlehem and the heavenly Jerusalem. God Himself wears Ekuphakameni as his cope:
> God the King of Kings
> We are thy poor children;
> Turn to us in thy grace,
> Thou hast put on Ekuphakameni
> as thy coat.
> *Chorus:* Come, come, Amen.[1]

And in such interpretations, there is a fusion of biblical and African images.

Here one notes an effect of translation of the scriptures into the various vernaculars. Many of the missionaries, naturally enough, were evangelical Protestants, and they therefore set

[1] Bengt Sundkler *Zulu Zion and some Swazi Zionists* (Oxford, 1976), p. 199.

great store by the Bible as the potent authority and Word of God. But the Bible, as such, could lead its own independent existence, as it had for many Christians elsewhere. In two ways this potent independence was especially dramatic in its impact upon Africa. First, the vernacular languages often identified whole peoples and so each translation could gain an ethnic identity, 'our' Bible in a very meaningful sense: it was in any case miraculous for non-literate peoples how sounds could congeal on to pages and then spring forth from them again when the reader made them move. Second, the Bible had been interpreted hitherto by missionaries who read out of it monogamy, various items of European morals and customs, a generally non-African perspective. But now it could be seen afresh through African eyes, and what they saw was often something much more akin to their own feelings than they might have expected. When Livingstone thought that the disintegration of traditional African societies was a precondition of their acceptance of Christian beliefs he was partly right. But he overlooked the 'African' echoes in the Bible. Strictly speaking, of course, they were not African, but, more, archaic. Even the New Testament was replete with events and ideas scarcely at home in Victorian England, but immediately relevant to African experience. The ethnic tribulations of Israel through to the casting out of demons by Jesus were full of new meanings when interpreted from within African religious experience.

The contact between Christianity and indigenous African cultures not only provided the latter with a dramatic and painful lesson in the need to change, as African worlds became disoriented; it also released a great new stream of religious experience. Many of the new movements of Africa have started in prophecy: in the strange visions and dreams, like those of Shembe just referred to. Possession by God and spirits was a strong motif running through much African religion (as indeed it runs through much religion across the world); and now the powerful feelings which once found expression through a narrower pattern of ideas were given a role within a cosmic dynamic infused with biblical imagery.

In a sense the old gods were failing, and this is a reason

why often the new movements were scarcely conservative, in the sense of reaffirming the old gods, albeit in new guise, or reintroducing features into Christianity, such as polygamy, which collided with the white ethos. Often they consciously turned upon the old values, and became a third force, hostile in many ways to native cults, but suspicious too of Christian establishment. Such a 'third force' movement was that of Simon Kimbangu, prophet in what was the Belgian Congo, and is now Zaire. Not only was his movement widespread and influential, but it happens to be the first of the independent churches to have gained membership of the World Council of Churches – and so made its peace with supposedly mainstream Christianity. Kimbangu's Church, now known as the Church of Jesus Christ on Earth through the Prophet Simon Kimbangu, is puritanical, and bans alcohol, tobacco, dancing and polygamy; it is also set against the use of what it regards as magic and witchcraft, and is pacific. By tradition (Kimbangu founded his Church in 1921) it was anti-colonial, and it played a meaningful part in the struggle against the Belgians – for which reason Simon Kimbangu was arrested in September of that year, and though his death sentence was commuted, he remained in jail till his death thirty years later. He was thus both prophet and martyr. As a Baptist catechist, he interpreted the Bible in messianic terms, and very differently from the Roman Catholic establishment in both the Belgian and French Congos. Partly because of its modernizing characteristics, for the Church is involved in education, healing, agriculture and so on, and because of the new wider struggle in which the Kimbanguists found themselves, the Church transcends tribal and other divisions. With a membership of a million or more it is the largest single independent movement in Africa.

In Africa and elsewhere the virtually simultaneous arrival of Christian missions and colonial rule has given an ambiguous air to the transactions across the white frontier, that is to say, the cultural frontier running invisibly between the various ethnic groups on the one hand and European culture on the other. The new Christianities of Africa reflect some of the different spiritual moves open to those living on the African side of the frontier. One move was to absorb as much as possible of Christianity and the attitudes of the white man. There were frustrating limits to this process – in South Africa, as we have noted, the growth of *apartheid* was one such limit, though paradoxically it could often give the black pastor a much more vital role to play than elsewhere, for missionary and general white control of the Churches was another sort of limit on complete integration of the Africans into the European thought-world. But with the increased flexibility of the European-based Churches, the rise of independence movements and the frequent association of Christianity with brotherly concern for the struggles and crises of the African political movements, a greater integration of Africanness into mainstream Christian life has been possible. It was very often the strains within Churches, because the white frontier ran down the middle of them, which brought on the independent movements, which some-times started without clear thought of separation.

Another kind of reaction is exemplified by Shembe, which was to effect a new synthesis between African tradition and Christianity, involving an extensive reinterpretation of the latter – especially in relation to the typical mainstream inter-pretation lying on the white side of the frontier. The word 'synthesis' here is meant to imply more than the weaving together of elements from both sides – probably all cases where a religion has moved into a new cultural area it has taken on something from the latter, however conservatively it may be interpreted. Rather, something can be counted a synthesis when it transmutes enough of the cultures lying on each side of the frontier to fulfil central functions from both. Thus Shembe expressed in new form the experience of God and Christ as brought explosively into contact with Africa through the missions, as well as a fundamental sense of identity with the preceding Zulu, and more broadly African, tradition. Such synthesis was helped by the fact that there were continuities between biblical Christianity and African feeling.

The Kimbanguist Church represents another reaction, in which there is a revolutionary Africanization of (in this case Protestant) Christianity. Christianity is appropriated through a black prophet, and is set over against official religion and government; but the price of such new strength is a rather uncompromising rejection of the major elements of past religious culture. The African reform remains, but the content is radically different. The discipline of the Church helps to create a new non-ethnic, African identity, mediated through solidarity with the prophet (who for this reason takes on some of the forms of the Messiah).

In these reactions the Bible was a potent force. The Protestant tendency to present it unmediated to the believer, with the implication that the individual could be inspired to interpret it in a true sense, was an invitation to ignore Church authority. The missionary was often himself blind to the effect of the Bible upon African converts. Already I have made some reference to the fact that most of the cultures of Africa were through the missionary enterprise and the colonial trauma moving from being preliterate to literacy. And so frequently it was the Bible which was the first book to be translated into the local language. It came therefore replete with a double miracle – the miracle of the potency of letters as they captured and made available the spoken word, and the miracle of the transformation of the person through hearing the Word of the Lord. In coming from afar and from another culture the Bible sounded strange: as being in the home tongue it was a treasured familiar. But the fact too that it was in possible contradiction with the preaching of the missionaries proved to give it a third potency. This arose from the dynamics of the situation: for what was on the agenda of the souls of many African converts was, obviously, the item of how to be both Christian and African, and how to appropriate what seemed good and powerful of white culture in a way which chimed in too with the perception that Europeans were exploiting the land and the people. The African Bible (that is the Bible interpreted in an African way) had the third potency that it was also European, but it was revolutionary too. The Bible spoke against the principalities of white dominance. It was like a gun: one could import it, but use it for freedom. Needless to say, such thinking was –

for the most part – not on the surface of consciousness, but creatively instinctual. It played its part independently in many different separate areas along the White Frontier.

There was, of course, also a band of reactions which moved far back in the direction of reaffirming indigenous cultures, in such a way as to be rather radically in conflict with white religion and culture. A political example was the Mau Mau movement which convulsed Kenya in the 1950s. More religiously oriented examples often look to the Old Testament rather than the New, in the reaffirmation of black values. An extreme case, stemming however not from Africa itself but from the African tradition in the Caribbean, is the Rastafarians, naming themselves after Ras Tafari (the princely name of the Emperor Haile Selassie): they see themselves as the true Jews, punished by being made black for their sins, whose original home is in Ethiopia – to which promised land they shall return. Puritanical, purity-conscious and militant, the Rastafarians shun physical contact with whites, yet shun magic and witchcraft; they spurn Western medicine, as well as most of the values of white culture. For them, Ethiopia is a symbol of their own Africanness. Paradoxically, Ethiopia is Christian, but it does have a strong Semitic strand in its culture.

Whether we look to a prophet such as Isaiah Shembe, or to those who went on the Great Trek, there remains in forms of African Christianity a strong sense of biblical drama: Shembe himself as it were enacted the life of Christ – shot through with the voice of God, fasting in the wilderness, the rejection of temptations, the healing of the sick in body and mind, the prophetic preaching; while the Boers could so easily see themselves as being led like the children of Israel into a new promised land. In Kimbangu's birthplace and his ultimate place of burial, there is a new Jerusalem, also to be found in Ekuphakameni.

At the same time the historical Churches in the decades since the 1950s have most markedly moved towards indigenization of worship and ecclesiastical control. Such a movement also poses the general question of what are to be the characteristic imprints of African Christianity. One can look on this question by considering African cultural forms as drawing up the agenda: the queries are African, the answers Christian, but not necessarily Christian as seen from the white side of the frontier. The agenda? Community, ancestors, brotherliness, health and sickness, prophecy, spiritual presence in nature and man.

In some ways the parallel with the dispersal of the Jewish people has force, save that for many African groups the exile was at home. The colonial experience, and above all the buying up and occupation of land by Europeans, caused a break in the umbilical cord binding men to the earth; and the new industrialism and city life, especially in South Africa, added powerfully to rootlessness. Of course too Europe brought some material blessings, in medicine and education (precisely areas where the missionaries were crucial). Yet here too there were ruptures in the fabric of life – the Western educated elite could easily come to despise both what was old and the religion of Christ; and as bitter experience often showed Western medicine could only go so far, and was poor especially in all those sicknesses of the soul which were a consequence of the radical upheavals all along the black side of the white frontier. The historical Churches could bind some of the wounds; the new independent Churches could bind others.

Livingstone, then, had looked fairly far ahead. What he could not altogether foresee, however, was the effect on Christianity of its indigenization. Neither the dour Calvinism of Scotland, nor the warmer missionary feelings of the Free Church, nor the psalms and preachings of the Dutch Reformed connections among the Boers were anything like a foretaste of the new Christianities danced out in high places or softly sung in the grey velvet dusk of the townships or preached practically along the vast sinuous Congo whose banks an inspired Stanley had trodden. Only in the modern era has Christianity made any strong incursion into the southern hemisphere. Now most of the world south of the Equator is Christian at least in name: in South America, in sub-Saharan Africa, in Australasia and many of the Pacific islands. Of all the southern regions the African is the most dynamic. It may be that a factor has been the explosive character of Protestantism, disintegrating and reintegrating; but underlying it has been the richness and plurality of many people coming to terms with great and extraordinary powers transmitted so forcefully into their homelands.

7

Varieties of Christianity
and its Offspring

We have traversed some of the varied waters of the delta into which the stream of Christian tradition has flowed, and now perhaps a broad geography of that delta can be sketched. It is not possible to define an essence of Christianity, beyond saying that the faith relates to Christ, either in historical continuity or through religious experience or both. However, it is possible to draw attention to some typical features of its main branches, mini-essences as it were.

Orthodox theologians sometimes write of their own Church as that of St John, Roman Catholicism as that of St Peter and Protestantism as that of St Paul. The idea is not particularly historical, but it does draw attention to certain differences of style and emphasis, and with this distinction I shall begin.

Eastern Orthodoxy may be regarded as primarily sacramental: it is the enactment of the liturgy that lies at its heart. A secondary emphasis is upon the monastic tradition and the interior illumination which spiritual life can bring. In both emphases there is a feeling of participation: the faithful share in the drama of redemption through the liturgy, and the contemplative participates in the Divine Light in inner experience. The fusion of the two motifs can perhaps be felt in the imagery of light which plays so notable a part in the liturgy itself. The idea of participation invites a dominant motif in theology – the deification of man through God's taking on human nature in Christ: 'He became man in order that we might become divine', as Athanasius put it. The historic destiny of Orthodoxy was first one in which, at Byzantium at least, there was a blending of Church and State, and so the attainment of what might be called a monistic Christianity. This was scarcely achieved in the West for any length of time.

But monistic Christianity, though it achieved a different embodiment in Russia, crumbled in most places before Islam and later Communism, so that Orthodoxy had the destiny of being ethnic, and often in captivity, under Turkish rule.

Generally speaking the other Eastern Churches, whether independent or affiliated as Uniate Churches to Rome, have the basic characteristic of being liturgy-centred, and in their most flourishing periods, as in the great days of Nestorianism in Persia and beyond, have experienced a vital monastic life.

Sacramentalism, though in a somewhat different key, has been the heart of Roman Catholicism. But the phase of Church-State fusion was short-lived in its early imperial form, and the Church acquired a spiritual centralism important for its survival, perhaps less for the realities of control than for the mythic reliance upon the traditional prestige of the holy imperial city. Additionally, Rome added certain other features to those visible in Orthodoxy: the rich growth of orders, including non-monastic ones, gave a flexible dynamic to its operations. Importantly too the Church managed to fashion a new doctrinal synthesis in the Middle Ages. So whereas the theologians of the East have been rather conservative, there was a growth of the fabric of Western doctrine and philosophy, fractured at the Reformation. Thus the main features of Catholicism can be seen as sacramentalism, doctrinal elaboration, centralism and celibate vocations as an abiding form within the Church. Much of this is under question, of course, in the period since Vatican II.

In its classical heyday Tridentine Catholicism can be seen as canalizing the numinous through the Church and giving it external expression. Thus divine power was, so to speak, directed into visible and concrete objects and actions: masses, holy water, relics, pilgrimages, penitential acts, blessings, vestments, cathedrals. The Church itself therefore became the largest visible concretion of divine power. It is unfortunate that there is no precise word in the English language to refer to this concretion of the numinous, this making substantial of the sacred. Without here wishing to enter a value-judgement by using the word, perhaps one could speak of the magicality of Catholicism in its classical form.

In various countries and times Catholicism also acquired a monistic form, as in imperial Spain and its colonies. For different historical reasons this monism no longer obtains in the old centres of Catholic power, and so the religion has acquired an increasingly denominational status. The incorporation also of many motifs from modern Protestantism has in many places therefore eroded various typical features of the Trindentine form: centralism and the sacramental emphasis remain, and the orders (perchance revitalized by extensive winnowing); but the doctrinal edifice has largely disintegrated, and the magicality has been greatly reduced.

Protestantism has of course had great transformations since its heady beginnings. For one thing, the simpler, more austere forms have largely died out – Calvinists now sing hymns, early Quaker egalitarianism has been overtaken by events, strict Sabbatarianism is less frequent. For that matter, persecution of minorities for doctrinal aberration has almost vanished among Christians. Even so, the main motifs of the Reformation can be still discerned.

The major shift in the Reformation can be seen as the rediscovery of the mythic heart of Christianity in a new form, as incorporated in a virtually autonomous Bible. The magicality was shifted largely from things to words. What happened to the various dimensions of Christianity? The old over-arching doctrinal synthesis of the Middle Ages was replaced by new constructions, which were not on the whole holistic though they could be impressively systematic – that is, not holistic in the sense of giving a continuity between divine and human knowledge. From this time onwards the split between revealed knowledge and scientific knowledge was real, though not always by any means a cause of antagonism. There was thus a shift from the doctrinal towards the mythic.

As for the latter, the autonomous Bible expressed a powerful story which was now repeated and re-enacted, less through rituals than through preaching. This in turn led to a new emphasis upon experience, for the magicality of Roman Catholicism and also its sacramentalism through the mass could bring about an invisible transfer of saving power independently of feelings. But preaching does not work without some conscious effect. Though Protestantism scarcely carried on the mystical tradition in its classical form, where monastic community or solitude formed the ambience of the contemplative life, it did learn from the mystics' lesson of inwardness. Thus in Protestantism there was a strong tendency for the myth to be re-enacted not so much in the ritual – in the sacrament and in the sacred cycle of festivals and holy days – as in the lives of individuals, and to some extent, too, the experience of groups. One could call this the *dramatization of experience*.

The ritual dimension of Christianity underwent concurrently a range of changes, from the moderate continuance of sacramentalism, but in a relatively non-magical context – as in Lutheranism and the Anglican Church – to its virtual disappearance. The worship service focussed on the Word, but after austere beginnings flowered into the more emotional form, garnished with hymns, which came to be a major expression of popular religion in Protestantism, notably for instance among the Welsh nonconformists. The effect of hymn singing is to emphasize lay participation in a congregational manner, rather than the more isolated devotions of the lay person within the magical ambience of sacramental religion.

Perhaps it was at the institutional and social level that the most difficult questions were posed by the Reformation. The solutions were various, now that the transnational monism of Catholicism was shattered. One type was the (largely ethnic) State religion; another was, more ambitiously, theocracy – conservative as in Geneva, revolutionary as in Münster. But the main destiny of Protestantism lay in denominational organization, which could exist satisfactorily once the principle of toleration came to be reasonably embodied in England, America and elsewhere. The fissiparous character of Protestant denominations and sects is largely the result of toleration, since the latter gives the State no interest in imposing uniformities, and Protestantism does, of course, reject that other 'external' authority, the papacy.

Though the doctrinal dimension of Christianity was from

the point of view of its outreach as a general philosophy somewhat diminished by the events of the Reformation, its details became vital as definitions of varying positions. The fusion between biblical interpretation and personal and group experience was marked through the dramatization of experience to which I referred, and consequently both personal and group identity were entangled in credal matters. On the other hand, at the outer edge of the Protestant movement there arose such movements as the Quakers and the Unitarians who in differing ways underplayed the doctrinal dimension, emphasizing more ethics and the need for social activism. And here we come to the shifts brought about by the Reformation with regard to the understanding of ethics.

By refreshing the myth of Christianity and giving it concreteness in the Bible, the Reformation gave the idea of the imitation of Christ a new vitality. As that myth was presented in the writings of Paul, the urgency of moral fruits was evident – an urgency reinforced in some phases of Protestantism through millennial beliefs. There was some tension between the new, sometimes puritan, ideals inculcated and the theory of grace and predestination: whether one was Lutheran or Calvinist one would not *achieve* anything by good works.

Though Protestantism had its main first impetus in Germany and neighbouring countries, it is perhaps useful to look at the varieties of Protestantism through the British perspective – partly because Britain was a main source for the transmission of Protestantism to the Americas and Africa, but chiefly because some of the main forms of Protestantism were evident there. Also it is of some advantage to pause to consider the Church of England and the phenomenon of Anglicanism as working out in its own fabric some of the main ideas flowing from the Reformation and the question of relationship to Catholicism.

The typical piety of the Church of England is represented by both the Catholic and Reformed strands which have been woven into its history. These cannot be understood in modern times without harking back to the evangelical and Anglo-Catholic movements. Both were revitalizations of the past, the one through pietism multiplied by ethical and social earnestness, and the other through a new sacramentalism and a reappraisal of the Roman connection.

The early nineteenth century was a convulsive period in England, compounded of rapid and often squalid social change, occasioned by the growth of the industrial landscape and the new politics of Empire. Evangelicalism, though primarily an upper and upper middle class phenomenon, was concerned with the improvement of those lower on the scale, and, abroad, with the slave trade, against which William Wilberforce ran a notable crusade. During the same period, Methodism was continuing to make headway, largely among the more skilled workers and the lower middle classes. Both movements converged, and sprang from a similar emphasis on religious experience and upright behaviour. In many respects the Evangelicals were a replay of the Puritans of Cromwell's time. Theirs was an inner-worldly asceticism, a theme in much biblical Protestantism. Such austerity related to the experience of the numinous Other and a sense of sin overcome through Christ, is rather different in style from the asceticism typically associated with mysticism: it might be described as prophetic asceticism (which is discoverable in another form in the Islam of the Wahhabis of Saudi Arabia).

By contrast the Catholic strand in Anglicanism presented a renewed emphasis on sacraments, above all the Eucharist, which was thus restored as something much more than a memorial of Jesus' death and resurrection. Here was Catholicism without the Pope. Not surprisingly in the twentieth century there have been rather warm relations between Anglicans and Eastern Orthodoxy. This is one of the reasons why Anglicanism has seen itself as in a strategic position in the movement towards Christian unity, since it contains, through the evangelical wing, an outreach towards the more radical kinds of Protestantism, and a corresponding outreach, through the Anglo-Catholic strand, towards the Orthodox and, of course, Roman Catholicism itself.

But if the temper of the Church of England was to try to comprehend the different styles of faith within its embrace, it was not altogether successful, as the existence of Nonconformism showed. Still, the internal pluralism of the Church has been important, facilitated by what may be termed orthopraxy: provided folk kept to the practice of the Book of Common Prayer, there was much latitude. But it should also be recalled that the Church has been an established one, so that it has had to function not just as an expression of the feelings and aspirations of various sorts of Christians but also as an identification of the national spirit. In this, as in some other respects, it resembles the State religions of Scandinavia – Lutheranism through different languages.

Curiously, the four main peoples of the British Isles evolved differing national religions: Anglican in England, Presbyterian in Scotland, Catholic in Ireland and predominantly Nonconformist in Wales. Presbyterianism was, as a national religion, somewhat doctrinaire, in that the duty was laid upon the rulers (king and parliament) to maintain the purity of religion, that is as defined by Presbyterian faith. The logic of the latter was dictated by the awful gulf felt to separate God from man, the 'Calvinist distance between heaven and earth'. The Reformed Churches stressed this separation in a new milieu. For Catholicism or for Orthodoxy the liturgy made Christ himself highly numinous, as bodied forth in the action and the Host. That was gone in the Calvinist arrangements, and it was natural enough that the weight of awe should be directed on to God as Father, and that a new emphasis should be laid upon the Old Testament. The fact that early Calvinism simply made use of psalms for worship, rather than more overtly Christian hymns, reinforced such feelings, so that in the Presbyterian dramatization of experience, the experience of being a fallen creature confronted by the awful majesty of God was a powerful element – yet coupled with assurance of being saved. All this was given strong intellectual shape through the doctrine of predestination. Calvin in this was not distant from the Koran – and the doctrines of both religions can be said to spring from the sense of dependence and otherness and mercy. The appeal of this Calvinist motif in much of later evangelical Christianity stems from the way in which it sharpens the drama of redemption. At the same time from a group point of view the Old Testament provided a relevant myth for various folk in the Calvinist connection, from the Covenanters to the Afrikaner Trekkers. But generally the more evangelical the interest (rather than group identity) the greater the tendency to moderate predestination, as with the Dutch Arminius.

All the types of Christianity we have touched on so far in this chapter (with the exception of Methodism, which however separated from the Church of England, in a sense unwillingly), conceived Christianity as a monistic religion. It and society were to be virtually coterminous if possible. Part of the inner dynamic of the Reformation lay in the fact that the Bible testified to states of affairs markedly at variance with much official Christianity – and whatever Luther or Calvin may have said, the picture in the New Testament is not, precisely, that of the faith as established, or national. The Old Testament was something of a different matter, for the history of Israel could always be allegorized into one's own history.

The radical Reformation, as we have seen, had a powerful early expression in the Anabaptist movement, partialforerunner of Baptism as it came to form itself in England. This can be said to be a type of Christianity which takes a rite of passage with utmost seriousness, but at the same time psychologizes it. The explosive part of the doctrine of adult Baptism lay precisely in the fact that faith was individualized (as it must have been too in the early Church). If individualized, then the monistic claims of the magisterial Reformers as well as of Roman Catholicism were challenged. It was logical that the Anabaptists were persecuted (even leaving aside the uncharacteristic violence of Münster). Nevertheless, much of Christian revivalism has been based upon a sentiment not altogether far from that expressed by the monistic arrangement – namely that the order of society depends on true religion. The revival integrates the twiceborn human atoms into a healthier social order. There is also the irony to consider that the Puritans who established a theocracy in Massachusetts were Congregationalists who, like the Baptists, believed in the Church as a set of congregations made up of the faithful voluntarily joining together.

Baptists and Congregationalists tended to take different paths, partly perhaps because of the former's adherence to the principle of total immersion as the only adequate symbol of identification with Christ's death and resurrection. The Baptists' more fervent path has tended more easily towards extreme conservatism over the Bible. Indeed one may see the products of the radical Reformation as polarizing towards fundamentalism and humanism.

While Baptists and Congregationalists retain sacraments, these are absent from the Christianity of the Quakers. Indeed the whole principle of the Society of Friends is that what is inside, not what is outside, that is important. Thus socially the movement was radically egalitarian, while religion had almost entirely to do with good works and the experience of the Inner Light. This is interpreted in a Christian way, for it is the Spirit of Christ which illuminates every man, so long as he seriously attends to it. One might see in Quakerism a lay mysticism. Something of the spirit of mystical Christianity is expressed individualistically and in the context of wordly life, rather than (as mostly elsewhere) collectively and monastically. Ritual, myth and doctrine are minimal; institutionalization is simple – but the experiential and ethical dimensions of the faith are everything. The Bible is not given that autonomy and power which it typically has in other Protestant movements. It may be noted that the mystical imprint of Quakerism gives its appeal to experience a quiet, inward air: the dynamic of the numinous, more overt in evangelical faith, is absent, and with it the violence and tendency to judgement which sometimes accompany prophetic kinds of Christianity.

If Baptism and Methodism stress conversion experiences, which in effect are dramatic reflections of the story of redemption, another motif of experience has come to play a role in Protestant (and latterly to some extent in Roman Catholic) religion – speaking with tongues, an effect of a kind of holy possession, together with other powers such as that of healing.

Indeed one may see the speaking with tongues as a sign of new life – it is the baptism of the Spirit. The strange tongue in which one so possessed speaks is unknown and rarely understood, but constitutes the loftiest praise of the Lord. It is as if the person blessed with this charismatic power has gone back to an original language, prior to the languages of man emanating from the Tower of Babel: in these pristine sounds there can be heard the unmistakable voice of God. The various Pentecostal Churches and congregations are a varied phalanx of ecstatic biblical religion, expressing a particularly emotional faith which feels itself true to Christian origins.

Modern Christianity has shaped itself more and more in ways that cut across denominational and organizational lines. Thus the ecstatic biblicism of Pentecostals can be found outside groups that label themselves as such, and there is even, in some areas, a vigorous Pentecostal outreach into the Roman Catholic Church. Moreover, the conservative type of biblicism, which overlaps with the Pentecostal movement, and is the consequence of a conscious reaction to, and criticism of, modern liberal ideas stemming from the historical treatment of the scriptures, the feel of modern science, and, often, a sense of human progress, represents one wing of many differing Protestant denominations and traditions.

In any case, there are various reasons for a convergence of many Protestant groups in the twentieth century – a convergence which is a main impulse behind the Ecumenical Movement through which the major part of modern Christianity is forming itself into a loose spiritual federation. One reason is that parallel influences have made themselves felt across Protestantism – a move away from strict Calvinism, the use of hymns in worship, a trend towards the formalization of worship among those groups, such as Presbyterians, who most stress extempore prayer and the like. Another reason, especially in the United States, is that groups of differing ethnic and religious traditions have become increasingly integrated in society, and widespread intermarriage helps to crumble the hard edges of old divisions. Furthermore, the denominations have consciously sought a greater unity, both because it seems genuinely the

Christian thing to aim at, but perhaps more importantly because the churches in Western societies have seen themselves on the defensive, and weakened by divisions: so working together has been perceived as a preliminary to a kind of spiritual counter-attack. And since, as we have noted, some vital polarizations run across denominational boundaries anyway, the boundary disputes between Churches appear to have less significance.

Christian ecumenism of the twentieth century has had two main features: one is the founding of the World Council of Churches through a conference in Amsterdam in 1948, and the other is the revolution effected in the Roman Catholic Church through Vatican II (1962–65). The latter has meant a vastly greater openness to Protestant, and to some small extent Orthodox, feelings and attitudes. The translation of the mass into vernacular languages has, furthermore, brought Catholic piety very close to that of traditional Anglicanism and Lutheranism. The ecumenical dimension of Christianity, however, can also generate new forms of exclusivism, since some groups fear a watering down of the faith: a reaction especially marked among the most conservative biblical kind of faith.

Pentecostalism has an affinity to the new African and other religious movements which we discussed in Chapter 5. As we have seen, however, only one of these has entered into the ecumenical circle, as a member of the World Council of Churches. They represent one aspect of the problem of the definition of the faith. Here we need to contemplate some of those offshoots of the parent stem of Christianity that incorporate a strong ambiguity with regard to the tradition. Since Christianity typically involved belief in Christ's divinity as sufficient for salvation, the ambiguous offshoots are those which in one way or another subtract from or add to this core.

A venerable movement stemming from Reformation times and indeed beyond is Unitarianism. Though persecuted, the Unitarians had some success – King Sigismund of Transylvania, for instance, in 1568 issued an edict establishing religious freedom there, and Unitarianism flourished in that country. Above all the promises and realities of freedom in the New

World gave Unitarian ideals vigour, and Unitarianism was a powerful religion of the elite in the eighteenth and nineteenth centuries: its influence was especially vivid at Harvard, and it animated the American Renaissance. In its modern form (after merging with the Universalists) it is remarkably open with regard to belief, not even demanding belief in One God, as the name Unitarian implies (by contrast with the word Trinitarian). One modern expression of the spirit of the movement indicates, however, its embodiment of certain central themes in the American tradition:

To become a Unitarian you should (1) feel within your own heart and mind the love of freedom of thought and conscience; (2) recognize the demand of the voice of reason, challenging you to examine the truths you would incorporate into the texture of your personal faith; (3) affirm and promote the dignity of man; (4) remain receptive to new knowledge; and (5) uphold the ideals of democracy.[1]

This statement reflects the theme of the perfectibility of man as a rational being which was so dominant a colour in the fabric of American hope; but it also is indistinguishable from an expression of agnostic Humanism. If Unitarianism starts from belief in one God, the ethics of Jesus and reverence for the human spirit, it also shades into Humanism. To this we shall return, for it is tied in with the question of the paternity of Christianity as to some of its modern rivals.

Though Unitarianism was influential in America, and helped to shape the framework of tolerance which allowed nineteenth-century America to draw into itself Catholics, Jews and a variety of Protestants, the American ethos was also open to, and indeed perhaps demanded, recurring waves and bouts of revivalism. Thus in the pullulation of new cults and rival preachings it was not surprising that a number of movements were born which were genuinely new, and partly for that reason remained in an ambiguous relationship to mainstream Christianity. One might think: If the twentieth century is the epoch of new Christian or semi-Christian movements in the Third

---

[1] Karl M. Chworowsky in Leo Rosten, ed. *Religions in America* (New York, 1963).

World, the nineteenth was the epoch of the New World.

Of these, perhaps the most surprising and heroic was the Church of Jesus Christ of Latter-Day Saints. It was surprising partly because of the originality of some of its teachings, at least in the context of upper New York State in the early part of the century, and partly because of the strange claims made with regard to the scripture known as *The Book of Mormon*. One of the strange motifs of the culture of that time and place was the belief that there was buried treasure to be found and that it could be found by a suitably gifted person using a peepstone. Joseph Smith involved himself in this searching, but in fact his greatest find proved to be at a different level of reality: it proved to be the gold plates received by him from the angel Moroni and which he translated by the means of a miraculous version of the peepstone into what is known as *The Book of Mormon*. This and other scriptures are added to the Bible, which Smith considered no longer to be in its pure pristine form, as the norm for Mormon beliefs. The amazing success of the new faith, after persecution and the great trek to Utah, makes it the most dynamic of the new faiths of America. But the novelty of its teachings have kept it sundered from the Ecumenical movement – teachings such as the distinctness of the three persons of the Trinity, the pre-existence of human souls, the evolutionary account of God and apparent polytheism, and the radical reinterpretation of Christian history. The idea that Christ after his Ascension visited North America, and that lost tribes of Israel migrated to the New World centuries before Christ, are part of a myth which gave special meaning to the goal of setting up Zion in America – ultimately, as it turned out, in Utah. Whatever may be thought of Smith's mysterious claims, he gave a new concreteness to the millennial temper in America. He made Christian hope in the last things to take on local colour, and provided a vividness of teaching which was to inspire a remarkable new experiment in living. Essentially he combined prophecy, a new myth and a capacity for creating the organization for a new style of theocracy.

Almost equally dynamic in their missionary activity are the Jehovah's Witnesses. Indeed in an important sense they have reduced religion to the practice of evangelism. Their meetings in a Kingdom Hall on a Sunday or a Thursday evening are not elaborate acts of praise, but rather means of furthering the enterprise of spreading the Word as they understand it. A certain growth in the teaching is built into the movement, in that the heart of it lies in the Watch Tower Bible and Tract Society, a publishing enterprise which does need some degree of novelty to justify the continuing production of pamphlets and explications of the scriptures. The Witnesses hold a doctrine of Christ which is very reminiscent of that of Arius; but their main preoccupation is with the imminent end of the world, and their missionary work is designed to give people a second chance before the last things. Their radical alienation from both Church and State leads them to be unwilling to fight in war, though they are not, strictly, pacifists – it is just that both Christendom (as they call mainstream Christianity) and the nations of the world are corrupt. If the Mormons represent a this-worldly and optimistic vision of the last things, the Witnesses are alienated and pessimistic about the possibility of a Zion established by human efforts.

Christian Science is another variant on the theme of Christian ambiguity. It is Unitarian, as befits a religion centred in Boston, but it concentrates on a particular aspect of the New Testament: the face which it perceives there is the face of Christ the Healer – Christ, not strictly God, but rather the great example who shows men that their true nature is immortal. Mrs Eddy's most distinctive contribution to the faith-healing tradition was to take it out (in her own view) of the realm of faith into that of science. The trouble with men is that they are confused – they suffer from a kind of cosmic hypnosis, which prevents them from seeing that sickness and all evil is basically unreal. The new science is expounded in a work which could be regarded as a sort of scripture – a parascripture: *Science and Health with Key to the Scriptures*.

It is not especially my intention here to evaluate these movements or to answer the question of how far they can be considered Christian or of how far they can be denied to be Christian. But they do lie along the edges of the Christian movement as a whole: perhaps in earlier days they would simply have been declared to be heretical. However, the heresies of the past often incorporated answers to questions which Christendom was unclear about or was unsatisfying about, at least for some. New movements are often ways of making concrete existential questions, and of taking seriously some aspects of the biblical myth which have become obscured.

From this perspective, let us look briefly at these new religions of America. Joseph Smith could be said to have resolved, in a certain special way, two dilemmas. The first was to do with the environment of the Second Great Awakening – the revivalism of his youth was a cacophony of differing teachings. Who could tell who was right? Prophetic vision settled the matter. (But the question remains: for why follow Smith's new prophecy rather than the other voices?) The second dilemma was: If America was God's own country, how was its new society to be given divine shape? Liberalism and democracy pointed to a plural solution – every voice being given its hearing. Smith chose theocracy, though of a populist kind.

The Witnesses fasten on to the apocalyptic aspect of the scriptures, and give vivid and literal importance to a dimension of Christian belief which has either proved indigestible or too vague to be of practical importance. But they have also carried the idea of mission to its ultimate conclusion: it becomes the only practical activity of religion.

Christian Science focusses on another aspect of scriptures not taken with great seriousness by much of mainstream Christianity (especially in its Protestant forms): the healing side of Christ. It goes, too, to an extreme: spiritual healing owes nothing to material methods.

Unitarianism, as found in the United States, tries to solve another problem, but one which is at the root of Christianity's modern weaknesses among intellectuals: how to maintain a continuity between traditional Christian values and the world of the religious sceptic – whose scepticism springs not from protest or alienation from the faith itself but from the acute tensions between traditional doctrines and modern scientific cosmology.

Was that scientific world-view itself indirectly a product of Christianity? It is possible, as some writers have done, to see science as partly a product of the Jewish-Christian conception of God as Creator. Such genealogies are hard to trace. It is perhaps more profitable to turn to contemplate the relationship between Christianity and Marxism, for here we have a vision of reality which functions for many both as an ideology or practical belief-system and typically as a potent rival to religion. Such antagonism is a good sign of affinity.

The vivid images of the Apocalypse complement the mysterious myth of Creation: they are the rise and fall of the curtain at the beginning and the end of the drama of human history. Some of the story in between is recounted, and above all the story of Israel, in the biblical narratives. But though so often men, be they Zulus or Voortrekkers, have figured their lives as patterned after Israel's, there is typically an uncertainty in Christian thinking about what to make of the period between the New Testament events and now. The discernment of biblical themes in ongoing events has been rather fragmentary. Yet Christianity is about a cosmic drama, and as men have become aware more clearly of the shape of their past, there comes the question of the significance of that in God's dispensation. In a word: Does history have a divine plot? Augustine attempted something in this line; but in modern times the two overshadowing figures who have assigned a plot to history have been Hegel and Marx. Both for Hegel and for Marx the religious issue was there, but in contrasting ways. For Marx, the thought of Feuerbach was vital – for it was he that had in essence invented the idea of religious projection: God was human nature, in effect, projected on to the screen of the universe. To understand God one has to understand the origin of the idea in human consciousness. Theology has then to be replaced by anthropology.

With Hegel we see the birth of a new myth of history, but a myth stated in rather abstract terms – the dialectical movement of Absolute Mind, in the waltz of thesis, antithesis and synthesis. Although Hegel's system was not theologically orthodox, it did grow in part out of his early concerns with a fresh look at Christian belief; and it saw human history as shaped by the rhythms of the Spirit. Marx retained something of the rhythms, but, of course, substituted Matter for Spirit. The new historical dialectic was formed against the backdrop of atheism, to be sure; but Marx's strong ethical passion, his vision of a new kingdom of man upon earth, his commitment to the drama of revolutionary politics – all these give a religious flavour to the system which he struggled to fashion.

Moreover, Marxism has come to function, in societies where it has become the official philosophy, as a monistic belief-system, echoing the Caesaropapism of earlier Christian days. The persecution of dissident intellectuals, the harrying of Baptists, the tight circumscription of Church activities – these features of a number of Communist regimes repeat in a new key the policies of Christian states of times gone by. One may thus see Humanism and Marxism as a polarity which reflects an earlier one, between the individualistic and monistic wings of the Reformation.

We may notice that both Hegel and Marx, in delineating the plot of the historical drama, are presenting us with a myth adapted to the modern condition – for the very abstractions which are used to describe the processes of history (dialectic, contradiction, feudalism, bourgeoisie, proletariat, exploitation, revolution, capitalism, socialism, false consciousness, projection, ideology, class-struggle) have a scientific air and at the same time a dark metaphysical force. In the highly charged interplay of these abstract forces we can play a part too, in rituals of solidarity, and have too a sense of self-sacrifice in the face of historic changes which swallow up the mere individual. Somehow to many modern men the thrust and counterthrust of the abstractions so concretely embedded in the untidinesses of history have more plausibility than the more personal and fanciful-seeming myths of the old Christian world – the struggles and mutual interchanges between God and Satan, Adam, Christ, the children of Israel, the saints, the Virgin, angels, devils. It is also of some interest that in China Marxism, admittedly in a Chinese adaptation, has proved successful in a way that Christianity was not able to: elsewhere too the Marxist idea has been geared to national liberation.

In moving to Marxism we have gone beyond the circle of Christianity and its penumbra. But even had we not stepped so far we would still have traversed a great variety of manifestations of religion. It is natural to ask for an explanation of this great diversity. It is true that most great religions change and develop different forms. In some, diversity is built into their prehistory and first appearances. One factor in Christianity's proliferation into varying forms lies at the very heart of the faith – the many faces of Christ that we can glimpse through the scriptures and the life of the early Church. And his words are similarly open to differing depths of interpretation. It may be the case that the very dogmatism which developed in the Christian tradition was precisely because of the inherent fluidity of the faith, for ever in danger of de-stabilizing the community of believers. Another factor lies in the contrasts of religious experience which the faith draws upon: it is sometimes awe-struck, replete with the numinous experience; at other times it is almost lost in the interior castle, the cloud of un-knowing; again it is often dramatically expressed in phases of repentance and conversion, in which the drama of redemption is re-played in the soul of the individual. And in expressing itself variously in experience it attracts a number of differing kinds of men who help to mould its diversity. Indeed it is worth observing how much the shapes of Christian traditions have been determined by individual heroes, thinkers, saints, missionaries – St Paul, Origen, Augustine, St Basil, St Benedict, Aquinas, Luther, Calvin, Fox, Wesley, and so on. In addition, Christianity has permeated and been permeated by such a number of diverse cultures – Hellenistic, Latin, Slav, Near Eastern, Germanic, Celtic, North American, sub-Saharan African, etc.

Still, there will be a desire to find the core, the heart, the essence. Yet every time we go beyond the gallery of historical pictures of the faith as etched in human history by the various traditions which go back one way or another to the early Church, we enter upon value-judgements. There is nothing wrong, of course, in making up one's mind in this way, Indeed for anyone seriously gripped by the faith, such judgement is imperative. Of all the pictures I can tell you which I like best, which seems to make most sense. But I know that there will be others for whom that picture is not the truth.

Is this too relative? I think not. From the perspective of the history of religions, Christianity is Christianities: it is how it is expressed in human history, in amazing variety. And it is obviously relevant to the person who wishes to make up his mind as to how he understands the faith – as to what the ideal essence is for him – that he should perceive how the river of the religion has bifurcated into so many streams across its mighty delta.

One other point about variety: let us not forget that there is a future as well as a past of Christianity. That future is as open as earlier futures were. There was no law that Christianity should produce Lutheranism: rather some possibility of Reform was present and it was given particular shape by Luther and his associates and successors. The future will hold new shapes of Christianity. This is so even if the movement towards Christian unity brings about a consensus. That consensus itself will be new in spirit.

And as we might learn from Christian history, every move to recapture the pristine Christianity results in a new expression of it. Perhaps there is something instructive to be learnt from the story of the Disciples of Christ. Starting in the frontier milieu, the movement was an attempt to cut through dogmatic and other divisions between Christians and to go back to a straight New Testament faith. It was a kind of Reform beyond the Reform, and a movement beyond denominations. This is brought out, in a way, by the following quotation, and yet something else is brought out too:

> Some will say that the Disciples of Christ are a great evangelical, Protestant denomination. Others will say that they are not a denomination at all, but the pure New Testament Church of Christ. Still others will prefer to describe the

146

Disciples as a brotherhood, or a communion. Perhaps the most favoured word among Disciples is movement – a movement back to the New Testament, and forward to ultimate unity under God of all who call themselves Christians.[2]

Thus writes a spokesman of the movement (denomination?). For a while my family and I lived opposite a church of the Disciples. It was in Madison, Wisconsin, and it bore the proud simple title: FIRST CHRISTIAN CHURCH. There were another three churches in the same street.

[2] James E. Craig in Leo Rosten, ed., *Religions in America* (New York, 1963).

8

Asceticism and Mysticism

I have a pebble with me, grey for the most part and rounded by the Irish Sea, and on it some white lines, nearly in the shape of a cross. I picked it up in Ninian's cave, on the Wigtown peninsula. To stand there and look out from the cave on the rather desolate coast, cold, wet and cheerless in winter, but flanked by beautiful woods and a fat burn or two, which are delightful in the spring and summer time, is to be reminded of several striking developments in Christian piety, even as early as the beginnings of the fifth century. First, in this outer fringe of the Roman world there was a counterpart to the Desert Fathers who had established the austere hermit-life in which was re-expressed the old battle between good and evil. The Celtic Church flourished and spread, and partly due to the *peregrini*, those wandering hermits and saints (who were briefly discussed in connection with the Scandinavian churches). Second, one recalls that not far from his cave, St Ninian, who probably did, despite what some scholars say, exist, had set up his *Candida Casa* or White House, a monastic foundation which was to prove to be an important educational centre in the life of the cultures flanking the Irish Sea. Celtic monasticism was to be one of the vital branches of this type of the Christian life which animated Latin Europe and the Orthodox East. There was a transition from the life of the hermit to the life of the monastic community, and it was the latter institution which proved so vital in projecting Christian values through the turbulent times lying between the crumbling of the Roman Empire and the formation of medieval Christendom. Third, in more general terms my pebble reminds one of the general problem of asceticism in the Christian life. Sometimes such worldly poverty and discomfort (pain even if one were to go in for flagellation and the like), seems in line with certain New Testament commands but at other times it seems strangely out of tune with the dynamic conviviality which Jesus and the disciples sometimes are depicted as displaying.

The three themes tie in with mysticism, that is the introvertive life of contemplation, culminating in such experiences and themes as are found in the classic writing of such figures as Bernard of Clairvaux, Bonaventure, Gregory Palamas, Meister Eckhart, Jan van Ruysbroeck, Theresa of Avila, John of the Cross, and many others. And also Jakob Boehme, the Protestant shoemaker, who stands as the greatest figure in the admittedly relatively thin annals of Protestant mysticism. Indeed, this represents a problem in Christianity which we shall come to: If contemplative Christianity had its typical home in the monastery, and if Protestantism affirms that the monastic life is unnatural in the context of Christian living (such at least was the attitude of some great Reformers, above all, of course, Luther), then is it that somehow the struggles of men such as Ninian, the Desert Fathers, Palamas and John of the Cross are irrelevant to the central spirit of the faith?

But a word first on the meaning of 'mysticism'. Some might have already bridled upon reading my words 'the admittedly relatively thin annals of Protestant mysticism'. For it could be argued that Protestantism gave immense impulse to the feeling that God's grace has to be tasted directly, that it is through inner experience of the risen Lord, through illumination in the heart, that the faith is to be known and apprehended. It could be thought that Protestantism involves a dialectic between inner experience and the words of scripture. From this point of view it can be seen as inherently mystical. But here we are entering a dispute which has to do with the meaning of the term. People have used it in differing ways. But a major way, and this is the one I prefer here, is to see mysticism in terms of a particular kind of experience, namely that which typically accrues upon the pursuit of the contemplative life. One can make here some comparisons with other religious traditions. The life of the Buddhist Order is in principle centred upon meditation and contemplation in which the mind is purified in certain ways. Similarly with Hindu yoga, and the major thrust of the Sufi movement in Islam. It is this meditative life which flourished most clearly within the context of the Christian orders of monks and nuns, and which is less in evidence in Protestantism precisely because of the latter's attitudes to monasticism. And since Protestantism in large measure saw itself as returning to the pristine Gospel message, it may be that there is a problem about the role of asceticism and mysticism in the Christian faith.

There are various roots of Christian mysticism and of the monasticism with which its life was so much intertwined. Consider again the cave. It already testifies to two motifs, self-abnegation and solitariness. The second motif has a certain logic to it when we are thinking of the contemplative life, and yet it bears with it a paradox. The logic lies in the fact that the person who turns inward in his spirituality, trying to find God in the depths of his soul (at its Ground, in the Spark – to use Eckhart's language), is on what is essentially a lone journey. This is brought out in a famous passage of Plotinus (a major influence himself upon Christian mysticism):

> This is the life of gods and divine and blessed men, deliverance from the things of this world, a life which takes no delight in the things of this world, escape in solitude to the Solitary.[1]

Thus contemplation has often been associated with the life of the recluse and (often) the wanderer. For the lone wanderer has no ties, and no base. The Celtic *peregrini* symbolized this condition well, as does also the figure of the roaming *sadhu* in India and of the Buddha-to-be, stealing away from home to live the life of the wandering recluse. And yet by a paradox the inner, solitary way often creates its own community.

Before considering this, however, let us look at the various grounds of Christian asceticism and their connection with contemplation. To some extent asceticism is evident in the writings of St Paul – for example, in his suggestion that those who have wives might live as those who have none. A certain austere other-worldliness was of course natural when people believed in the imminent Second Coming. Time was short:

[1] From *Enneads* VI.9.11, translated by A. H. Armstrong in his *Plotinus* (London, 1953), p. 160.

spiritual matters pressed. But of course the urgency had somewhat worn off by the time of St Anthony, struggling with sexual and other temptations in the desert. On the other hand, the very success of the faith in penetrating to the vitals of the Empire had brought with it a relaxation of moral attitudes, and it was partly to balance this that the eremitical and monastic ideals gained influence. They were a new form of voluntary poverty. Further, Christianity, though it rejected them as heresies, was not unaffected by dualist views which treated the body as evil – views which were current in various kinds of Gnosticism and in Manichaeanism.

But asceticism, of course, was not just conceived as a negative thing – the refraining from various actions, foods and so forth. For it was geared to the spiritual life, and this was a matter of prayer and sacrament. In that Christianity's central rite was a communal one, there was an inevitability in the predominance of the monastic ideal over that of the hermit. As for prayer, which would of course be solitary, this was the chief activity for which the things of the world were given up. The ascetic could look to St Paul's image of the athlete, who has to get into training. If one multiplies the ascetic life by prayer, one inevitably enters upon a form of mental and physical training, so that there is both a causal and a logical connection between the growth of the ascetic goal and the development of the contemplative life. Moreover, though from a popular point of view an ascetic might be thought to gain power (this being a common motif in religions, especially with regard to the concept of *tapas* in the Indian tradition), the Christian emphasis upon grace made it less likely that asceticism would become a path independent of worship.

As well as the image of the athlete, early Christian asceticism also used the image of martyrdom. There is a nice story of a brother who practised self-mortification as a hermit but heard of the monastic life initiated by Pachomius of Egypt. His great ambition, as was that of many committed Christians, was to 'bear witness', that is, to become a martyr. This was to the early Church a second baptism, the baptism of blood, and a sure entry into Paradise; and the blood of the martyrs was the seed of the Church. Admittedly later times were to overdo the memory of martyrdom, and to exaggerate Christian suffering and witness in this respect. But it was a vital motif in the life of the community as it emerged from under the period of insecurity and sporadic, but often dreadful, persecution into the light of Constantine's reign. It was during this new period, after (as our text has it) 'the blessed Constantine . . . had put on Christ', that this brother was received into Pachomius' monastery. He kept pestering his senior to pray for him that he might become a martyr. But opportunities were not what they were, and Pachomius evidently became a trifle impatient. He admonished him: 'Brother, if you can put up with the quarrelling of the monks in a firm and blameless manner, and live your life straightly in accordance with what will please Christ, you will have the companionship of the martyrs in heaven.'

Mortification of the flesh was, as the name implies, a kind of death, and Christianity has been shot through with the idea, derived from Christ's death and implicit in the rite of baptism, that one must die in order to rise. One dies to the old Adam in order to acquire the nature of the new Adam. Now the way in which the contemplative life came to be interpreted (and more than interpreted, lived) through specifically Christian models helps us to strike a balance between those who say that mysticism is everywhere the same – a teaching which happens to have been fashionable in the last two or three decades under the spell of the attractive idea of a 'perennial philosophy' running through all the great religions and expressed most luminously in mysticism – and those who draw a very clear line between Christian contemplation and that found in other faiths. To this question of the place of Christian mysticism in the world's religions we shall later return.

The ascetic struggles of the Desert Fathers and early monks were often fierce. One rather typical example (typical in spirit at any rate) is this: A brother was tormented by the memory of an attractive woman. Another monk came to join the group to which he belonged, and told him that his wife was dead – for she was the woman he lusted after. Hearing where she had been buried he went there, dug down and smeared his robe with the blood of the corpse. He then returned, and addressed his temptation: 'Look, this is what you desired, and now that you have it, enjoy yourself.' The blood stank more and more, and his passion died down. This was grim heroism, indeed. But as monasticism emerged it took a middle path between extreme asceticism and indulgence, and this was one of the main achievements of those who, like St Basil (330–379) and St Benedict (late fifth to mid sixth century), formulated rules for the control of the new communities.

Basil listed some of the advantages of the communal over the eremetical life. That he had to do so was an indication of the high esteem in which the solitary life was held. One reason was about self-sufficiency – this could be achieved by a community but not by a hermit. But much more importantly, Basil saw a contradiction between the lone quest and the Christian ideal of love. For the former ultimately was self-centred, while love is directed towards others. From a practical angle also, there are advantages in the common life, since the hermit has no one to guide him if he deviates from the right path, does not have the check represented by communal censure and can easily become smug and self-satisfied. Nevertheless, there was an assumption that it is an honourable thing for a monk to progress through the life of the community to a stage when he might become a hermit. Such an ideal has remained active in the Eastern Orthodox wing of Christianity; and it was not repudiated by Benedict when he drew up his rule, which was to have a profoundly formative effect on monasticism in the West.

Nevertheless, it was a Benedictine assumption that the monk would live in his community until his death. And the notable thing about the rule is its practicality in details, and its quiet warnings that following the rule is just a beginning. Indeed it was criticized by those under the influence of the more heroic Egyptian ideals for being rather soft. A monk's life was full and governed by a daily rhythm, but it was not all that austere by the standards of the times. Thus the rule provides for a pound of bread a day, two dishes for the main meal, plus fruit or young vegetables if available. About half a litre of wine was the norm. But quantities could be varied at the discretion of the abbot. The labour of the monks was divided between working in the fields, reading and meditation and the performance of the Office. Thus worship always played a central part in Christian monastic life, and for this reason humility was a virtue prized very greatly by Benedict. The attractiveness and commonsensical nature of this framework in Christian living was such as to ensure a sufficient supply of recruits to the monasteries during the centuries following the formulation of the rule.

Now though the life of asceticism, supplemented by communal discipline, could be a vital instrument of that turning away from the senses and from entanglement in worldly concerns which is a typical condition of the contemplative life, other forces were at work in fostering the interior life. Notable were the effects upon Christian thinking of the philosophical traditions of the Graeco-Roman world, and in particular the tradition going back to Plato, which had, by the start of the Christian era, moved towards that set of teachings which has come to be known as Neoplatonism.

In absorbing ideas from 'pagan' philosophy, Christianity trod somewhat warily, and there has been a constant pattern of renewed resistance to an opening out to non-biblical sources of inspiration. Tertullian could ask what Athens had to do with Jerusalem. Still, the Platonic tradition had an undoubted appeal, especially for those of mystical inclination, for not only had Plato held the ideal of ascent to the contemplation of the Form of the Good, but Plotinus (205–270) had given an even more explicit place to contemplation as the goal of philosophy. At the same time one cannot help but be struck by the relative impersonality and seeming abstraction of much of the language of Plotinus and many others who have sought to express the higher principles with which the mystic believes himself to be in intimate contact. An understanding of the polarity between the personalism of biblical Christianity and the impersonalism of some mystical language is important for understanding the nature of Christian mysticism. But let me first rehearse two examples of the latter type of approach, one being that of Plotinus, the other being the writer thought to be Dionysius the Areopagite, mentioned in *Acts*, but in fact someone who composed his influential works around 500.

Writing about the One, the Ultimate Principle, according to his system Plotinus says:

> Since the nature of the One produces all things It is none of them. It is not a thing or quality or quantity or intellect or soul; It is not in motion or at rest, in place or in time, but exists in Itself, a unique Form; or rather It is formless, before motion, before rest; for these belong to being and make it multiple.[2]

This One in Plotinus, though so negatively described and (apparently) abstract is doubly significant from a spiritual point of view. For first it is in the nature of perfection – and the One is supremely perfect for unity, oneness, is the form of all forms – it is in the nature of perfection to flow over into creative activity; and so there eternally emanates from the One the Nous or Intellect, which is the realm in which forms are contained; this in turn gives rise to Soul, the universal Soul of which our souls are fragments. This in turn produces, as its lower half, the soul which animates and guides the universe, known as Nature. Below this lies matter, so weak in power that it gives rise to no further level of being. The aim of the wise man is to ascend upwards in the opposite direction to the downward emanations from the One.

In fact, bald statements of the Plotinian system cannot, of course, evoke its richness, majesty and (one could say) spiritual charm. But they can perhaps stimulate in us a question about the function of this strange ballet of principles – One, Intellect, Soul, Nature and so forth. Perhaps in modern times we may after all have some affinity to this way of thinking: consider the grip of Marxist accounts of history, which depict a gavotte of thesis, antithesis and synthesis, and the promise that an understanding of this interplay will contribute to our own exalting participation in history's more hopeful thrust. Of course, sometimes Plotinus slips into referring to the One by

[2] *Enneads* VI.9.3, translated by A. H. Armstrong, *Plotinus* (London, 1953), p. 58.

the personal pronoun: the It sometimes seems like a He.

Something of the spirit of the work of Pseudo-Dionysius can be captured from the following passage:

> The Scriptures themselves teach us that no being may take in the meaning of this Super-Essence that transcends all Essences, this Good defying the description of all words, this Mind that eludes every mind, this Word beyond Experience, Insight, Name and Category, this Cause of all being that does not itself exist, this Super-Essence that is beyond all being and Revelation save its own self-manifestation.[3]

The author goes on to say that though the Good in Itself is not in any way to be got at or understood, it does out of its isolation send forth a Super-Essential Ray which illumines creatures, and draws them to him, to contemplate the Divine Goodness and be in harmony therewith. Elsewhere by a paradox he refers to the divine illumination as a kind of dazzling obscurity – a paradox also found elsewhere in the Christian mystical tradition, notably in the writing of Jan van Ruysbroeck, to whom I shall be referring later.

Five different motifs can, I think, be perceived in such passages. First, and obviously, such language has been influenced by the Greek philosophical tradition, and this not unnaturally tended towards abstraction. (In modern times an analogy would be where the attempt is made to wed religious belief with scientific theory – as in Teilhard de Chardin's noosphere and Omega Point, etc., or in Capra's *The Tao of Physics*.) Second, less obviously in Plotinus but more explicitly in Dionysius, there is concern to describe the highest Being in a way which transcends the anthropomorphism of mythic language, whether we are looking to Greek mythology of the old religion, the mystery cults of the Empire, or the biblical revelation. Thus though it is less misleading to call God wise than it is to call him drunken, it is still misleading – hence one reason for the negative way in theology, the 'description' of God by saying what he is not. Third, there are aspects of

---

[3] Translated by R. S. Petry from *De Divinis Nominibus*, 1: 1–2, in his *A History of Christianity: readings in the history of the early and medieval Church* (Englewood Cliffs, N.J., 1962), p. 146.

the mystical way which mean that descriptions of the contemplative states in which one 'sees' the divine are highly inadequate or impossible. Thus the very fact that the contemplative withdraws his senses and stills his imagination, in the quest for the depths of his own being, implies that the ordinary language of perception, memory and so forth does not apply. And because terms such as the One, Goodness in Itself, Being and Super-Essential have a certain abstract emptiness, it means that they chime in with the sense of emptying implicit in the contemplative path. It sometimes seems to be a fine point, in mystical writings, as to the difference between Being and Nothingness, Oneness and Emptiness – and even between light and darkness and knowing and unknowing.

The fact that the mystic tends to transcend the forms of the religion of worship and sacrament, and of easy talk such as one may find in catechisms and reach-me-down texts, opens the way to the thought that perhaps after all the various paths of the mystics, Eastern or Western, lead to the same place. Maybe so, and yet also maybe differences remain, in that the paths come from different directions, and even leave their marks upon their goal. Since the notion of spiritual wedlock is an image recurrent in mystical literature, I can perhaps use love as an analogy: love is in a sense the same the whole world over, and yet the significance of a loving relationship varies according to individuality and milieu. To milieu, in that love within Hindu, Muslim, Christian or Jewish marriage, or outside marriage, has its diverse outer meanings; according to individuality, for it also has its very special place within the life of the two, or more, people involved.

A fourth motif in the above type of mystical language is connected with ineffability. The latter arises, as we have seen, at least in part from the fact that the mystic searches inwards in such a way as to transcend the usual processes of the mind, which is normally much engaged with its social and natural environment. If the individual was thought of as having memory, intellect and will, then what the mystic penetrated to in his own soul seemed to be beyond these. Sometimes this something was called the ground, spark or abyss in later mysticism. But it suggested that there was an analogy between this 'true self' and the unity lying behind God as a personal being. This tendency was reinforced by the Platonic principle that like is known by like. There is, then, in religious traditions which centre upon belief in a personal God, a trend among some mystics to speak of some kind of summit or Godhead behind God's personal activity. Thus mystical theology has some drive towards a geography of the transpersonal, and on this territory there can sometimes be depicted a ballet of the metaphysical. But it should not be mistaken for mere speculation, in that its apparently speculative character arises out of a desire to explain experience.

A fifth motif is about knowing. It is a curious kind of knowing – a learned ignorance, entering a cloud of unknowing: ignorance because it goes beyond what we ordinarily think of as knowledge, which typically involves a division and categorizing of things, analysis, explanation of one level in terms of another, and so forth. The life of pure knowing-which-is-unknowing suggests various metaphors, of which light is the most common and powerful. The mystic is illumined by the Ray of which Dionysius speaks. Much later this metaphor was to burn on as the Inner Light of the Quakers. In using such models as knowledge and illumination, the mystic sometimes looks on his experience as the highest activity of the intellect, and again there seems something appropriate in using non-personal forms of language.

In line with all this, it will be worth while later considering how far Christian mysticism does and does not converge with some major kinds of Eastern contemplation.

The thought of Dionysius was directly relevant to the development of the theology of mysticism in the Greek-speaking half of the Church. In the West his impact was, until his writings were translated and interpreted by John Scotus Erigena (ninth century), less immediate and profound. But Neoplatonism had strongly affected Augustine's thinking, and through that Western theology.

The early Middle Ages saw the emergence of a powerful monastic system, mainly under the dominance of the Benedictine rule; but power could also mean laxity, and near the end of the eleventh century the Cistercian order was founded as a centralized, reformed movement, whose most influential figure was the formidable Bernard of Clairvaux (1091–1153). Thereafter a number of new orders were to be formed, ranging from the Franciscans, to the Knights Templars. The notion that an order might specialize, say in preaching and education, as with the Dominicans, or fighting and tending the sick, as with the Knights of St John, was to become a vital means whereby the Western Church renewed its forces. No such specialization occurred in the East, which maintained more consistently the contemplative ideal as the heart of monasticism. Nevertheless, the ferment of the next five centuries or so after the Cistercian reform was to prove the major epoch in Christian mysticism in the West. Here, though, it is worth mentioning two developments which were deviant; for their rejection by the main tradition illustrates something about the values implicit in Christian asceticism.

That the religion of the Cathari (literally 'pure ones'), otherwise dubbed Albigensians after the city of Albi in Languedoc, should have become, in the twelfth century, so influential in south-west France, not to mention in Lombardy and parts of central Italy, was perhaps due to widespread dissatisfaction with the spiritual standard of the Christian clergy. Contact with the Bogomils in Bulgaria, from whom possibly the Cathari originated, reinforced the movement, the last fling in the West of the once great religion of Manichaeanism. The Cathari's faith involved a double dualism – a dualism of standards and a dualism of good and evil. The former arose because of the latter. The belief that matter was evil – for this world was under the dominance of the Prince of Darkness – and that men's soul must be freed from entanglement with matter induced a severe asceticism forbidding the eating of meat, sexual intercourse and so on, which could be followed only by the elite 'perfect ones' or *perfecti* who underwent special initiation. The rest of the followers had a laxer life. The movement in effect formed itself into a counter-Church, which inspired considerable loyalty, partly because of the undoubtedly noble spirit of the *perfecti*. The crusade launched by the papacy against the Cathari, culminating in the catastrophic capture of their principal fortress at Montségur in 1244, was an index of the threat both to Church government and to orthodoxy. But why should mainstream Christianity have reacted so strongly against dualism, seeing that in many respects the Cathari's doctrines bore some excellent fruits in the contemplative life which the perfect ones pursued?

Basically, the Manichaean ideas were in opposition to two fundamental themes: first, the drama of redemption, and second the relative goodness of the created order. If the world was under the dominion of the antigod Satan, then a radical reinterpretation of the Old Testament was required, as well as of the incarnation. How could God voluntarily take on evil flesh? Thus heroic as might be the perfect ones, the thrust of their inner life was negative – its aim to escape into purity, rather than to help in the redemption of God's marred, but still good, creation.

Thus Christian mysticism was not to be conceived as apart from the practice of love. If any figure in Christian history stood as a contrast in spirit to the *perfecti* it was Francis (1182–1226). But if the Cathari were too good, the problem was the opposite with the Brethren of the Free Spirit.

This movement was not an organized Church which in effect the Albigensians had been. Rather it was a trend, a loose confederation of people, an informal order, a fashion. But it was real enough and attracted considerable persecution. This was not unnatural, for although it did not have the systematic menace borne by the Cathari, it was undoubtedly subversive. And it has remarkable echoes in other religions, by which the movement could not have conceivably been influenced.

The logic of the position of the Brethren of the Free Spirit was something born of their inner experience, though to it were added some eschatological ideas. The logic turned on the fact that these mystics, who underwent a considerable novitiate, considered that they had attained the highest mystical experience – the experience of God – and that in that state there was no differentiation of consciousness, to demarcate the soul from God. No: they were God, and in that mystical union they perceived the eternal nature of the soul and its essential identity with the Divine Being. But if a man or woman was God, then he or she could do no wrong. Consequently, they were perfectly free, and not subject to moral rules. As a sign of this they sometimes went about naked, to demonstrate their free and innocent state; and at other times involved themselves in sex and orgies, as signs of liberation. Having realized Godhood they were superior to the common man, and though they might attract disciples who could gain a kind of vicarious superiority through closeness to their divine human masters, they need have no particular sense of obligation to the masses.

The echoes of other traditions resound – nakedness as a symbol of freedom was common in ancient India and still sporadically persists among certain ascetics; the notion that sexual intercourse is a means of liberation is found in Tantrism; the mystical anarchism of the movement has correspondences in early Taoism; the absolute obedience of disciples to masters reflects the institution of the guru; the dissolution of any sense of difference between the soul and God is reminiscent of Advaita Vedanta.

The eschatological ideas gave their elitism a peculiarly disturbing twist, disturbing that is to the orthodox. For they saw the world as having three ages – that of the Father, that of the Son and now the age of the Holy Spirit. This new age in which they participated and helped to inaugurate. In the first age of the world the Father acted alone; with Christ there was inaugurated a second age; now a third age was starting in which the Brethren were divine, even surpassing Christ. These elite souls had realized their essentially divine nature, a realization not achieved by the unillumined mass of people.

Naturally such teachings aroused deep opposition from Church authorities. The wandering Brethren and Sisters were a turbulent counterpart to the mendicant orders, and often outshone the regular monks and friars in austerity. And because their sanctions and authority came from their inner experience of unity they were essentially anarchistic. But they teach us an important lesson on the mainstream Church's treatment of mysticism. The lesson contains three elements.

First, there is the problem of how Christianity can contain within its own fabric freedoms based upon inner experience. To some extent the medieval Church, through its begging orders, such as the Franciscans and Dominicans, and later through the further proliferation of papally sanctioned orders for various tasks, tried to provide a flexibility of vocations which to some extent offset the appeal of such as the Brethren of the Free Spirit. Second, the latter raised again in acute form the question of the interpretation of mysticism. Even those who were in intention orthodox in their spirituality came close to saying that in the mystical experience they actually 'became' God; and it was no coincidence that the language of deification became so strongly entrenched in Eastern Orthodox mysticism. If in the higher states men enter 'a cloud of unknowing', a 'dazzling obscurity', and the dissolution of the sense of contrast between subject and object, then why not say that they become united, even identified with God? The answer seems to lie in the whole context. The interpretation of inner experience must relate, if it is to be Christian, to the rest of Christian teaching and life. Thus the amoral anarchism of the Brethren of the Free Spirit seemed to be in contradiction with the commandment to love one's neighbour. And identity with God is in tension with the whole notion of the gap between God and men implicit not only in the language of worship but also in the doctrine of creation. So the issue: What is mystical experience like? is already more complex than might be imagined. Even if it were all alike in certain respects (such as imagelessness, timelessness and ineffability) it would still need to be seen in context. Its meaning does not lie in itself alone but in the mode in which it is embedded in a person's life.

Third, the Brethren had their own eschatology, and illustrate the way in which a number of reforming and revolutionary movements of the period were experimenting with new theories of history. In this they were forerunners of the radical Reformation. And though their new doctrines were to many shocking and to official churchmen dangerous they were part of a restlessness which has been frequent in Christian history, and this stemmed in part from the vision of a renewal from within.

Meanwhile the mysticism of Eastern Orthodoxy had continued very much under Neo-Platonist influence, but had also developed a characteristic type of spirituality through the Hesychast movement, formulated by St Simeon the New Theologian (d. 1022), in which techniques of stillness were applied, including breathing exercises, together with the use of the Jesus prayer 'Lord Jesus Christ, Son of God, have mercy on me a sinner'. The prayer has a wide use in Orthodoxy, and is held in itself to sum up the whole of the faith. Thus, regarding 'Lord Jesus' – no one can say this, as St Paul says in I Corinthians 12:3, except by the Holy Spirit. And as for 'Christ, son of God', according to Matthew's Gospel, to say this is to say something revealed by the Father, and 'not by flesh and blood'. 'Have mercy' expresses God's mercy as it is exhibited through Jesus. 'On me a sinner' – for God comes not to the worthy but to the unworthy. And in the name of Jesus all things are to be granted. The prayer puts Christianity in a nutshell. The prayer can be considered in three ways.

It can be considered as a brief means, easily to be repeated, for helping the Christian to lead the good life. In this respect it does not differ in principle from much of prayer as it has been traditionally conceived. But in the context of contemplative mysticism the prayer has a further meaning: for it is through serious repetition so 'built into' the consciousness of the person that it is powerful in bringing him beyond ordinary prayer to that which prayer tends towards, namely the practice of the presence of God. This awareness of divine presence is the state of mind which the various techniques of Hesychasm are relevant to. Third, the prayer is typically thought of in the Eastern Church as connecting the interior life to the glories of the Liturgy. The power expressed there is also, so to say, found in the words, in the name of Jesus. It is in this respect like the *mantra* of the Indian tradition – a holy formula which may be used both in ritual and in the spiritual life. The Hesychasts with their whole imagery of divine light (reminiscent of Dionysius' Ray) would appreciate that great formula from the *Upanishads*

– 'Lead me from darkness to light'. It was highly appropriate that I should receive this on a Christmas card just lately, sent to me by an Indian priest of the St Thomas tradition. Indeed, Hesychasm has many affinities with the Indian world, even if also in its secure anchorage in the liturgy it bears too the unmistakable stamp of Orthodoxy.

Just as through the Jesus prayer the contemplative goes beyond words, and finds himself in the constant presence of the Divine, so too contemplation is not, as a number of Eastern Orthodox writers say, meditation *about* God. So there is also a strand of thought here that theology itself is not really the quest to find the right propositions about God, but really the quest for union *with* God. That Orthodox theology has on the whole been remarkably little concerned with issues (say) about science and belief, modernization and so on has been in one way a re-expression of this old spiritual tradition (though it can present problems in adaptation).

However, it was in the late Middle Ages particularly that Western mysticism had its richest life. It is highly selective to pick out just one or two figures. If I pick out Eckhart and Ruysbroeck it is because they represent different motifs in Christianity which are relevant to a rounded estimate of this phenomenon, at least in the context of the general phenomenon of mysticism.

As a Dominican, Eckhart was at differing times student, teacher and preacher; but he was also, and most inwardly, a contemplative – and one moreover active enough to be the superior-general of his order for all Germany. In his later years, his lectures attracted some criticism concerning their soundness, and after his death a number of propositions of his (or supposedly his) were condemned as either heretical or rash by Pope John XXII. This was in 1329, one or two years after the Master's death (he is commonly referred to by this title in German, *Meister*). A major aspect of his theology – an aspect which seems to derive in part from his inner experience – was the distinction between the Godhead and God (*deitas* and *deus*). The latter is the divine being in personal and active form, as the Trinity. But transcending God is the pure One, also referred to on occasion by Eckhart as Nothing – on the ground that existence is grounded in the One, which is prior to it. Thus though God acts, as Creator and so on, Godhead does not. The interior life consists in turning away from created things and transcending the functions of the self, to attain to the essential soul, which Eckhart refers to as the 'Ground' and as the 'Spark'. This is where the Godhead is present in the soul. But Eckhart did not consider this a kind of achievement on the part of the individual, but rather a result of God working in the soul – for God is 'born' in the soul, and so to speak takes over a man's active intellect, directing it towards the Godhead. Now much of this was expressed in the language of philosophy. Nevertheless the parameters were set by experience and by commitment to the Christian interpretation of life.

We may see Eckhart as partly at least in the tradition of Dionysius. At any rate he reflected in his notion of *deitas* that impersonal idea – or suprapersonal idea – which we have noted already as a constituent of Dionysus' conception of God. But also, because of this, Eckhart has been seen by a number of commentators, from Rudolf Otto to the former President of India, Sarvepalli Radhakrishnan, as having much in common with Sankara (8th century AD), the great exponent of Hindu monism. We have already touched on issues related to the question of whether there is a perennial philosophy – a mystical philosophy – running through the great religions, in that the claim of the essential unity of mysticism is centrally what that perennial philosophy expresses.

Now though the question is in large measure one for evaluation, it also has a historical or descriptive aspect. From this point of view it may be worth commenting on the question here. It is a still unresolved issue, both factually and conceptually, as to whether there is an essential unity with regard to mainstream mystical experiences. But as I have already argued, even if such a unity can be established, the context still remains vitally important, as it does in the case of lovemaking which I cited as a parallel. Further, how central is the contemplative life in Christian experience? For many – for example for most evangelical Christians – it is not central, and it is perhaps only barely recognizable as a theme in the New Testament. Unless, of course, one takes the line, from which some modern commentators have not been averse, that Jesus' 'I and the Father are one' is a monistic statement indicating that Jesus had a mystical experience not unlike that which animates much of Hindu teaching. There would be a paradox in holding to the perennial philosophy as vital to Christian interpretation but denying that Jesus was a mystic in the required sense. Now as we shall see in the chapter on the Faces of Christ, Jesus is unavoidably enigmatic; and so we may have latitude to see him as a mystic. But by the same token, this would only be drawing out one possibility from a number, and only one aspect of Jesus at best. In short a dogmatic assimilation of Christianity to other esoteric traditions is not easy: more strongly it is not historically justifiable. But, of course, this is not to say that a person (coming to Christianity from another standpoint) might not see the mystical strand as the most important and significant; this can be held no more unjustifiable than the converse selection by the Christian, who might see certain strands of the Hindu tradition (Ramanuja's theism, for instance), as being the most meaningful for the interpretation of the Hindu type of spirituality.

To return, however, to Eckhart. Even if there were aspects of his thought and mysticism which attracted suspicion, especially where he uses language to suggest that the spiritual aristocrat goes beyond God himself to the ineffable union with the One, he set his experience in a strongly Christian frame. Thus, writing of the self-mortification through which the body and mind are disciplined, he says that the most effective subjection of the flesh occurs by love: 'With love you may overcome it most quickly and load it most heavily.' He expounds this with typically Christian imagery:

> That is why God lies in wait for us with nothing so much as love. Love is like a fisherman's hook. Without the hook he could never catch a fish, but once the hook is taken the fisherman is sure of the fish. Even though the fish twists hither and yon, still the fisherman is sure of him . . . To hang

166

on this hook is to be so captured that feet and hands, and mouth and eyes, the heart, and all a man is and has, becomes God's own.[4]

The emphasis upon love is, naturally, a strong motif running through much of Christian contemplative writing. It is especially clear in the outlook of Ruysbroeck, whose community, founded with a colleague when he was fifty, not far from Brussels, became an important centre of spiritual life, attracting a number of disciples and visitors. The loving mood is captured in the following verses:

> Those who follow the way of love
> Are the richest of all men living;
> They are bold, frank and fearless,
> They have neither travail nor care,
> For the Holy Ghost bears all their burdens.
> They seek no outward seeming,
> They desire nought that is esteemed of men,
> They affect not singular conduct,
> They would be like other good men.[5]

Ruysbroeck also stresses humility in following the mystical path, in accord with the example of Christ, whom he sees as doubly humble – first, because as God he willed to become human and so to take upon himself that very nature which had been banished and cursed to the bottom of hell – consequently any man good or evil can call Christ his brother. (By implication, Ruysbroeck is saying that compared with this worldly esteem is nothing, and by a paradox the humble following of the humble Christ brings the greatest glory.) Second, Christ, not content with taking on human nature, does so in lowly and obedient circumstances – he was humbly subject to the old law, and did his religious and civil duties like any other Jew. And he was a servant of all the world. Thus for Ruysbroeck the self-emptying which is part of the life of interior questing has a powerful moral and mythic dimension. Hence he is never weary of criticizing those who relapse into a sort of quietism – finding as they think an inner peace and

⁴ Sermon 4 in R. B. Blakney's *Meister Eckhart, a Modern Translation* (London, 1941), pp. 223–4.
⁵ Quoted by Evelyn Underhill in *John of Ruysbroeck* (London, 1916), p. xvii.

bliss, they remain passive in the world. He saw mysticism as a creative dialectic.

In this he harks back to notions of God's creative activity as an outpouring of divine love. He sees the contemplative's way as being an oscillation, so to speak, between rest in God and activity in the world; and this mirrors God's own dual existence of rest and work. And though Ruysbroeck's language sometimes emphasizes the deep union in the highest state, there is also a dialectic between identity and otherness: this is why in his major work *The Adornment of the Spiritual Marriage* he uses the image of earthly love. The mystical state is, as the penultimate paragraph of that work declares, the dark silence in which all lovers lose themselves. But, he adds mysteriously:

> If we would prepare ourselves for it by means of the virtues, we should strip ourselves of all but our very bodies, and should flee forth into the wild Sea, whence no created thing can draw us back again.[6]

One may see Ruysbroeck as a mystic who includes typical elements of that 'cloud of unknowing' and 'dazzling obscurity' which characterize the higher mysticism, but at the same time implants them in a soil of Christ-like good works and self-sacrifice. It has, of course, been often remarked that the most influential Christian mystics have been active in the world, and despite Ruysbroeck's withdrawal to his hermitage-priory outside Brussels he was always outward looking. He thus resolved the tension which can easily exist, and to which his own writings attest, between the (almost seductive) peace of contemplation and the concrete expression of love in the outer world. One may see here something of a parallel with the ideal of the Bodhisattva in Mahayana Buddhism, which overcomes the contemplative temptation in Buddhism, namely the concentration upon one's own liberation to the exclusion of true concern for other beings.

If Eckhart and Ruysbroeck represent facets of Catholic mysticism in its medieval flowering, one can point too to another great period in the tradition, during the sixteenth century in Spain, which saw such great figures as Theresa of Avila and

[6] ibid., p. 178.

168

John of the Cross – major fruits in the revival of the Roman Church. Perhaps too the second half of the twentieth century will be considered a vital era in the development of Christian mysticism, with the interplay between Western and Eastern varieties of the spiritual life. But before coming to that, let us look at two other developments of great significance: one is the effect of mysticism on Protestant interiorization of the faith; and the other is the use of spiritual disciplines among more specialized orders of the Catholic Church to effect work in the world. Here the Jesuits can stand as expressing in clearest form the instrumental use of the interior life.

Jakob Boehme is probably the most influential of the Protestant mystics, though he differs from most of the figures we have considered as being typical of mysticism in that he was more of a visionary, less of a contemplative. In 1600, when he was twenty-five years old, recently married and set up as an independent shoemaker in the town of Görlitz which is now in East Germany, he had a remarkable experience. It had come upon Boehme after a period of struggle, for he took a deep interest in spiritual, cosmological and scientific matters, and he felt the contradiction between the soaring gothic edifice of medieval cosmology, with heaven conceived as hundreds or thousands of miles above the earth, beyond the blue empyrean, and the new naturalism of the Renaissance. He was troubled too by the presence of evil in the world; and he was doubtless disturbed by the times, since his own city was typical of some major German centres of the time in finding itself at the crossroads of different movements – orthodox Lutherans; those who professed Lutheran commitment but had been influenced by Calvinism; Anabaptists and so on. Slicing through the religious divisions was the new humanism, and some other more mysterious currents. One of these was the gnostic teaching associated with Paracelsus, the maverick physician (1493-1541) – such ideas were subversive of official medicine and other orthodoxies.

The essence of Boehme's complex teachings could be summed up in two motifs – one was the picture of a dialectic within God himself and through into the creation; the other was a psychic interpretation of the dialectic. As to the former, for Boehme there was the issue of good and evil, wrath and love, and he found these in part explained through eternal processes within God's nature – for the highest and last aspect of the divine being is the original *Ungrund*, a kind of nothingness, which yet evolves into the Trinity. But this evolution takes both an outward-going form (love) and an inward-returning form (where God goes back in on himself and appears to us as wrath). The inner dynamic between love and wrath, though it involves a dialectical 'Yes' and 'No', is harmonized through the Divine Wisdom, presented by Boehme figuratively as the virgin Sophia. However, in the created order, the Yes and No appear as good and evil because of a precosmic catastrophe, the primal Fall of Adam, an eternal event preceding time. The redemptive process involves a knowledge of Wisdom and the restoration of the true Adam. Boehme wove into these notions an apocalyptic seeing in his own age and experience an anticipation of the last things. In this psychology, he stresses the divide between the essential nature of man and his actual condition, brought on through the Fall. He also stresses men's will and freedom, so that catastrophic as the Fall may have been it is an expression of freedom.

These ideas, so vividly written in a number of works (usually privately circulated to a growing band of friends and disciples), were both an attempt at a new cosmology and an expression of his root vision, which incorporated simultaneously a perception of both the Yes and the No. In his *Aurora* he wrote both that when the Light arises there is love, brilliance, joy, pleasant and sweet taste, without end; but also too there is fire, for

> If all trees were scribes and all branches pens, and if all hills were books and all waters ink, they could not give a sufficient description of the sorrow which Lucifer has brought into this place.[7]

Yet his apocalyptic vision was optimistic – he saw a new age dawning, and he an important prophet of it. This optimism went with his acknowledgement of the divine spark within

[7] *Aurora* xvi, 26, translated in John J. Stoudt's *Sunrise to Eternity, a study in Jakob Boehme's life and thought* (Philadelphia, 1957), p. 67.

man. Indeed the imagery of light which suffuses his thought, and is derived from his experience, was given new impetus by him in the imagination of the Christian world – a notable influence being upon the doctrine of the inner Light among the Quakers.

On the whole, the most important continuity between medieval mysticism and the religion of the Reformation lay in the stress on inwardness, and this inwardness could take a visionary, almost prophetic form. Thus there was something of the interiorization of the *Theologia Germanica* in Luther's piety, while the thought of Boehme has found an influence in modern times through the writings of Paul Tillich (1886–1965). But also Boehme's illumination was a charter for a certain spiritual egalitarianism – he could write that even if he might be criticized as being a poor shoemaker, was it not just a lowly monk who purged out of the German churches the Pope's greed, idolatry, etc.?

If the Reformation released new forces of lay piety, the Catholic response, the so-called Counter-Reformation, saw the creation of a number of new orders, such as the Capuchins, who were reformed Franciscans, the Oratorians and so on. But there can be little doubt that the most profound impact belonged to the Jesuits. If the Protestant visionaries could move from the old mysticism towards a new inner-worldly illuminated piety, the Jesuits demonstrated in sharply outlined form the birth of a new Church-oriented instrumentalism – that is a movement which could use the techniques of spiritual self-training to create a highly educated force at the disposal of the Pope. The accent was, above all, on obedience. From one direction it took its inspiration from the contemplative orders; from another direction from the military ones. But these new soldiers of Christ were not to be Teutonic holy warriors with horse and mace, nor occupiers of great northern and Levantine castles. They were to be an elite mobile priesthood ready to act on behalf of the Church in its struggle and opportunity (struggle, of course, against the Reformation aftermath in Protestantism – and opportunity through the great new dominions falling within the grasp of Catholic Spain and

Catholic Portugal both in the New World and in Asia).

Ignatius of Loyola was born one year before the final expulsion from Spain of the Moors, and by the same token one year before Columbus's discovery of America. In the year that Luther posted his theses at Wittenberg, Loyola entered the military profession as a knight in the service of a relative, the Viceroy of Navarre. In 1521, he was wounded at the siege of Pamplona, and it was a consequence of his enforced convalescence that he turned towards the spiritual life. It is interesting that a decisive mark on his mind was made by a *Lives of the Saints* in which the service of God was compared to the vocation of knightly chivalry (Ignatius' head was full of the knightly ideal). His enforced idleness not only gave him leisure to read; it also brought him a recognition of the unworthiness of his former life – which was perhaps not especially sinful, but full of knightly ambition. He saw all that as vanity now, and, giving up the world, he turned to begging, austerity and pilgrimage, to do penance for his sins. Though his pilgrimage took him to Jerusalem and back – he was prevented from staying in the Holy Land as he desired – Ignatius decided to train his mind at university, and his long studies, in Barcelona, Alcalá and Paris, culminated, after a dozen years, in his ordination in 1537, together with some companions, destined to be the nucleus of the Society of Jesus, founded after some papal hesitation in 1540.

In many respects the instrument which Loyola forged was revolutionary. First, his 'Spiritual Exercises' formed an extended initiation based on the imitation of Christ which could be used to train members of the Order. The military model remained, and the exercises were a kind of spiritual drill. They were an effective counterpart to the more haphazard initiation through conversion which dominated the Protestant imagination. We see a contrast which could also be perceived in the polarity between Ruysbroeck and Boehme: in the latter there is less sense of disciplined works. Likewise the Spanish mystics saw the religious life as involving a discipline as well as grace – the distinction being made between ascetical or active prayer on the one hand and supernatural or mystical prayer on the other hand. But in the case of Loyola the ascetical practices were not so much a possible prelude to the higher reaches of contemplation as to the battle in the world for men's souls under the generalship of Loyola and the authority of the Pope.

The idea of a discipline of conversion was important. So too was the ideology of obedience. The strong emphasis upon this in the Order was backed by the assurance of the member that in obeying orders he could do no sin – he did not need to worry about right and wrong within that framework. Mistakes could be made in plenty, but in principle obedience gave confidence. A third revolutionary feature was the devising of the rules in such a way as to free members from some of the traditional forms of the religious life – the long daily chanting of offices, for instance. The Jesuits were to be mobile, and also detachable – they could act on their own if necessary, as would be required of far-travelling apostles. In Loyola's own lifetime, missionaries went out into Germany, India, China, Japan, the Congo and Ethiopia.

Beyond all this, the Jesuits were given exceptionally long training, and became well equipped as educators. Though in early days Loyola did not think of the Order as primarily drawn to teaching, it found a highly effective role to play here; since as well as being well trained the members tended to be upper class, the Jesuits could gain great influence for the Church by teaching the sons of influential people. In an age of princes, evangelism from the top could be important.

But the whole movement, partly because of these innovations, partly later on because of its very effectiveness, partly because it gave the Popes a special and sometimes unwelcome task force, attracted much hostility and criticism. However, our main concern at this point is to see it as a case of the more instrumental use of spirituality. Though it had some roots in late medieval mysticism, the Society of Jesus had the military model, and in having that it perceived Christian duty by analogy with those who in earlier times had gone on crusades against the infidel. It was a fusion of several themes – of spiritual self-training, of learning, of holy war, of missionary zeal.

Though the Protestant spirit was for the most part directed against monasticism, some changes have occurred in the nineteenth and twentieth centuries. For one thing, the revival of Catholic sentiment in the Church of England led to a concern to re-establish the communal life. In fact, the earliest communities were for women, such as that of St Mary the Virgin in Wantage. Probably the best known male foundations were the Society of the Sacred Mission based until recently at Kelham, the Cowley Fathers at Oxford and the Benedictine Abbey at Nashdom. In a somewhat different, but related, spirit there were established the Iona Community in Scotland, and the Taizé Community in Burgundy. All these various communities were variations on the theme of a revived concern for living together in service to God. Many of these institutions also played a vital role in the growing Ecumenical Movement, which helped to promote understanding between the different traditions of monasticism and the contemplative life. More recently, the contact between Christianity and the great Eastern religions, in a new spirit of tolerance, has infused into Christianity some beginnings of a new willingness to experiment with Oriental means of meditation. Thus there has been some feeling towards such notions as Christian yoga, on the grounds that faith in Christ is compatible with (and maybe even demands) a learning from the variety of men's spiritual experiments.

Yet in the mid sixties and the seventies, the remarkable revival of religious concern, and especially of that kind which focusses upon inner states – upon transcendental meditation, Buddhist self-training, Taoist techniques, Zen and so forth – has tended to turn East rather than back to the Christian mystical tradition. The reasons seem to be various.

The first is that much of this movement towards mysticism in the modern West has taken place in North America and (to a lesser extent) in northern Europe. Broadly it has occurred in the countries where a Protestant traditional influence predominates. But as we have seen, there has been by and large a neglect of the mystical, contemplative side of the faith among Protestants, and especially among evangelical Christians.

More than that: there has sometimes been a latent hostility to mysticism for various reasons – its association with Catholicism to which most evangelicals have been opposed; its association too with non-Christian, and so supposedly non-salvific, religions; its appearance of world-negation; its seeming lack of biblical warrant (at least as the Bible is typically interpreted from an evangelical point of view). Indeed, modern Protestantism, with its strong revivalist strain, has been suspicious of any thought that one can somehow gain the truth by manipulating the mind – rather conversion happens supernaturally, unpredictably, from without, and God confers his grace on the faithful without their having to undergo special religious works. The emphasis has been much more on the numinous God, the Other, the sinfulness of man, the intervention of the Saviour – all solid Christian themes, to be sure, but leaving a very different impression from the style of the contemplative religious movements, especially Oriental ones. Another factor in the popularity of Eastern mysticism has been its very novelty and its cultural freshness. Alienated young folk will more easily accept truth from abroad than from home. But in addition we must also recognize the intrinsic attractions of such wonderful spiritual movements as Buddhism, a faith with a very different flavour from that of Christianity, but impressive in its nobility, richness and intellectual power. It has not surprisingly proved a magnet of hopeful affection among Westerners in the first main epoch of world history during which it has been available for a deeper acquaintance among Westerners.

Now we are in some position to begin to sum up the distinctive characteristics of Christian mysticism. First, it has most typically though not exclusively grown up in the ambience of the religious orders. It is true that there have been experiments which have brought together people in other ways for the practice of the meditative life, such as Nicholas Ferrar's experiment at Little Gidding in the seventeenth century. Still, both among the Eastern Orthodox and in the Western Church the main mystical milieu has been monastic. The rationale for such a way of life has been sometimes instrumental, where religious orders have been specialized towards various kinds of social service, such as education. But the main rationale has been to combine prayer and work in a context of poverty. In so doing the monastic community has provided a special kind of witness in the world. Where the Church was a minority group and subject to persecution or disadvantages, its witness was more transparent; with its triumphal acquisition of the soul of society, the monastery becomes a counterpoise to worldliness, and a reaffirmation of the central end of man, the adoration of God. Now within this situation, the growth of mystical experience, as in the great periods of German and Spanish mysticism, can be interpreted as illuminating the meaning of Christ and of the Trinity. Thus the 'negative', emptying side of mysticism also brings a kind of union with the divine, and a supreme peace; but dialectically it also is seen by most Christian mystics as showing the nature of love and therefore it has a relational aspect – cosmologically it is because of the outflowing of his love that God creates; psychologically, the unitive life also is one in which the mystic affirms his loving relationship to the world and to his fellow men. Further, the mystical experience has been seen as a kind of birth of Christ in the soul. In these ways, psychological pilgrimages are depicted as reflections of the cosmological dramas of creation and redemption. Moreover, in Eastern mysticism most transparently through the use of the Jesus Prayer, but everywhere in the Christian tradition, the active prayer – the active means of contemplation – has been intertwined with the Christian liturgy and piety. In other words, somewhat as *mantras* in Indian religious life have been relevant means of training the psyche towards the attainment of contemplative insight, so Christian mystics have used Christian *mantras*, formulae of the devout life. This has given to Christian contemplation some of the properties also of devotional awe before God as numinous Creator.

The demands of awe indicate that God is other; but most Christian mystics have spoken in one way or another of a kind of union. This has naturally chimed in with the idea of Christ whose human and divine natures were united in one person.

This has given a powerful impulse to Christ-mysticism in the Christian tradition – and it has helped to generate pieties in which Christ is found within man.

It is easy for mysticism to burst the bounds of orthodoxy, although the fact that it has chiefly been nurtured within communities themselves fairly strictly organized within the framework of church life has kept its tendency to disturbing language and (sometimes) revolutionary conclusions in check. But modern Christianity, in most Western countries at least, does not live in a situation where orthodoxy can be imposed or where it matters so much any more. Consequently as we have seen many of the older impulses sending men and women into the religious life send folk in many directions, and mostly not towards the Christian tradition. It may be that for the fore-seeable future the importance of a rediscovery of mysticism within Christianity will lie in its forming an intelligible bridge between the tradition and the various movements inspired from outside it. This is maybe just a reflection of the more general point that all great religions either start from or draw into themselves a strong mystical element.

9
Worship and the Numinous

There was a paradox about the effects of the Reformation on Christian worship. The whole movement was, of course, an attempt to purify the faith and to restore something of its pristine spirit. It was based on a rediscovery of the New Testament and the Old, and of the early Church as at least perceived through the lens of scripture, if not through the glass of historical enquiry. Yet if one asks oneself what is the heart of early Christian worship – what made it distinctive – one would have to answer: the Lord's Supper. Christians continued the practice of the synagogue, and as Christianity grew away from its Judaic origins the general shape of synagogue worship was retained, albeit with somewhat different 'fillings'. Increasingly, the scriptures became Christian ones, rather than the readings from the Old Testament. Now the shape of Jewish sabbath worship was the prelude to something distinctive: to the second part of the service, the Supper. The division between the two parts is still evident in (for instance) the Book of Common Prayer in England. The two halves were referred to respectively as Syntaxis (coming together) and Eucharist (thanksgiving). So, then, the Eucharist was the climax, and was uniquely Christian. But the paradox of the Reformation lay in this, that often it emerged that the Eucharist was what diminished in importance; the Syntaxis was what increased therein. To put it more concretely: a service which consisted of psalms or hymns, readings from scripture and prayers and a sermon was what came often to dominate the ritual of Protestant Churches, rather than the service culminating in the communion. The former became the typical public service of Presbyterians, Methodists, Baptists, Congregationalists; and assumed strong importance in much of Anglicanism and Lutheranism. The paradox then was that in restoring an earlier Christianity, Protestantism seemed to be increasingly neglecting its distinctive rite. The stage was set for the yawning gulf which exists between, say, the Baptist Sunday service and the Eastern Orthodox liturgy.

The explanation was twofold. First, the Reformers' attack on what they saw as magical aspects of the priesthood and strong regard for grace as coming to the faithful unmediated were in the long run bound to tend somewhat against an emphatic belief in the real presence of Christ in the sacrament. They tended towards treating the Eucharist more as a means of remembering Christ's work than as channelling Christ to the people through the rite. Second, the inward thrust of Protestantism, especially among the radicals, made the operation of God's grace perceptible within, psychologically. In the heart, rather than 'out there' in some priestly action – this was where the power of God worked. If there was a new type of worship foreshadowed, it was one which centred on the preaching of the Word. The pastor and preacher displaced the priest. The upshot was that of the three main branches of Christianity, Orthodox, Catholic and Protestant, two were strongly sacramental and the third was (at least in traditional terms) much less so.

The Reformers were reacting against late medieval worship; the Counter-Reformation improved and refurbished it. It was this mass, fortified by a better-trained clergy, embellished with Mozart and organs, decorated with baroque art and dark ornate churches, expressed in vestments and incense, which penetrated into modern times as the heart of Catholic piety, to be transformed only through Vatican II. How did it compare with its distant predecessor, the Eucharist of the Church as it was in Rome just before the conversion of Constantine?

Let us scan the scene in the courtyard or atrium of a well-to-do man's house as the Eucharist is celebrated. Well-to-do? A poor Christian's room in a tenement would be too small for the crowd gathering, secure behind the gate, looking across the courtyard to the stone table behind which the bishop and other priestly persons were ready. The bishop was seated where once the household gods had been. The ornate vessels and cups were ready. There was a lectern set up for the readings from the scriptures. Among the crowd were those apprentice Christians who would be dismissed at the end of the Syntaxis. The community had already made the transition from the synagogue and was poised on the threshold of the more elaborate ceremonies of the basilicas and converted temples which would house the Eucharist in not-too-distant times.

The community would not be prepared for the transformation which was to come over the service during the next thousand years. Could they foresee that the clothing of their times would become the specialized and archaic vestments of those later priests? That Latin would have become the language of learning and ritual, but not of the ordinary worshipper? That men would kneel, not stand, at communion? That the bishop would not be there most times; that priests would mutter masses to themselves virtually at side altars; that anybody could attend the mass; that it was held in a huge, specialized building; that the celebrant had his back to the faithful as though he somehow represented them rather than mingled with them; that there would be much moving to and fro, processing, the carrying of candles, and general drama; that the lay folk would be seemingly mere spectators; that the bread would be held high for all to see and adore; that folk would regard it good just to hear the mass, without partaking of the communion?

In the thousand years or more the language changed. People went to *hear* not to *do* or *make* the Eucharist. And they went too to see the Host, and to experience in awe the magic moment when the bread and wine changed their substance into the very body and blood of the Saviour. In a sense the whole of the Roman Church was centred on that moment. It was for this above all that the great regiment of priests existed, canalizing through their sacred function the saving sacrificial merit of Christ. It was for this that the apparatus of faith existed, to ensure that men and women would worthily and eagerly accept from the Church this incalculable benediction; it was for this magic moment too that the Pope in a sense existed, for he was the Vicar of Christ who organizationally was the mediator between heaven and earth, who stood at the heart of the living Church which dispensed salvation. Rulers and poor men, barons and monks, the learned and the peasants – all these in their differing way thought of the mass as a sacred protection against disaster, and a means of both heavenly and earthly welfare. If priests were corrupt, sensual, illiterate – well, it was cause of much uneasiness and cynicism; but the Church still had the keys of the kingdom. And the mass in a great building could be a scene of majesty and glory, a wonderful evocation of the high Fatherhood of God and of the paradoxical power of his dead and risen Son. And if many lay folk did not often take communion, it was partly because of the very power of the ritual, since so much dynamic merit emanated in pulses from the Host and from the relics of the saint enshrined behind the altar. The whole dark smoky air was redolent of acted out redemption.

The logic of the mass derived from the following thought. Whatever Christ meant by instituting the sacrament, it was the Eucharist that was, as we have seen, distinctive of the early. Church. It caused her much trouble: without it there might have been no need for the perplexing doctrine of the divinity of Christ and hence of the Trinity, nor for wearisome divisions about the two natures, wills and so forth of Christ. It was the heart of the Christian religion. If so, then (and here comes the logic of the mass) something really happens at the Eucharist. It was not a fancy way of remembering the Founder of the faith – just as baptism was not mere symbolism (symbolic however it really was). If something happened then it was a presentation once again, a making real here and now, of the true Christ and his work. The breaking of the bread was the breaking of his body, and that meant the Cross. The Eucharist, then, was giving to Christians here and now the very power which Christ exhibited in his death and rising again – actions which brought redemption to mankind. In brief, the logic of the mass implied: Something happens here, in the community and (so to speak) deep inside the bread and wine. For the medieval Church, and for its successor after Trent, this repeated miracle required a valid context, and that context was made concrete in the priest and his actions. It was a priestly miracle, and it was real, whether clothed in a humble low mass or in the pomps of the high altar.

The arrangement of the atrium was a conservative reflection of the peasant's hut, and the courtyard of the farm in front. The table before the hut by an appropriate symbolism was the chopping board upon which carcases could be carved: now in its polite disguise it became the altar. Its final apotheosis on its voyage from freeholding to cathedral was the high altar. But the offering of the mass was, of course, no animal sacrifice. However, it had the spirit of the animal sacrifice in it. For Christ was offered anew, and Christ seen as the lamb, who by his death on the Cross abolished God's wrath against sinful men. The mass was the later world's access to the redemptive midpoint in the history of the world – that blessed midpoint between Fall and Second Coming. It short-circuited the years, channelling into the cathedral or the chapel, the priory or the church, the battlefield or the sickroom, the power of the old event.

The dynamic and sacred power of the Eucharistic miracle gave a focus to the building, and constituted the nucleus of benign radiance which gave meaning to Gothic arches and baroque spirals. The building itself could in being the theatre of the sacred drama also help to sanctify the whole area. The building of proud cathedrals was not just a beautification – it was a way of giving substance to the saving work and protection of the Lord, in the midst of Christian society.

In brief: the medieval and post-medieval mass was a dynamic, almost magical institution. Modified and put into the vernacular it became the Eucharist of the Church of England, and given a different power through the marvellous language of the Book of Common Prayer. Embellished and heightened by the Anglo-Catholics of the nineteenth century, that rite converged with the renewed mass of the Roman Catholics. It has a shape which has often been considered as the 'norm' of the sacrament – the typical ritualized Eucharist of the Christian tradition. But does not our brief glimpse of the atrium suggest that the high mass is a long way from the Eucharist of much earlier days?

Clearly there had been much development, and we could

see similarly a great elaboration in the East. The evolution there was indeed more rapid in some respects. Thus by the fourth century the sanctuary was hidden by a veil. St John Chrysostom, that golden preacher, around 390 at Antioch, declared: 'When the sacrifice is carried forth for the communion and the Christ Victim and the Lord the Lamb, when you hear the words: "Let us all entreat together . . .", when you see the veil drawn aside, then reflect that heaven is rent asunder from on high and the angels are descending.' Perhaps naturally in Syria, with its old equation of holiness and danger, stretching to pre-Christian times, the Eucharist was perceived as the locus of mystery and the fount of awe. Later the veil congealed into the iconostasis, the barrier between sanctuary and congregation on which ikons came to be hung, and which had been perhaps first introduced in the great church dedicated to the Holy Wisdom, the Hagia Sophia in Byzantium (later to be converted into a mosque), built by Justinian. With its doors the screen corresponded to the backdrop of the theatre of the times, with its three sets of double doors. In a sense the Eucharist was thus turned into a drama, but a rather special one, for the crucial action took place out of sight, behind the screen. Only at the processionals such as the Great Entrance were the actions behind moved forward into the midst of the laity. Thus we see a nice contrast between East and West. For the Easterner the consecration should *not* be seen: indeed there is something almost indecent, to the Orthodox mind, in the very public celebration of the rite in the West and the exposure too plainly of the sacred drama. The hiddenness enhanced awe and mystery. In the West the Host was elevated precisely so that it *could* be seen by the laity.

Still both styles could be seen as different approaches towards the same goal – the expression of the highest reverence to the focal point of faith as expressed eucharistically – the coming-to-be-present of the divine Saviour.

There is perchance a congruity between the styles of worship and the styles of architecture. The Byzantine dome was the symbol of heaven, and being placed over the temple signified the descent of the heavenly to earth. On the other hand, the

Gothic spire soars. It follows the motion of the upraised hands of the priest as he holds the Host. The movement is upwards, for the Victim is offered up to God in heaven. Both styles in East and West see the Eucharistic liturgy as a meeting-point of heaven and earth, but there is almost a sense in the case of the Eastern rite of seeing the earth from the standpoint of heaven. The bright candles, the mysterious screening, opened up though in light and mystery, the brilliant gilt and the pictures' translucent haloes – the combined effects are to suggest indeed that into the sanctuary the very light of heaven has descended. Which in a sense it has, for Christ is truly present in the Liturgy: the procession outwards from the sanctuary is Christ coming to the people. So though in some respects the whole scene is priestly, elaborately artificial, an acted out drama, a performance, it can also be seen from the other direction, as a coming into the world of the divine and heavenly presence. God's initiative is, so to speak, expressed by the mysterious arrangements.

However, the full use of ikons was inhibited for a long period by the Iconoclastic Controversy. It was one of those outbursts which has occurred at different places and times in Christian history over whether the sacred image, whether picture or sculpture, is legitimate. Indeed perhaps there is a more or less continuous puritan strand in this regard running down through Christian history. At one level, the clash represents the tension between Classical and Semitic culture. The pressures of Islam had something to do with the iconoclasm of the eighth century in Byzantium, and Islam has most consistently maintained a puritan, ikonless art, especially within the context of worship. In this Islam was carrying on the Jewish ban on graven images. Yet there was a rich, non-puritan side to Jewish ceremonial – in the Temple. It was easy for Christians, by the second century, to think of the celebration as in some manner carrying on the sacrifices of the Temple, but in a new context. Herod's great Temple, twice the size of Solomon's, was one of the wonders of the world. Thus perhaps it is necessary to make one or two distinctions, in order to be clear about some of the issues about the nature of Christian worship as it has been conceived by puritan and other groups.

One division is between those who use images and those who do not. Another is between ceremoniousness and simplicity. Another distinction again is between ideological and other practice – that is, whether a Church or movement adopts a given practice for an ideological reason or not. Those who wanted to remove the ikons from Byzantine churches did so for ideological reasons. Let us now consider the types yielded by these classifications.

First, there are those who use images ceremoniously, such as typically the Churches of Eastern Orthodoxy and much of the Roman Catholic tradition – again, there is a strong strand of this type within Lutheran and Anglican Protestantism. Second, there are instances of simplicity in the use of images (much of renewed liturgical practice in Roman Catholicism since Vatican II has turned in this direction, for instance in university chaplaincies, new churches and chapels, etc.). From another direction, some Protestant Churches previously ideologically imageless have in these latter days got stained glass windows and the like on which images appear. Next, there are cases of ceremonious ritual which is imageless, as in Judaism and as for a while in the Byzantine Empire (during the iconoclastic period). In Christian puritanism, as under Cromwell, and in most of Islam, the worship has been simple and ideologically imageless.

The ceremonious kind of worship means money, both for the fashioning of ornaments and fine buildings, but typically too for the maintenance of priests. It thus has sometimes been resisted by those who protest that the Church needs a simpler life, to return more to the holy poverty of Christ; and it has been criticized likewise by those who feel that there is bred, in ceremoniousness, too great a distinction between priest and laity – the latter becoming passive spectators. So anti-cere-moniousness is a recurring motif in the Christian community's critique of itself.

However, there are two further factors of perhaps deeper importance in the puritan protest. They have to do with prophecy and a certain conception of spirituality. The ceremonious type of religion, especially where it uses images freely, tends to be integrated with the rhythms of life – the seasons, the holy year, the faith of ordinary folk seeking visible and rhythmic signs of God's activity and presence. It also easily integrates into a hierarchical view of the world and society. In being available to ongoing society it also may be corrupted by it. In being warm, it may be soft; in its beauty it may be too comforting; in its need for wealth to sustain it, it may be bought. Against such a mood in ceremonious religion, the puritan rebels, in a prophetic manner. The Calvinist reformation, for instance, injected a renewed sense of ethical prophecy into religion. Both consciously and unconsciously, such a protest, in Christianity, harks back to a kind of Old Testament faith, and it presents an austere counterbalance to the luxuriances of a ritually complex tradition.

The idea of spirituality to which I referred involves a deep suspicion of externals. They were an obstacle to true worship, which is essentially a mental activity – it includes focussing the attention upon the one God, who is Spirit and who is imageless. So representations of God tend towards blasphemy. Moreover, since God's self-revelation is discovered in the Bible, and the Bible is in the form of language, it is through words alone that we should, strictly, pray to and adore God. This theory is partly a derivative of course, of the ancient Jewish tradition, and yet the puritanism of Calvin and his successors would easily have found itself in collision with much of the living ritual of Judaism. Calvin himself was logical and sincere in his rejection of externals, but there was also an animus against the Catholic system which led him to a very ruthless condemnation of its symbols. He went so far as to claim that in the Roman mass 'all that a criminal godlessness could devise is done', and he swept away a whole apparatus of piety – bishops, the liturgy, the vestments, the pictures, the candles, the incense, crosses, crucifixes, processions, chants, choirs, organs. The utter plainness of the true Calvinist church building left only two things: seats that showed people gathered together, and a pulpit to show that there was preaching. The sacrament of the Word, prophetic, no-nonsense, biblical, unvarnished – this was the heart of the puritan public service.

The puritan outlook also had an effect on another dimension of worship – the sanctifying of time through the Christian year. This practice of an annual cycle of celebrations was, and remains, important in most cultures. In Judaism, the practice represented the various 'D-days' of Jewish sacred history, and in principle early Christians recognized such a cycle; but in addition it was not unnatural to begin to remember vital dates in the story of Christ – above all Easter, the day of the Lord's resurrection. Indeed every Sunday was a commemoration of the latter.

The point needs a little expansion. The Jewish sabbath was, of course, the Saturday, the last day of the week, when God rested after his creative labours. The Christians chose Sunday, the first day of the week, as their day of celebrating the Eucharist, for it was on the first day that Jesus rose from the dead, and the Eucharist is inescapably entangled with that event. It was thus natural to have both Saturday and Sunday as significant days, though only the first of these was a day of rest. Only gradually was there a conflation between the idea of the Jewish sabbath and the Christian Sunday, leading to the later conception, most obviously expressed in the more conservative wing of Protestantism, of Sunday as the day of rest. This conflation was facilitated by the fact that Constantine made Sunday the official day of rest. This was in effect a revolution for Christians in that until the fourth century there had been no idea of Sunday as day of rest.

Basically Christianity came to be involved in a double cycle – the one weekly, in which Sunday was the chief day and indeed in a sense the fount and origin of the week, for it was out of one's sense of service to and gratitude to God that the rest of one's life – one's life of labour – was undertaken in the spirit of worship. The other cycle was the year – in its full form rolling onwards from Advent, when the coming of Christ is heralded, through Christmas when the birth of Jesus is celebrated, towards Lent, when the Lord's passion is re-enacted and the Christian fasts as a sign both of this and of preparation for the great central feast of the year, Easter, then through Pentecost towards the Ascension and the long summer months when the Trinity is remembered and contemplated: and so once again to the misty fruitfulness of the time of Advent. Not only were there these great D-days of the year – but there were crowds of saints and martyrs populating the calendar: Stephen, slap after Christmas, death after birth (the hand that rocks the cradle gives place to the stones that batter the martyr); St George of England conveniently foreshadowing Shakespeare's birthday; St Josaphat, unknowing reflection of the Buddha; St Anthony of the desert; St John of the Cross, mystic; St Athanasius; St Bede; St Pellegrinus . . . they come in clouds through the calendar. Traditionally they help among other things to hook individuals into the sacred year – one celebrates one's name day, when one's name is seen as reflecting something of the saint.

Naturally the evolution of the Christian year owed something to preceding religion, and such religion paid much attention to the unwinding of the year. The solstices, the advent of spring, the lengthening day, the increasing darkness, life, death, growth, sun, mysterious moon – the rhythms of planetary existence were deeply woven into human life and above all sustenance and fertility. Therefore the classic Christian calendars (differing a little between East and West but in spirit similar) fitted well with the mentality of northern and eastern Europe, so heavily implicated in rural existence. If the cycle has diminished in relevance in more modern times it is partly due to the substitution of other rhythms for that of the countryside: the beat of repetitive production processes, rolling indefinitely without pause save for human rest, and the sheltered city rhythms of transaction and entertainment. Just as archery has made the transition from the serious business of killing to the polite ambience of games, so the seasons are for most people no longer the matrix of survival but rather the concern of poet and tourist. But though these are factors in the modern decline of the religious year, another has been the puritan attitude to it.

For Calvin was hostile too to the practice of the Christian year. For one thing he objected to the Church's insistence on Easter communion. This was an attempt to get lay people at least once a year to make their communion, since the piety of the late Middle Ages, as we have seen, was one of hearing and seeing rather than partaking in the mass. And incidentally when they did partake it was in one way only – eating the wafer but not drinking from the cup. Calvin with his theology of inward relationship to God and outer rectitude considered that all life should express obedience to God's will, and thus there was no special place for holy days. Except, in a sense, the Sabbath, as we shall see. Thus Calvin forbade Easter communion and in doing so removed the central feast of the Church's old year. The other feast days likewise had to go. The whole rhythm of Catholic commemoration and of rustic dependence was swept on one side. The saints? Saints are not folk to be revered through relics: all the chosen of God are equally saints. There was importantly a sense in which Calvin's community was (to borrow the Mormon title, itself borrowed) a church of Jesus Christ of latter-day saints. So radical was the change that in Presbyterian Scotland, fashioned on Calvin's principles, popular enthusiasm was shifted from Christmas to the New Year, a purely secular date (though with undertones of the 'pagan' past – so even now the Scots wassail tremendously and even unchristianly on this feast: commerce, though, and the softening of old scores against Popes and Englishmen, have meant that Christmas has crept back on to the Scottish scene).

Thus the old Christian year has crumbled in the West substantially under the twin onslaught of industrial rhythms and the path of puritanism. If Christmas in modern times seems to flourish as never before it is because the merchants find it lovable: it pumps new life into the economy, as once the winter solstice promised the coming of spring, and in effect the start of a new growing year.

The conflict then between ceremonious and austere worship was worked out, then, with regard to the mentality of the sacred calendar. But the conflict here leads to some reflections about time in worship. And it may be useful to pause at this point for a short side trip on chronology.

A date is a way of ordering days in a series. The dates, or as we say, the days, of the week are in some languages numbers: Day One, Two, Three and so on. For reasons of convenience we chop our total day sequence up into these seven date dollops. In the older situation of a six-day working week, the day of rest had added significance. But serially it has only one property – of coming after Seven and before Two (though psychologically, with the notion of the weekend, it figures as between Six and before One: the first working day, Monday, being in the modern world the first day of the week from a psychic point of view). If we select out one day as being special then the name or number of the day takes on a special value – in the case of religion, a sacred value. In theory in Christianity, Sunday is also the time when the time of the Resurrection is re-presented; but it can also, as we have seen, be linked to the idea of a holy rest day. But each Sunday really has no other property than its place in the sequence.

But where we move to the annual rhythm of the year, there are two new factors coming into play. First, the major feasts that a religion may celebrate, and this applies in particular to Catholic/Orthodox Christianity, will occur rather bumpily over the plain of time. If we visualize time as a flat line with bumps in it where time becomes emotionally and ritually charged, large or small in relation to the amount of the charge, then the Church's year has some peaks and lesser bumps in it as it goes wavily through the calendar. And these are rather irregularly spaced out in terms of the whole year. This irregularity is enhanced by the fact that fixed dates such as Christmas wander through the week, so that sometimes it is on a Sunday, sometimes on a Monday and so on. So though the calendar is macroscopically regular (or nearly so – Easter wanders and with it a train of other feasts), in the sense that it repeats itself from year to year, microscopically it is irregular. This property of irregularity both arises from and helps to express the given nature of history.

For history itself is not repetitive (except in the Hindu and

Buddhist imaginations, where there are world-epochs or kalpas, like super-histories in which there are sequences of histories of the world). History can be represented as a linear sequence of dates upon each of which various clusters of human events occurred. In addition, some dates are more important, or more psychically charged, than others – 1066, 1492, 1517, 1776, 1789, 1917, 1933 and so forth. History too is bumpy, rather irregularly. There are of course those who try to 'explain' such bumpiness in terms of some underlying regularity – hence the attractions of numerology in history. At any rate, history's bumpiness can be represented in compressed form in a bumpy annual calendar in which the 'D-days' are registered. From this point of view the Church's year helped to keep sacred history present to people's imaginations. But this may have been somewhat offset by the other main factor which comes into play in an annual cycle rather than (say) a weekly one.

This other factor has to do with nature. Planetary beings, whether whales or finches or men, are immersed in the rhythms imposed by the earth's yearly voyage round the sun. If man is less immersed now, it is because he has gone indoors rather radically. He has built his own solar system round him: his heat is from coal and cracking plants, his light from electricity, his food from supermarkets, his sports in astrodomes, even his wars at consoles. But still he has some sense of seasons, and it is that rhythm which the annual cycle evinces, so that Christ's birth picks up the power of the winter new year; Easter acquires the overtones of the spring festival, and so on. The annual calendar could make the Christian year also into a pre-Christian one. The irregularities of history become tailored somewhat to the regular rhythms of the shrinking and expanding sun and moon.

If Judaism and Christianity celebrate a myth of history it does not mean that, as ceremonious religions (or *in so far as* they are such), they differ quite radically from other more rhythmic faiths. It is rather that their rhythms incorporate irregularities as well as regularities: more purely 'nature' religions have a more regular pattern. Also, a ritual which represents a completed past act, for instance the birth of Christ, is a species of time travel. The harvest ritual, on the other hand, has a more timeless aspect, as it plugs into a force which is there in principle from year to year. The priest is trying to canalize that force beneficently towards his clients and towards the community. One is like my birthday, re-presenting my coming into being as a determinate individual; the other is more like St Valentine's Day, when we plug into personal love, in general.

The effects therefore of the Calvinist sweeping away of the ceremonious Church year were ambiguous. It removed traces of the pre-Christian from the faith and so (presumably) superstition. It removed a potent aspect of the priestly operation. But it also could be thought to weaken the sense of sacred history. Or at least it weakened the feeling that history was available to us objectively. It had, in puritanism, to be made vivid within. The force of history was given a definitely psychological meaning, in line with the whole theory of puritan worship.

Calvin and Knox's reforms put, of course, great weight upon the preaching of the Word: it was through this that the history of man's salvation was given a new dynamism. The prayer too would, for the most part, be rather unstructured, prepared or spontaneously uttered by the minister. In the eighteenth century both in Scotland and in much of the Church of England, where this still exhibited strong puritan influence, the grip of a more rationalist approach to the faith contributed to a dryness in worship: it was through the late eighteenth-century and nineteenth-century revivals that new fervours were to be injected into Protestant worship (and at the other end of the spectrum the Anglo-Catholic revival was one factor in a rediscovery of the more classical Christian approach to the Eucharist). The new fervours were substantially expressed in the growing importance of music and hymns. Indeed, after the Bible and preaching, the hymn came to be the most potent means of expressing and stimulating Protestant piety. Not of course that the hymn had been absent from the Christian tradition – far from it. But the Protestant worship service provided a good setting and a stimulus to a sense of shared faith. But before coming to this fecund modern period of Christian hymns, let us glance briefly at the evolution of such praise in the history of Christianity.

The Christian community had, of course, inherited the great songs known as Psalms of David, and these played an important role in worship from early times. But they were not (for obvious reasons) very explicitly Christian. At a much later time paraphrases of the Psalms would deal with this problem. The great hymnwriter Isaac Watts could turn the 72nd Psalm's lines, about King David:

> He shall have dominion also from sea to sea and from the river unto the ends of the earth

into:

> Jesus shall reign where'er the sun
> Doth his successive journeys run;
> His kingdom stretch from shore to shore
> Till moons shall wax and wane no more.

There are, as well as psalms, traces of other hymns in the New Testament, such as the words of I Timothy, iii.6:

> He who was manifest in the flesh, justified in the spirit, seen of angels, preached among the nations, believed on in the world, received up in glory.

But it seems to have been St Ambrose (*c.* 340–397) of Milan who introduced the office hymn, a song that is for inclusion in public worship. Augustine remarked that the practice of singing hymns and psalms in the Eastern manner was begun in the church at Milan, while the people were keeping vigil in the church with Ambrose, during persecution by Valentinian (whose mother was an Arian – this was a Christian-Christian persecution): the hymns were to keep them awake and free from anxiety. It is thus appropriate that one of the hymns of Ambrose which has come down to us is 'At Cock Crowing':

> Dread framer of the earth and sky
> Who dost the circling seasons give
> And all the cheerful change supply
> Of alternating morn and eve!

Loud crows the herald of the dawn,
Awake amid the gloom of night,
And guides the lonely traveller on,
With call prophetic of the light.[1]

The growth of a full participation of the laity in the liturgy
through hymns was inhibited, however, in the early Middle
Ages by the increased clericalization of worship, and by the
establishment of choirs in cathedrals and large churches.

The Reformation, by pruning the liturgy, and by returning
to what were perceived as biblical norms, moved in two directions. One was that which stemmed from Luther's hymns –
towards a new vernacular flowering of hymns for all to join
in. Another direction was that which confined singing virtually
to the Psalms. Still, they were made metrical, and they were
often interpreted as closely pointing to the troubles and joys
of the men who sang them. The Puritans had struggled through
many troubles before their victory in the Civil War, and they
were to know further difficulties, both in England and Scotland.
The Psalms appealed to their sense of the majesty of God,
their identification with his righteousness and his identification
with their warfare and struggle. The most militant of the Psalms
were their favourites. And even in the England of the Restoration the general Puritan line was taken regarding the undesir-
ability of the use of non-biblical language, and it was not effectively until the eighteenth century that hymns could become
widespread.

But the fashioning of the metrical Psalms had already had a
large impact. It was borrowed from the style of Geneva, where
English Puritan exiles had encountered the solemn togetherness
of the French psalm-singing. Already in 1564, too, there was
printed the Scottish Psalter, and a new version came out in
1650. These were to have an incalculable effect in giving
Scottish religion an Old Testament stamp, and to give the Scots
a sense of identity with the embattled and faithful Israelites of
old. And Geneva contributed some of those seminal melodies

[1] Quoted in Ray C. Petry, ed., *A History of Christianity – readings in the history
of the early and medieval Church* (Englewood Cliffs, N.J., 1962), p. 148: trans. E.
Caswall, *Hymns and Poems*, 1849.

that have echoed solemnly down to us today, notably the famous Old Hundredth.

There was a line, though not altogether a straight one, leading from Luther to some of the greatest writing of the English tradition, that of the Wesleys. The German Reformation had been both a stunning success and a dark tragedy, looked at from the perspective of the second half of the seventeenth century. It had transformed the face of German Christianity, but it also had been a major factor in the bloodshed and division which had found its long and weary apogee in the Thirty Years' War, concluded exhaustedly in 1648. The time had come for a new kind of renewal, in which the Protestant mind could rediscover more deeply the personal devotion, high conduct and outward-looking charity which the New Testament seemed to call for. A major expression of this was pietism, initiated above all by Jakob Spener (1635–1705). As we have already seen one of those influenced by pietism was Count Nicolaus von Zinzendorf (1700–61) who gave new life to the kind of devotionalism stemming from John Hus and the Bohemian Brethren. The Count composed some two thousand hymns, a prodigious, if on the whole not tremendously distinguished, output. They were the staples of community worship in the holy village founded at Herrnhut: this commune, so seminal in the spiritual fortunes of the Moravian Brethren, important in early days in America, was visited by John Wesley, who was impressed by the warmth of religion expressed through the hymns, some of which he translated.

The net result was a fusion of motifs in the growing chorus of the English hymn tradition – the pietist strain, mediated through the Wesleys; the Calvinist strain, as it came through Isaac Watts and the earlier psalm tradition; and the general tide of English popular poetry. The hymns and translations of the Wesley brothers came at a propitious time, for it was in the second half of the eighteenth century that the Church of England was preparing itself for a new situation – the legalization of hymn-singing in church (which remained officially banned until 1820, though already hymns had been used at prayer-meetings, in the charity hospitals, where evangelicals had been active, and elsewhere).

The flowering of the English hymn in the nineteenth century (and by this I mean the hymn written in the English language – for American hymn-writing began to assume a significant part) was in part due to revivalism and piety; it was partly due to the fact that singing congregationally was the one major point where the laity could be active; it was also partly due to the fact that hymns could express much more directly and feelingly the meaning of Christianity, in an age when men were becoming at times alienated from the older structures of the faith. So vital has the hymn become that those who edited the *Pilgrim Hymnal*, 1958 edition, could write as follows in the Preface:

> The hymnbook has a central place in the worship of the church. The psalmist invites us to 'sing to the Lord a new song'. St Paul urges the churches to praise God 'in psalms and hymns and spiritual songs'. The Reformation began in a burst of congregational singing. In our worship the people have always taken an active and significant part, and a zeal for corporate worship has featured every period of renewal within Protestantism.

As our brief historical survey has indicated, these words conceal from our gaze the revolution which has occurred in Christian piety through the substitution of the modern hymn for the diet of psalms and canticles which was more characteristic of the medieval church. And what does the revolution mean? Perhaps three things chiefly.

First, it has meant a strong accent on sheer praise as being an integral, indeed dominant, element in the congregation's part in Christian services. It has reinforced the accent on awe and the glory of God expressed more austerely through the Calvinist psalm tradition. Second, it has been the vehicle of a warm *bhakti* (see p. 217) religion – the devotional atmosphere of Christianity has been suffused with the spirit of love for Christ. Third, hymn-singing has contributed to the sense of Christianity as a congregational religion. Perhaps these three motifs can be illustrated by parts of three well-known hymns.

First, then, the sense of awe and the numinous aspect of the Godhead:

> Mine eyes have seen the glory of the coming of the Lord;
> He is trampling out the vintage where the grapes of wrath are stored;
> He hath loosed the fateful lightning of his terrible swift sword;
> His truth is marching on . . .

Here there is a powerful echo of the wrathful terror of Isaiah lxiii. The Lord is never to be underestimated, and Christianity is by no means all sweetness and life: there is punishment for the transgressor, and God's anger is to be felt in the thunderstorms of life.

Charles Wesley's 'Hark! the herald angels sing' well incapsulates Christian *bhakti*, and the theology of redemption is expressed very simply in:

> Hail the heaven-born Prince of peace!
> Hail the Sun of righteousness!
> Light and life to all he brings,
> Risen with healing in his wings,
> Mild he lays his glory by,
> Born that man no more may die,
> Born to raise the sons of earth,
> Born to give them second birth . . .

And based on the Old Hundredth, the following gives a strong sense of Christian collectivity in the act of praise:

> All people that on earth do dwell
> Sing to the Lord with cheerful voice;
> Him serve with mirth, his praise forth tell,
> Come ye before him and rejoice.

I have emphasized the importance of the hymn, especially in Protestant worship, but it must always be seen not only as a relatively new development but also as taking place in dialectic with other things – with the Eucharist in many cases, and in more radical Protestantism in dialectic with the sermon and more generally the ministry of the Word. Probably the great growth of the hymn in the late eighteenth and the nineteenth centuries testifies to the fact that the austere shape of Puritan worship, and the rejection of ceremonious ritual, left a gap, which was very appropriately filled by the hymn. For the hymn expresses emotion easily, and so was a way of bodying forth those inward changes upon which Protestantism so warmly insisted.

A consequence of the Protestant style of worship, especially in the Calvinist and radical traditions, has been the central place of the preacher. The shifting of the sacrament of the Word into the key place in the service has meant that some of the feelings which hymns express – awe, loving devotion, fellowship – have also found expression in the sermon, and by implication in the life and personality of the preacher. In addition he has served as a guide to morals: indeed more than a guide, considering that he deals with an authoritative message. Thus it is not possible to consider the ethos of Christian worship without seeing in it a strong commitment to certain patterns of behaviour. By the same token, everyday behaviour can be thought of by the devout Christian as itself a kind of worship – men praise God as much by their actions as by their hymns.

We may now discern some patterns of Christian worship. First, both in its inheritance from Judaism and through its own sense of mystery, a strong component is the expression of numinous awe. But this is characteristically achieved by different means: there is the more ceremonious and sacramental style; and the austerer Puritan style – the one using much drama and visible actions to convey the heavenly nature of the occasion of the liturgy, the other personalizing awe through the preaching of the Word and the use of hymns of praise to the Almighty. Second, at some periods Christian worship, through the mass, has expressed what might be described as concrete potency – the sacrament pulses as it were with holy power, and from it the laity can tap grace. The medieval and Tridentine mass had some analogues in the whole theory of the *mantra* or sacred formula in the Hindu tradition, in which the priest helps in canalizing the divine mysterious power in ways which are favourable to his clients. Third, however, the Christian liturgy, whether of East or West, has differed from the ritual sacraments of other faiths in presenting not just the power of God concretely to the faithful, but God as, so to speak, in motion. That is, God acting in history, through Christ's death and resurrection. Thus Christianity represents the unrepeated crucial events of salvation history. Fourth, Christian worship has divided between the ceremonious and puritanical, with the former being typically integrated into the cycle of the Christian year, which in its regularities echoes the rhythms of nature (common to non-Christian religiousness) and in its irregularities reflects the givenness of the historical events which it re-enacts (in this it is like the ceremonious cycle of Jewish observance). Fifth, Protestant worship has returned somewhat to the spirit of synagogue worship, but has, both in the centrality of preaching and in the growth of hymn-singing, sought to express both the awesomeness of God and the nearer sense of loving devotion also present in much sacramental worship. Sixth, Christian worship has provided a model for daily living, through seeing ordinary duties as a kind of service or praise of God if performed in the right spirit.

The differing motifs of worship have been frozen into architecture – the sense of the descent of heaven in the domes and onions of the Eastern Orthodox churches, the aspiring cathedrals of the West, the plain chapels, pulpit-dominated, of the radical reformers, the restrained colours of the Lutheran churches of the European north.

The divergences between styles have diminished in modern times, partly because of the Ecumenical Movement and partly for other reasons. The mass's new lives in the vernacular languages have been accompanied by a great deal of experimentation which has drawn on Protestant experience. Contrariwise the austerer types of worship in Protestantism have tended to be embellished by a certain liturgical revival. It is not now all that easy to know from the appearance of a new church building to which denomination it belongs.

But Eastern Orthodoxy has been comparatively little affected. This is partly because of its natural conservatism, partly because in Eastern bloc countries it is less easy to experiment, but mainly because the liturgy has come to have a much deeper significance than it has elsewhere in the

Christian movement. Thus in (say) the Roman Catholic milieu it is possible to vary the ritual while holding to the doctrine and the Church commitment. But the teachings of Orthodoxy *are* in a sense the liturgy. To vary the latter in a substantial way would be in effect to destroy it.

When one adds to the main varieties of Christian worship the other factors sometimes apparent, the complexity of the Christian tradition reasserts itself. Passionate Pentecostal movements, snakehandling, services of healing, Coptic rites, the African independent variants, Mormon piety, the quietness of the Quakers – these and many more phenomena embellish the Christian scene. But they tend in their differing ways to exhibit *bhakti* religion, varying between the polarities of ecstasy and formalism, between simplicity and ceremony, between the psychological and the objective drama, between the numinous and the ethical.

Also, it must not be forgotten that public worship in the Christian and related traditions has had an outreach into various means of encouraging and expressing personal piety – the rosary, the ikon in the house, the crucifix, the text over the mantelpiece, the family Bible, grace said at meals, the annual visit of the priest to bless the house, the family prayers, and so forth. However, in great measure Christianity has displayed itself as a congregational religion, and this makes it different in its emphasis from (say) Hinduism and Buddhism, which though strongly rooted in communities, are less concerned with people gathering together at a special time and place to worship.

In brief, Christianity is predominantly devotional, sacramental and congregational. It has therefore in recent times needed to consider how it can present as meaningful the idea of a personal God, the sense of God's having saved men (but from what?) and the reality of its community concern.

10

The Faces of Christ

By definition, Christianity is the religion about Christ. Jesus is its central focus. But since the earliest times there has been mystery about him. The Gospels are both frustrating and, in their own dark way, illuminating, for they present glimpses of Jesus which tell us something, but tell us something which seems to us very incomplete. So there is a problem about what can be made of the enigmatic hero of this early drama – a problem, that is, which can be looked at as a historical conundrum.

Yet it is hard to disentangle the historical conundrum from the question of the experience of Christ in the tradition. For it is of the nature of Christianity that not only is Jesus the central focus, but he is conceived dynamically, that is as capable of entering powerfully, gently or both into people's lives. Let us look at this for a moment in relation to Paul's conversion, as he was making that momentous journey to Damascus.

One could say that there is no one more insistent on the vital character of the Resurrection than Saint Paul. Jesus' rising from the dead, however, appeared to take differing forms, for even the risen Christ showed, characteristically, different faces, at least if we follow the traditions recorded about him. Thus there is on the one hand the picture of Jesus who let Thomas feel his side and who ate broiled fish: transparently Jesus, and bodily. On the other hand, there is the Jesus on the way to Emmaus, incognito and (also) physical – one would not fall into such a natural conversation (albeit about matters somewhat spiritual) with a shimmering ghost. Then there was the appearance, out of due season it seemed, to Paul, which turned round his whole life; and Jesus was present but not precisely in a physical way, yet transparently and clearly, as far as Paul's consciousness of him went.

Thus between ourselves and the purely historical conundrum about Jesus there lies something vivid in the life of the early community which in one sense transcends history and in another sense does not. It transcends it in the sense that it is the interpretation placed upon it by the Christian community which is important rather than the raw details of what actually happened, if anything. But it does not transcend history in the sense that the importance which it does have, arising from the interpretation, is historical importance – that is, the experience of the risen Christ was a new factor in the historical process which in essence gave rise to the distinctively Christian way of life (as distinguished from the Jewish). The ambiguities of the Resurrection experiences – ambiguities as to its physical and other aspects – add, then, another layer to the mystery of the human Jesus. But formative as the Resurrection events may have been, they are only the beginning of a sequence of occurrences proliferating through Christian history in which Christ occurs within human experience. Moreover, both in the early period and onwards into history, Jesus is not either just the historical figure or just (so to speak) an inner experience: he is also interpreted in such a manner as to stand as the focus of faith. That is he is also defined by beliefs, of varying kinds, needless to say. So we have three layers: Jesus of history, Jesus of experience (beginning with the Resurrection) and Jesus as focus of faith. Christianity tries in varying ways to fuse the three together, so that belief in Christ has had to involve some affirmations about historical events, some also about the actuality (or at least relevance) of Jesus in personal experience and some too about his wider cosmological place. In the complexity of this situation, Christ has thus presented many faces. I shall try to delineate some of these as they have appeared in Christian history, and beginning with the life of Jesus himself. But before doing so, it may be useful to note the contrast between Christ and some other seminal religious figures – Muhammad and the Buddha. It may help to highlight something of the unique shape of the Christian focus.

Muhammad (of course) is not regarded as divine, but is a human Prophet. Still, he is the Seal of the Prophets, and stands as an example to Muslims. There are some problems about his biography, but in essence his career is clear, and the revelation accorded to him came definitively during his lifetime, so that the Koran has not the composite and sometimes contradictory character of the New Testament. Thus though Allah may indeed transcend human comprehension, his religion does not: it is well-defined, as the career of the Prophet is well-defined. The essence of Muslim ritual, law, ethics and teaching was all laid down from the start. Even if Islam developed, which it, as a historical phenomenon, was bound to, nevertheless it has a clarity about its origins which is lacking in the Christian case.

Or is it so lacking? There are those who see the literal meaning of the Bible as plain, and the Bible as inerrant; so that perhaps my judgement of the ambiguity of Christian teaching is open to challenge. Still, it is clear that where recourse is had to the Bible as the sole authority for doctrine, sects have multiplied, and myriads of interpretations have abounded. Clarity is in the eye of the beholder.

The particularities of Islam are a great contrast to the picture of Christ too. Muhammad was a successful politician, general, diplomat; he helped found a new political community. None of these things apply to Jesus, as portrayed in the New Testament. This is not to deny, of course, that Jesus seems to have taken positions on matters pertaining to politics, war and so on. However, if Jesus is a contrast to Muhammad, he is much more so with regard to the Buddha.

Admittedly there are mysteries about the Buddha, and the quest of the historical Buddha is even harder perhaps than that of the historical Jesus. But the life described in the Buddhist scriptures, notably the Pali canon, is fairly clear. He was brought up as son of a rajah, got married, fathered a child, left home to look for the spiritual truth, eventually attained enlightenment, went around preaching, founded an order of monks (and nuns), at length died at the age of eighty of a digestive complaint. Not only does this contrast in most ways with the brief and stormy career of Jesus; but its fabric is contrasting. The Buddha may have taught through parables and similes, but there is also a strong analytic and philosophical stamp upon his message: four Truths, eight elements in the Path, five constituent factors in the make-up of the individual, the three marks of existence – the flavour contrasts with the strange flashing images of Jesus' apocalyptic utterances, or the mysterious paradoxes of the Sermon on the Mount. Further, for the Theravada Buddhists especially, the work of the Buddha was to inject the Teaching into the flow of human life, or rather to reinject it (for the Dharma is everlasting, but fades from men's understanding as history takes one of its regular downward slides). The Buddha is above all Teacher. But more centrally, in most Christians' understanding, the work of Christ was not so much his teaching as his very career, in particular his death and coming to life again. It was through his self-sacrifice that the alienation between God and man was overcome.

Now admittedly in the Greater Vehicle the evolution of the ideal of the Bodhisattva brought into prominence the notion that the Buddha-to-be is self-sacrificing in his service to other living beings, and can even transfer some of the merit he thereby acquires to effect the salvation of other beings, otherwise unworthy and so tied karmically to the round of rebirth. But there is no historical anchorage to this notion. This is not to make a value-judgement (whether it is good or not for a sacred story to have a historical anchorage or not is a matter on which differing spiritual perspectives can be brought to bear). By contrast to the Bodhisattva ideal, the picture of Christ's self-sacrifice is a historical one, in the sense that human salvation has to do not just with psychology, spiritual relationships and so on, but also with the particularities of the historical person Jesus. And in calling him 'historical' here, two things are being said: first that his actual character and acts have to be reckoned with; and second that they are to be seen in the context of the history of the Jewish people and of the world.

In a sense Jesus stands at a midpoint between Muhammad and the Buddha. On the one hand, he is like the Buddha in himself effecting a revelation, but on the other unlike him in that he is embedded in a quite different theory and actuality of history. He is like Muhammad in standing in the light of that Semitic understanding of God's revelation through a series of events happening to the Jewish people and beyond; but unlike him in being more than a prophet, but himself somehow the God about whom he speaks. And while Muhammad's life is, as we have seen, historically rather clear, a whole forest of questions surround Jesus' life. And these questions have not merely arisen in the last century or two – the period during which the methods of modern historical criticism have been brought to bear on the text of the New Testament – for the ambiguities surrounding Jesus have always been there, and they account in part for the varieties of interpretation of the faith which have made themselves manifest in the course of the history of the Christian Church (and of the heresies surrounding it). Indeed the difficulties which were ample enough in the framing of the correct doctrine about Christ's divine and human natures are a testimony to a certain instability and paradoxicality in the root ideas out of which Christian doctrine came to be formed. And for all the achievements of modern ways of probing the texts, contemporary scholarship does not settle the issues, but rather transposes them into a different key. As we have hinted too, those who reject ambiguity in the name of faith and certainty ironically attest another type of ambiguity, because of the very variety of the certitudes.

Differing conclusions could be derived from this situation. It could be that the facts of Jesus' life were transparent enough, but that they have become overlaid by a confusing tissue of interpretation, selection and misunderstanding. It could be that this tissue is there anyway but Jesus' life was by no means transparent. But it may be that there were fundamental ambiguities in the life and acts of Jesus which are quite well reflected in the tradition. Of course, in order to face the evolution and impact of Christianity we do not finally have to make up our minds about the character of the historical Jesus, but have rather to consider simply the pictures which men had of him. Still, it may be that some account of the historical Jesus can itself explain something of the diversity. The theory which seems to do this best may be called the theory of category-transcendence. I shall explain this in a moment. In any event it is a useful device to delineate some of the earliest faces of

Christ. But before going on to it I want to add a further remark about the relationship between the Jesus of history and the Christ of experience. It is part of Christian doctrine (for the most part), and it is an observation drawn from the history of religions, that believers perceive the truth out of their own experience and context (are guided by the Holy Spirit, to put it theologically). Thus a given datum in a religion has a future as well as a past. It is put, as it were, to new uses, and it is perceived afresh. A datum is like a move in chess: its significance lies partly in the future, on what moves are going to be made next. Thus not only do we need to see something of the earliest faces of Christ but also the perceptions of later times. But I shall begin with the theory of the historical Jesus as being involved in what I have called category-transcendence.

Various concepts and religious movements were, of course, present in Jesus' day. Some of them more, and some of them less, intimately entered into the making of the early Christian community. Jesus made use of some of these concepts, but gave them a new context, or indeed broke them up. He accepted the ideas in a sense, but transcended them. In other words, the ambiguities of Jesus' career arose from category-transcendence. Thus it was not so much that there was a 'Messianic secret' – Jesus' keeping the fact of his Messiahship secret; but rather there was a trans-Messianic role which Jesus played.

It is in line with this interpretation that Jesus managed to align a remarkable coalition of enemies against him: the Sadducees, Herod, the Pharisees, the Roman authorities and one of his own disciples. And it is also significant that though his movement had roots in the preaching of John the Baptist, there persisted a group of the latter's followers independent of the early Christian community. It is also significant that there should be debate about the whole issue of the mission to the Gentiles. The fact that Jesus brought a reaction among the coalition I have referred to may be explained by the fact that the person who is 'betwixt-and-between' is so often, and throughout human cultures, treated as especially dangerous (and indeed powerful). It may be worth expatiating a little on this before

206

returning to the problem of the trial of Jesus and of the coalition against him.

Part of the task of concepts both inside and outside of the religious context is to classify events, people and so forth in such a manner that, given the classification, appropriate behaviour can be generated. In short, many concepts have a ritual and behavioural dimension. Drawing lines can thus be invested with a strong emotional charge. Thus the differentiation between man and woman, child and adult, affords a preliminary clarity in the matter of sexual relations. Hostility is likely to arise with regard to those who for one reason or another are betwixt-and-between, like the adolescent and the homosexual. One method of dealing with the problem is to create some new category to cover the intermediate case (such as *teenager*, *gay*, etc.), with itself a positive emotional charge to win acceptance. Rites of passage are a way of shifting a person clearly from one category to another (hence if a dead person does not get proper last rites he becomes dangerously intermediate – a haunting ghost). But sometimes the strange person who is neither quite this nor that can, because of his power, become not so much a danger as an extraordinary help – consider such great leaders as Churchill (half American), Napoleon (Corsican), Hitler (Austrian), de Valera (part Portuguese), Stalin (Georgian). Thus too with Jesus, to whom some emotionally charged titles might be applied but who transcended them, and so displayed a dangerous ambiguity. For reasons which must remain partially obscure, the ambiguity which brought him death brought him, through the Jesus movement, unprecedented power in the hearts and imaginations of men.

One can perhaps see where Jesus' closest links were by noting how strong are the criticisms, in the Gospels, of the Pharisees. The strongest criticism is reserved for the alienated brother. Many of the motifs of Jesus' teaching and that of his disciples were drawn from the thought-world of the Pharisees: the sense of the last things (apocalyptic), belief in angels, hope of resurrection and so on. But though Jesus may have affirmed his loyalty to the Law (coming, he is supposed to have said, not to destroy but to fulfil), his attitude to the tradition was ambiguous. Not only did he from one point of view infringe the Law (healing on the Sabbath and the like), but he uttered prophecies about the destruction of the Temple. So his outlook could seem dangerously antinomian to Pharisees, and even politically threatening to those conservative collaborators, the Sadducees (clearing out money-changers could look like a prelude to more violent action). Here again, Jesus' attitudes were two-faced, it might be thought. His Messianic role, such as it was, could by implication be thought anti-Roman; and yet the saying about rendering unto Caesar the things that are Caesar's was an endorsement of those who tried to save Jewish religion in the face of Roman power by acquiescing in collaboration with the latter. And what had Jesus to say to the Zealots? One or more of his disciples seems to have been a Zealot (maybe this lay behind Judas' disappointment); but Jesus, though he may have had something of the emotional intensity of the Zealot, chose the opposite way to that of armed resistance. The other main movement of the times, the Essenes, are not mentioned in the New Testament; but one can see some elements of their thinking both in the Jesus movement and in its immediate precursor, that of John the Baptist. Regarding the latter, one can see that Jesus both did and did not endorse the teaching of an imminent kingdom, and though his followers carried on the practice of baptism, it was given a new meaning.

If we turn to two or three of the titles used of Jesus in the New Testament, we can see further ways in which Jesus attracted certain interpretations but still failed precisely to fit them. Thus he is referred to as a prophet, and not only this – there was the question as to whether he was *the* prophet, the eschatological one, who would return at the beginning of Messianic times, and commonly identified with Elijah. At the scene of the Transfiguration, however, Jesus is represented not as the prophet, though with Moses and Elijah, but as going beyond that role: he is 'my beloved Son in whom I am well pleased'. If Jesus had many of the properties of a prophet, still there were some significant differences. Thus like other prophets, he had an inaugural vision, at his baptism; he knew the secrets of the other world; he predicted his own death and resurrection; he used symbolic actions in order to express and illustrate his teachings (like causing the fig tree to wither); he knew the deep meaning of the scriptures; he spoke in the name of God; he transmitted God's judgement; and foretold the future of the kingdom. All this was in the style of the prophets of old. But yet in the scheme which Jesus sketched out it seemed that he was not *the* prophet (that role was played by John, it seemed), and though he might speak the words of God he did so not only as a transmitter. For no prophet could claim to forgive sins. Thus in the upshot, the status accorded to Jesus burst the bounds of prophecy. Or at least, the status accorded to him in the Christian movement: the Muslims by contrast retained the picture of Jesus as a prophet, though of course not so important as the Seal of the Prophets. From this point of view Islam was a logical continuation of the Jewish tradition in one direction.

For there were indeed differing directions in which the Judaism of Jesus' own times could develop. It could stay within the strict confines of its own tradition. Here there were basically three options, two of them fatal. One of them was Zealot resistance; another was collaboration in the style of the Sadducees, with the attempt to retain the ongoing viability of the Temple cult. The other was Pharisaism, which could maintain Judaism through the Law, even after the destruction of Jerusalem. Another general direction for Judaism was towards a universal monotheism based on the prophetic ideal, and this, in a sense, was the direction which led to Islam. Another direction was also universalistic, but which made use of various strands of religious imagery within Judaism, but fused them in a new and revolutionary synthesis. This was what happened in the case of Christianity. It was not enough for Jesus – in this direction – to have the face of a prophet. He also had the face of the Messiah, and then as it turned out not even that.

A great deal of attention is paid in the Gospels to the whole series of events leading up to and including the trial and execution of Jesus. Indeed to the dispassionate observer, coming to the books for the first time, it would seem that this was the most significant part of Jesus' biography. It makes it reasonable to think that Jesus deliberately courted the death which overtook him: that the whole was a new drama of Messianism. But though Jesus might be the Christ who would restore Israel by overthrowing the oppressor and creating a new kingdom, he did it all by analogy with the more usual Messianic expectations. He was indeed of David's line, as befitted the Messiah, but important as this might seem, and it was much insisted on by early Christians, Jesus' origins and upbringing were rather humble, and he turned out to be King in a special sense. For the kingdom was not of this world, and the new Israel was the community which followed on in faith from him. It was to be the Church. And the victory over the oppressor was a highly paradoxical one, since it involved crucifixion as 'the King of the Jews'. So Jesus took all the Messianism seriously and then exploded it through a series of lived analogies.

Another face of Christ was that of the Suffering Servant – a face made familiar to us through the Crucifix. But whereas that figure stood for Israel, in the case of Jesus it partly did not. That is, Jesus himself was the suffering servant, though he was also representative of humanity, in that he seems to have used of himself the mysterious title Son of Man. This figure was sometimes seen as idealized man concentrating in himself also the divine presence, who will judge the wicked and rule the righteous. What Jesus may have perceived (or at least his followers attributed to him) was the identification of idealized humanity with his own suffering to come. Thereby a new constellation of ideas was born. Jesus was not the Son of Man as usually understood, nor was his interpretation of the role of the suffering servant traditional. Again, older categories are made use of, but transcended.

The way in which the figure of Jesus came to emerge into early Christian history involved a set of teachings which were in essence simple, even if the situation within Judaism out of which they came was rather complex. The clearest systematization of these notions was in Paul's writings. They looked to a scheme of history in which there were three main junctures:

the creation and covenant with Israel as the first juncture; the coming of Christ as the second juncture; and the last things when Christ will return as the third juncture. The Messianic role of Christ was clear, but now it is a new Israel (the Church) which is constituted by a people in solidarity with ideal man (Christ) who is the second Adam, and who has won victory over the oppressor (sin) through his own sacrifice in which he is both priest and victim. This sacrifice makes obsolete the whole system of the Temple cult. All the assumptions of the old Israel, though accepted, are now transcended. They point beyond themselves. It was indeed not unreasonable for most Jews to find this set of ideas too revolutionary (even alien and subversive) to count as a plausible reinterpretation of the Jewish heritage in a new key. But it provided a picture of a Christ whose face could be universal, for though its physiognomy was very particular, Jewish in fact, its gaze was directed towards all men. Christianity was thus given its special dynamic.

But the ambiguities of Jesus remained, and the development of Christian experience was long and complex. Thus we see some very special faces of Christ continuing to emerge.

The faces of Christ can, for instance, be seen in Christian art, and up to a point they mirror differing doctrinal views. Christ has to be seen as both divine and human, but sometimes the former is on the verge of taking Christ away from history altogether, as in the mysterious ikons of Christ Pantocrator, or ruler of all. On the other hand, the Renaissance introduced a realism which could easily fail to capture the numinous. One wonders sometimes what to make of those so realistic pictures of Jesus ascending to heaven, hovering so it seems as though kept up with the thrust of invisible jets. One feels the force of an impending unitarianism.

The whole doctrine of salvation seemed to require that Jesus should be both God and man, and so there is a dialectical character to the way Christ is looked at. It is dialectical because indeed the character of God is revealed as having a certain polarity. Thus God is awe-inspiring, given to wrath, great judge, thunderous creator; yet on the other hand he is merciful and forgiving, and he is, too, beautiful, drawing men to him.

It is useful at this point to draw out the implications of the doctrine of Christ as redeemer or saviour. (It is also a question as to how far Jesus may have thought of himself as involved in the act of reconciling God to men, but this perhaps was implicit in the fusion of the images of Son of Man and Suffering Servant which he effected.) Much of the thought of the Church on the matter was summed up by Aquinas when he diagnosed that Christ's Passion brought about men's salvation in various ways. One way is through merit, for Christ's merit, acquired by his life and by his self-sacrifice above all, could be transmitted to the faithful. This picture of Christ's work is a rather formalistic working out of the logic of such metaphors as that Christ is the vine. In such metaphors there is a sharing of life, so that the Christian, in a state of solidarity with Christ, shares Christ's merit. Christ, as divine, has infinite merit, and can share it inexhaustibly.

Another way in which salvation is effected is by satisfaction, for Christ pleased God more by his passion than men alienated him by their sins. Here Christ can be seen as the second Adam, and so as perfect man – man as we were meant to be. Sometimes in a weakened form, this picture of Christ is that simply of the ethically perfect person who can save us by his example. But this scarcely brings out the dialectical nature of religious experience, and it is to this in part that the figure of the second Adam appeals.

For on the one hand, God is judge, and if judge then justice comes into play. It can be terrifying. Thus Luther could write: 'Then God appears dreadfully angry, and with him the whole of his creation. There is no possibility of escape or relief, either within or without . . .' This picture of God as judge is also the picture of Christ as judge. It is there in the New Testament: the mysterious face of Jesus on the mountain at the time of the transfiguration is that of the Ancient of Days, the Judge, present with his two assessors (Moses and Elijah), and the frightening countenance is reflected in the words ascribed to Jesus in Matthew x: 11–15: 'And whatever town or village you enter, find out who is worthy in it, and stay with him until you depart. As you enter the house, salute it. And if the house is worthy let your peace come upon it. But if it is not worthy let your peace return to you. And if anyone will not receive you or listen to you, shake off the dust from your feet as you leave that house or town. Truly I say to you it shall be more tolerable on the day of judgement for the land of Sodom and Gomorrah than for that town.'

The judgemental character of the Lord is more vividly depicted still in Revelation, where the author writes: 'I saw a great white throne and the one who sat upon it; from his face the earth and heaven fled away . . .' The terror of damnation and the wrath of God are, however, balanced by the sense of forgiveness which flows from God through the merit of Christ in which the believer participates.

But Christ's pleasing God by his death can be seen as the effect of sacrifice. Thus John's Gospel refers to the Baptists' introduction of Christ: 'Behold the lamb of God, who takes away the sin of the world.' Here Jesus is identified with the paschal lamb, perhaps; and the image of the blood of the lamb has entered deeply into the language of acceptance of salvation.

The use of the image of sacrifice points to a certain paradox in the Christian message, in that the logic of sacrifice has to be understood if this idea of Christ's saving act is to work, and yet on the other hand the point of the new Christian dispensation is that the old sacrifices are over. In other words, one has to accept the serious meaning of animal sacrifice in order to see that such animal sacrifice is now quite irrelevant. This is one aspect of the general problem which has recurred from time to time in Christian history as to how much weight to put on the preceding Jewish religion itself. However, let us pause for a moment to consider something of the general logic of sacrifice.

At its most basic, a sacrifice involves the destruction of something which is of value to the person who makes the sacrifice. Additionally, that destruction may have particular symbolic value – e.g. in the killing of an animal the blood, the life-principle, is poured out and offered in a certain way. The destruction however is a transition which makes the sacrifice like a gift: the animal is offered (for instance) to God. At a crude level it may be just a matter of pleasing God. But more importantly it is a concrete symbolic gesture which (if acknowledged by God) is a sort of communication with God, supplying a certain mutual benignity. The sacrificer means well, and God in acknowledging the sacrifice responds and so too means well. An analogue at a non-sacrificial level is the proffered handshake. In effect, then, Jesus' sacrifice is a concrete communication by man to God which in the nature of the case re-opens benign communication between God and alienated man.

Another picture of Christ, however, which draws the outline of a different understanding of the atonement, was that of Christ the Victor, who overcomes the Devil. Indeed, in many ways it is the figure of Christ defeating Satan which was the most vivid in the mind of most Christians until relatively modern times. Thus it is hardly feasible to enter into the thoughts of such men as St Paul and Luther without recognizing the vitality in them of the figure of the Devil. Christ is, then, the anti-type to Satan. But who was the latter?

Considering the important part he has played in Christian history he is remarkably little regarded in modern Christian theology. The Enlightenment saw the decay of ideas of both hell and the Devil: such aspects of the Christian myth were seen as medieval exaggerations and concretions of the symbolic language of the Gospels. However, the New Testament was itself involved in such concretion, and indeed inherited ideas of the Evil One which go well beyond the picture of Satan as drawn in the main part of the Old Testament. There, for instance in the Book of Job, he is a sort of partner of God, whose job is to put people to the test: he is not so much Tempter as Tester. The Satan who is the leader of angels and antagonist of God is a later figure, but a singularly impressive one – so much so that he definitely caught the Christian imagination, and turned the drama of history into a scene of warfare between God and the righteous on the one hand and the Devil and demonic forces on the other. In the New Testament he is prince of this world, the evil one, the tempter, the adversary of Christ, variously known as Satan, Belial and Beelzebub.

In all this the legacy to which the New Testament was heir itself owed something to Zoroastrianism, with its dramatic picture of the universal struggle. The Devil is the prototype of pride, for he wishes to set himself up as the equal of God, and his continual task is to try, with his demons, to seduce men in the same direction and so add to his army. In all this he is highly cunning. But as it turns out (so thought some early Fathers of the Church) God is cleverer. Through the incarnation, God is disguised in the form of a servant. His human nature is the bait, his divine the hook, and it is on this that Satan is caught, thinking that the (human) Christ is in his power.

Still another image was that of Christ as redeemer, in the sense that he freed the slaves of Satan by paying the price, though not to Satan but to God. Or again: he was a ransom for many. In such metaphors, Christ is again seen to be divine in his action, but identified with man. It was this insistent requirement that he should have this amphibious nature which made the problem of defining Christological doctrine so difficult. And these difficulties marched with the problem of monotheism. How could the Christian faith remain true to its Jewish heritage while seeming to add an extra God, namely Christ? We have already seen (Chapter 3) the consequences of the attempted resolution of the various problems at the Council of Chalcedon.

It is perhaps not surprising that Christ's dual nature should cause problems in understanding something of what it was like to be, or to encounter, Jesus. How do the triumphant pictures of the victorious Pantocrator fit in with the human realities? And what has Christianity made of the miracles? Were they not signs of supernatural power? Here was another ambiguity in Jesus: he performed miracles of healing and so forth and yet was reticent about his powers. Still, a significant part of the portrait of Christ in the Gospels is the picture of him as healer and caster-out of demons. Nevertheless, an important motif from earliest times was the theory of the self-emptying (*kenosis*) whereby Christ as human being is divested of his divine attributes, and so does not need to be conceived as omnisciently knowing what would happen next and so forth. This portrait is one which has appealed particularly to the modern age.

And here we meet a wide ranging question, namely how the traditional faces of Christ fare when the older cosmology and mythology appear to have broken down. What are we to make of the second Adam in the absence of the first? How is Jesus' human nature bait if there is no Devil to hook? Such problems in modern Christianity have been compounded by those arising from scepticism about the historical value of much of the New Testament accounts of Jesus. It is easy in these circumstances for the face of Christ to become an elusive abstraction. Probably therefore a considerable degree of reconstruction will be necessary before a modern equivalent of the classical framework in which the work and nature of Christ was set can take a grip on men's imaginations. However, it is a notable feature of modern Christianity that it renews itself through critical self-appraisal. A number of other religions one can think of would have difficulty in being so radical in applying vigorous critical research to their origins.

What can be said to have emerged from the foregoing analysis? Three things, chiefly. First, Jesus appears to have used a range of available categories but to have transcended them. This failure to fit may have been part of both his power and dangerousness. It would, incidentally, be relevant to the question of his divinity, since it is typical of the divine that it eludes categories. Second, the faces of Christ relate strongly (and not surprisingly) to the theory or theories of salvation, and hence to a conception of a historical drama. Perhaps more strongly in Christianity than in any other religious tradition there is a sense of an earthly, and not just a cosmic, drama. Third, however, this drama has been played out against a cosmology which has been most effectively expressed in the medieval synthesis but which has been in course of fairly extensive change and decay since then.

But as well as the historical drama there is also the psychological one. Thus Christ has not only appeared as redeemer, victor, prince of light and so forth: he has also entered into men's experience. Thus the whole idea of deification in which man becomes like Christ has an inner application in the mystics' notion of the birth of Christ in the soul. Similarly the story of Jesus' death and resurrection is mirrored in the death of the individual to sin and his sense of being reborn in Christ. So Christ can be seen as it were at different levels: as triumphant intervener in history, as present in the sacraments which recapitulate his saving work, and in the inner experience of those who have faith.

The worship of Jesus has another dimension – and that is its personalism. Christianity is in a central respect, as we have seen, what would be called in the Indian tradition a path of *bhakti*. But whereas this personal devotion there relates to forms of the divine being that are on the whole rather remote from concrete historical processes, Christian *bhakti* is tied to a very definite, if rather mysterious, historical figure. And where that *bhakti* is expressed by, and related to, a strongly sacramental religion, the polarity between the numinous God and the man Jesus becomes heavily charged, as in the hymn:

> Let all mortal flesh keep silence
> And with fear and trembling stand;
> Ponder nothing earthly minded,
> For with blessing in his hand
> Christ our God to earth descendeth,
> Our full homage to demand.

Christianity's Mythic Dimension:
The Bible

Since, for Christians, the Bible centres on Christ – the New
Testament being explicitly about him, the Old foretelling him
– the discussion of the faces of Christ has already carried us into
biblical territory. But the book itself warrants separate treatment. And the way we look at it will determine our attitude
to Christian myth and history.

Myth? Should we use the word? There are those who would
only use the term of what occurs in some other realm of time,
a 'once upon a time', and not of what occurs in history. There
are those who use the word for stories which are fanciful and
symbolic, not for stories of hard history. And certainly in the
Old and New Testaments there is a lot of the latter (how much
is a matter of some debate, of course, among modern scholars).
Then again there are those who, like the oratorical Baptist
Straton, whom we encountered in New York in the early
twenties, would not wish to use the word concerning what is
recorded in the inerrant scriptures. There are several different
issues here, partly conceptual and partly factual. Let us try
to disentangle them.

First, as to historicity. To say that something is a historical
fact can mean one of two things. It can mean that an event took
place which can be established by the use of the historical
method, that is by the means through which modern historians
try to determine what did and what did not happen, in view
of presently available documentary and other evidence. To ask
whether Judas' betrayal of Jesus is historical or not is to ask
whether it can be shown or plausibly argued to have happened.
But second, to say that something is a historical fact may mean
that it is a fact about that flow of events (or set of streams of
human events) which we refer to as history. There are lots of

facts which are not historical in this sense. The moon is cratered, but this is not strictly a historical fact, unless we are perhaps talking metaphorically about the history of the solar system. But it is not a fact within the flow of human, earthly events.

There is a wide division of opinion among scholars as to how much of the New Testament narrative, especially in the Gospels, can be considered historical in the first sense. But the writers tell the story as if the human events they describe are historical in the second sense – belong to the flow of human events. For most of the history of the Christian community they have been taken as real events. For the sake of clarity I shall use the following convention. When events are taken as real, for instance by Christians, I shall refer to them as real happenings. When they are provable or otherwise, I shall refer to them as provable (impossible, etc.) happenings. Thus Jesus' first miracle at Cana in Galilee is (for most Christians) a real happening, but to many historians it is unprovable or impossible.

One of the issues about the historicity of the Gospels is: How many real happenings have to be provable or at least probable for a person reasonably to have faith in Christ? To this we shall come back. Meanwhile let us reconsider the question of the use of the term *myth*.

One major use for this term in the history of religions is for a sacred story, typically involving a god, God or transcendent being in relation to men and/or other living beings, or to the world. Some myths are about events predating man – namely cosmogonic myths describing the origin of the cosmic order. But mostly they relate to men. Since real happenings set in intelligible chronological sequence is what we mean by history, those sacred stories which include such real happenings can be considered to be myths, but myths of a particular sort. We can call them historical myths. They differ from creation stories, which do not strictly involve historically real happenings. Thus, and given we stick to this understanding of the matter, there is no reason why we cannot use the term *myth* to refer to the happenings of Jesus' life, death and resurrection.

But of course a sacred story is not just a story. What does the sacredness add? It adds an extra dimension which we can call symbolic depth. Thus Jesus' crucifixion was not just the death, on a criminal charge, of a particular religious leader. That is, incidentally, a real and provable happening, provable that is by reasonable historical canons. The crucifixion is seen biblically as having a crucial meaning in relation to the salvation of man. Its symbolic depth is its significance with regard to God's drama of redemption.

There is therefore a certain gap between history and faith. If faith is acceptance of the myth of the crucifixion, that is the crucifixion seen in dramatic depth, then the depth-aspect transcends history. One cannot by documents prove or make probable the fact that Christ died for our sins, but only that Jesus, called the Christ, died – and that some people thought that he died for our sins.

But (it may be countered) if the Bible is the infallible Word of God, and if it states that Christ died for our sins, a document, namely the Bible, can in fact prove the fact that Christ died for our sins. This is, so far as it goes, rational enough; but it needs to be tempered by the reflection that assurance is transitive. If A implies B, and I am sure of B because I am sure of A, then the degree of assurance about B cannot be greater than my assurance about A. If I am sure I am going to win $1000 because Diablo Canyon is going to win the Kentucky Derby and if he does I shall get $1000, then a lot depends on how sure I am that Diablo Canyon is going to win. How sure then can I be about the infallibility of the Bible? If it is a matter of faith-commitment, then I am producing not proof, but faith.

A property of history, as a flow of real happenings, is that it is linear. Sometimes men have thought of it as unilinear, as though we have one swirling stream from early times through Christian origins to the modern era: from Abraham to Jimmy Carter, so to say. Actually planetary history is multilinear, with relatively independent histories going on, over long periods, in China, Europe and so on – with occasional rivulets criss-crossing from one river to the next. With modern communications, basically since the time of the great voyages of discovery, planetary history is becoming unified – the rivers are forming a single mighty stream. Now part of what is sometimes meant by saying that Christianity emphasizes history is that it sees the divine drama as linear and embedded in the process of real happenings. The contrast is sometimes drawn with archaic and Oriental religions, which see happenings either as not linear or as definitely cyclical (with cosmic history repeating itself, as in the Indian vision of recurrent creations and destructions of the world). The contrast is somewhat overdrawn, but it nevertheless has a point. More consistently and dramatically than in other religious traditions Judaism, Christianity and Islam see God as involved in a linear process of real human happenings.

To say that the New Testament describes happenings with symbolic depth, and so in that sense is mythic, implies that it has, in Christian use, more than a descriptive function – and indeed this becomes immediately apparent when one looks into it. Its narratives sometimes break into hymns (or, as in the case of St John's Gospel, begin with a hymn); and many of the passages are for celebratory or other use. It is not there to have the facts on file: it is there for a set of community functions; and notably for using within the liturgy. This is natural, in that a myth typically is for telling, and through the telling an emotional charge is transmitted and a happening is re-presented, re-enacted. To put it another way: the Bible is not just mythic, but it also has a ritual dimension.

From this point of view, the New Testament can be said to have arisen from the need to supplement the Old in the growing services of the Church, especially in the Gentile world. Early Christians, as faithful to the Jewish tradition, participated in, and then transferred the forms of, synagogue worship, and this incorporated readings from the old scriptures. The need for the formation of a set of specifically Christian scriptures arose partly therefore as a means of extending the readings from the Jewish aspect of the weekly gathering into the Christian communal meal aspect. It is thus not all that surprising that such a large part of the Gospels is taken up with the events leading up to, during and after Jesus' trial, since those apparently tragic days had their meaning focussed in the Last Supper, now ritually re-presented among the faithful.

It is important to recognize that even if the scriptures became, naturally enough, objects of study and commentary, they were primarily encountered, in the life of the Christian, as the basis of public liturgical acts and preaching. And since the New Testament was that which was distinctively Christian (at least once it had moved towards being authoritatively established as a canon) it is not surprising that gradually it acquired much greater liturgical weight than the Old. This tendency had its expression for instance in the Eastern Orthodox liturgy as it evolved after the great councils: the reading from the Old Testament was displaced, there being two readings from the New, including, of course, a Gospel reading, honoured by a procession from behind the iconostasis known as the 'Little Entrance'. Here in very clear form was expressed a way of looking at the Gospels as more than a set of books, or more even than readings.

They were, and are still, seen in this act as bringing to us the Redeemer. Christ is made present again to the faithful in the reading. The procession, the hymns, the candles, the kissing, the whole numinous occasion is replete with the glory of Christ himself. This reverence for the Gospels recognizes in them something of the substance of Christ himself, and goes even further than the honouring of the scrolls by procession and so forth in the synagogue service on which the Christian worship was partly modelled. As we shall see, some modern Protestant uses of the Bible represent an experientializing of this ritual use of the scriptures.

Now the liturgical use of the Bible, and its functioning as a matrix for the coming into being of an authoritative canon, are logical counterparts to the fact that the writings themselves refer to happenings which have symbolic depth. That depth is conveyed by the writings, but conveying here is more than description, since it is the wonder and power of God (among other things) which intendedly shine through the narratives, etc., and wonder is not just to be referred to – it has to be evoked if it is to be effectively conveyed. So part of the symbolic depth consists in a revelatory element which is to be evoked or expressed by the reading. (This is partly why in latter day revivalism the preacher, without the ambience of a glorious liturgy, has to use the alternatives of rhetoric and acting to convey feelings of power.)

The shift to the use of Christian scriptures in the liturgy was completed with the exclusion of the readings from the Old Testament, even if the use of the psalms and other elements retained a Jewish anchorage in the services. Theologically the Church had rejected the challenge of Marcion (who flourished in the mid second century and who was supposedly son of a bishop from the southern shores of the Black Sea), who argued for a much more dramatic eclipse of the Old Testament. He posed in dramatic form the question of the relation between the myth of Christ and that of the Chosen People.

When Marcion came to Rome in 138 or 139 he joined the Christian community and despite his views he was a member for five or six years before being excommunicated. The fact that he was excluded, however, helped to determine later Christianity's attitudes both to scripture and to the nature of Christ's redeeming work. Very probably Marcion was a Gnostic and as such represented a slant upon life which in varying forms had and continued to have a powerful effect on the imagination of the late Roman empire. Marcion endeavoured to give Christianity such a slant, and to lead it far from its Jewish origins. For, according to him, the supreme being was not to be identified with the evil God, the Demiurge, who was the creator of men and of the world and who was the God of the Old Testament. The Demiurge was prone to order men into battle, demand bloody sacrifices, require arbitrary obedience to his rule and to the law and to choose favourites. The supreme being, God of Love, sent down Christ from the highest heaven, and yet this Christ was not actually human, only having the appearance of man. Since flesh is the creation of the evil God, Christ could not be born of the flesh.

Marcion's teachings were by no means unpopular and he organized a large number of widespread Churches, some of which persisted into the fifth century (surprisingly: sexual intercourse was forbidden among married converts, as it helped to propagate the evil fleshly work of the Demiurge). The fact that the doctrines never captured mainstream Christianity may be partly because of their austerity and world-negation. But also so drastic a rejection of the Jewish background to the redemptive work of Jesus made the latter's work unintelligible. It is true that Jesus transcended the categories of his times; but it was an affirmative transcendence – that is, it took the traditions and currents of thought of contemporary Judaism with the utmost seriousness, and then extended them in a revolutionary way.

The fact that Marcion, in order to establish his position, had to argue that much of the Christian literature circulating and in use was a distortion, led him to produce his own set of genuine writings – an expurgated Luke and a pruned Paul. Such a challenge was an important factor in moving the Church towards settling upon a canon of New Testament writings. Necessarily a primary criterion of authenticity had to do with the way in which the symbolic depth of the happenings of Jesus' life and of the earliest community was treated. In part, the choice was a theological one. Despite Marcion, a dialectical continuity between Old and New Testaments was the outcome.

There was also a dialectic between the Church and its foundation documents. The canon's settlement took a long time. As late as the eighth century Revelation was not universally accepted among the Greeks. The epistle to the Hebrews was not Pauline, though acknowledged as such after the Council of Carthage in 419 (Augustine who was there was certain it was not Pauline, however). The whole process was effective in the long run in providing a rather wide-ranging set of documents about Christ and the early community, which could serve as a doctrinal norm. But the whole thing too was a spiral: the Church teaches true Christianity because that is what is to be found in the documents; and these are the true documents because this is what the Church determines. And once the scriptures were fixed, the collection could congeal into a hardened corpus, to be transmitted down the centuries, and destined therefore to be a formative influence on the new culture which emerged in the turbulent period after the break-up of the Roman Empire.

What the Bible came to mean in Western Christendom can be seen by viewing it from the perspective of Athanasius and Jerome in the fourth century and then from the perspective of the 'finished product' in the Middle Ages. The fourth century was important in that doctrinally the Church was largely formed, even if some major disputes would recur. In line with a measure of uniformity of creed there emerged a growing consensus on the authority of the New Testament: the twenty-seven books were listed in the Easter Letter of St Athanasius to the Church in Alexandria in 367. Such other works as the *Didache* ('Teaching') which had been in long use were also commended for the instruction of converts.

But once scriptures reach a canonical position one needs an approved version of them, and in the West what was needed was an agreed Latin version. It was primarily through Jerome (*c*. 342–*c*. 420) that the Vulgate came into being – the dominant version for the Latin-speaking half of the Church. A man of gloomy and tempestuous austerity, he devoted himself with great learning and single-mindedness to the problems both of getting the right text and the words to translate it. His version was not without opponents: by taking a critical look at the variant texts, by translating the Old Testament from Hebrew and by consulting Jews on matters of translation, he was bound to diverge from more conservative and less learned peers. But his labours won out. His Bible was already strong in influence by the late sixth century and the time of St Gregory the Great, and in the thirteenth it acquired its name of 'Common Bible', namely Vulgate. But both in its early days and more especially in its later spreading its aim of accuracy and uniformity was partially obscured by the fact that for all its freshness it was written in a language which increasingly diverged from the tongues of everyday discourse. The Latinization of mass and Bible had various effects. One was that the Bible as a ritual medium of the expression of the Christ myth was highly controlled. It required learning, typically under Church auspices, if one was to understand and interpret scripture; moreover, the economic and cultural circumstances of the production of Bibles were highly important.

Until the invention of printing with movable type, the cost of a Bible was great. A large one would take the skins of about twenty-five sheep; there would be the binding, illuminating and, of course, the immensely long labour of copying the whole manuscript. Thus Bibles were not very widely available, and generally their possession was a mark of wealth. Even if only rather plainly bound in leather over wooden boards, it could attract the attention of a thief; and thus in churches the Bible was usually chained. Moreover, because most scribes were monks, the supply was mediated through the Church. It was not surprising that the chained Bible became for the Reformers a symbol of the papacy's authoritarian attitude towards the Word of God. But it also represented another kind of piety. The Bible had become integrated into a whole hierarchical world, both civil and spiritual, and into a ritual of mysterious power, in which the use of Latin helped to augment the mystery.

There had been demands for vernacular scriptures because of missionary endeavours and successes. Thus parts of the Bible were translated into English from the seventh century onwards. It was said that the Venerable Bede finished dictating his translation of St John's Gospel on the eve before Holy Thursday, 735 AD, and then expired. Already in the fifth century a written Bible in Armenian was produced. But such developments were within a framework of authority. Later the translation of the Bible could have an explosive effect, in bypassing the mediation of the priesthood, as in the fourteenth century revolutionary Christianity formulated by Wycliffe, who among his other acts translated the Vulgate into English.

The relative unavailability of the Bible to lay people, except among the well-to-do, gave the Church a virtual monopoly of interpretation. The increasing complexity of methods of analysis, and the use of allegorical interpretations, were factors in enhancing a trend which goes back to the earliest growth of the faith – namely the radical divergence between Christian and Jewish interpretations of the Old Testament.

This is one of the remarkable ways in which Christianity is unique in the history of religions – its takeover of the main sacred corpus of a preceding, but different, tradition. Or at least, it is the sharpest case: one could perhaps argue that the interpretation of the Vedic hymns by later Vedanta represents a similar 'takeover'. Nevertheless, it is a remarkable situation where the Bible of the Jewish tradition is recognized so solidly, and yet seen so differently. Paul set this movement in motion, and in medieval times it added to prejudice against the Jews – there being something wilful in their refusal to see Christ foreshadowed in the Old Testament.

The distinction between literal, allegorical and moral senses of the text was partly rooted in the fact that much of the language of religion cannot be taken literally, for its very symbolic depth depends upon metaphor and analogy. But of course there was the problem of how to reconcile the different parts of the Bible – not just as between the Old and the New, but within the Gospels and so on. All this derived from the view, implicit in the very name of the scriptures (the Bible) and much encouraged by the widespread use of Jerome's text bound between covers, that the scriptures form a single work, rather than a collection of rather diverse works built up over a long period and with varying degrees of coherence, either internally to each other, or among one another. There arrived in Christianity a holistic concept of the Bible. It is reflected in a lot of modern phraseology as when people talk of 'the biblical view' of – whatever: man, the creation, redemption, homosexuality, the end of the world. This holistic view almost inevitably precipitated a crisis later on, after three main developments overtook the Bible, as a consequence of the events surrounding the Reformation. These three were: democratization, experientialization and secularization. Or to put matters more plainly: the Bible became open to everyman, a potent source and interpreter of religious experience, and (conflictingly) dissected and read as a set of ancient documents, to be treated like any others.

Behind such a revolution lay the Reniassance and the invention of the printing press. The former gave new impetus to the work of editing the Greek text of the Bible and to the philological vigour which rediscovered some of the classical sources of Christianity, The latter made possible the cheap dissemination of the book, and in a manner which it would be hard for ecclesiastical authority to control. This can be seen from the life of William Tyndale (1494–1536). Already only five years after Luther's critique of indulgences, the mood of reform had spread to England, and with it the thought that the Bible should be freed from its Latin bondage. Using Erasmus' text, he translated the New Testament, and had it printed on the Continent, by the famous printer Peter Schöffler who had been involved in the epoch-making production of the Gutenberg Bible. No less than six thousand copies were brought into England, though many were seized and burnt. But this only triggered greater effort to bring more in. Tyndale became in effect a noted smuggler, a bible-runner. After his arrest in 1535 and before his execution in the following year he went on with his translation of the Old Testament. His work left its imprint on the ultimate fruit of English scriptural genius, the King James version.

The wide availability of scripture, together with the belief that it was authoritative, effectively shattered the priestly monopoly. Only by a thorough reform of its own fabric and a renewal of holiness could the Roman Church begin to confidently reassert its own magisterial descent from the first apostles. A new, post-Trent ideology had to be fashioned to take the place of the old medieval hierarchical vision of the world and society. On their side, the Catholics recaptured the Bible, though by submitting the new scholarship to Church authority the Church was to cause trouble for itself in the late nineteenth century. But at that time the modernist crisis lay far in the future.

In the more conservative branches of the Reformation – in Lutheranism and in Anglicanism – a remarkable synthesis was achieved between democratization and symbolic depth. Luther's translations were clear, strong and numinous; as also was the language of the English Bible. But though the text might be inspiring, the problem of inspiration, of how the

Bible was inspired, rather than how it was inspiring (though the two were connected), was clearly to be acute through the very process of democratization. Was every reader to be capable of knowing God's truth by a simple reading of the text? If so, there were great advantages in holding that the Bible, as understood according to its plain meaning, is inspired and so inerrant.

At first, Luther for one could be rather free on the interconnected matters of inspiration, the canon and inerrancy. He had, notoriously, referred to the Epistle of St James as an epistle of straw. In 1522 he declared that he did not think Revelation prophetic or even inspired by the Holy Ghost. The test of whether a book should be included in the canon was not, however, authorship but whether it preached Christ. So he left Revelation in, even though his own private judgement, which he did not wish to impose upon others, was that it did not know Christ. He was also to remark that God is in every syllable of the Bible, and that no iota in the work is in vain. The logic of the Reformers' position on the authority of scripture led them to this holistic attitude.

But the effects were bound to be explosive, and that was recognized by the irony of such tests as the Thirty-Nine Articles. One of these reads:

> Holy Scripture containeth all things necessary to salvation; so that whatsoever is not read therein, nor may be proved thereby, is not to be required of any man, that it should be believed as an article of the Faith, or be thought requisite or necessary to salvation.

The irony is that this article should make all the others unnecessary. But the fact is the Church of England, quite naturally, wished to control the limits within which biblical interpretation could be tolerated.

Democratization pushed interpretation towards the literal or plain meaning of the text. But it also was accompanied by a strong emphasis upon the experiential dimension of Christian faith. If scriptures had been inspired by the Holy Spirit *then*, when they were composed, they also need interpretation *now* through the Spirit. That at least was the position taken by

Luther and other reformers. But this 'subjective' component could be taken in three ways at least. One way is to take it as meaning that the scripture must light a flame in our hearts. This means entering emotionally into the life of the Bible, and is well described by a modern writer, concerning Luther:

> How Luther suffered with Joseph in the house of Potiphar, with Jonah in the whale, with the virgin Mary when the child Jesus was lost, with the Syrophoenician woman when Christ appeared to have called her a dog, and with the Lord himself as he cried out upon the cross 'My God, my God, why hast thou forsaken me?'[1]

The text, then, is not flatly descriptive, but stirs the reader, and it is in the light of such understanding that the reader interprets. This first way of getting at what the meaning is of the 'subjective' component is moderate. It sums up the ethos of those who have in the modern period, especially in the nineteenth and early twentieth centuries, found in the family Bible and in private Bible reading a source of illumination in ordinary living. It also relates to modern attempts to interpret biblical Christianity in terms of modern existentialism. But if there is as it were to be an interplay between the text out there and the reader's inward feelings, the integrity and other-ness of what is out there must somehow be preserved. This is, as we shall see, one of the basic roots of a conservative view of the Bible.

The second way is to interpret the text much more intellectu-ally, in the light of reason. This was the preferred way of eight-eenth-century rationalists, such as Locke in his *The Reasonable-ness of Christianity*. But there were troubles for such an approach lying in wait, once the eighteenth-century view of the cosmos was to be fractured by the discoveries of the nineteenth century.

Thirdly, the interpretation of scripture might have a heavy visionary component – the Spirit working through men in dramatic fashion. Along this path lay the fragmentations of the radical Reformation and the proliferation of prophecy. Ultimately inner experience could come to outweigh the actual

---

[1] Roland M. Bainton in S. L. Greenslade (ed.), *The Cambridge History of the Bible, The West from the Reformation to the Present Day* (Cambridge, 1963), p. 23.

words of scripture.

As far as the main stream of Protestantism is concerned, the attempt to maintain a balance between objectivity – the Bible 'out there' – and subjectivity – the faith within me – ran through such movements as English Puritanism, German pietism, Methodism and the Evangelical revival. It involved a kind of sacramental experientialization of the scriptures, and since this is a characteristic element within Christianity it may be useful to see the matter against a wider background.

Different motifs can dominate a set of scriptures. Incidentally, some scriptures (as we now view them) were essentially oral traditions, as with the Veda. The notion of a holy *book*, most obvious in the Jewish, Christian and Islamic traditions, is rather special, and suggests something mysterious and powerful about the very notion of writing: words are made concretely manifest. It is interesting that a holy, authoritative text has a different dynamic from a set of oral formulae – the latter have to be handed down invariantly by exact repetition; the former, however, has a greater detachment from a priestly tradition. The book is more exoteric. It is no accident that in the esoteric tradition of India the major later texts are in the form of *sūtras* – so aphoristic that they need extensive exposition by a teacher. But let us return to the question of motifs.

One dominant motif can be that of the scripture as a set of injunctions. The chief emphasis then is upon the imperatives for daily action, etc., to be derived from the text as a whole. This motif can be seen in the Jewish tradition, and in the *Mīmāṁsā* ('Exegesis') school of Hinduism, which sees the whole of the Veda as a set of injunctions about ritual and other action.

Another dominant motif can be didactic. Thus much of the Pali canon is taken up with the description and analysis of the world and living beings with a view to showing how liberation is possible. The Pali scriptures are scarcely sacramental or magical, though they may occasionally be used in practice for these purposes.

But the centre of gravity in the New Testament is neither to do with injunctions nor analysis. It is perhaps nearer (in one way) to the dominant motif in the *Upanishads*. Here the major problem is: What is the inner meaning of the sacrifice? The sacred text expresses a mysterious picture of the universe and its inner and outer powers, and in so doing exhibits a path (or paths) of liberation. It is both about the inner meaning of sacrifice and a means for its realization in experience. One might see the New Testament as both about Christ and as providing a key to the realization of solidarity with Christ.

Now the *Upanishads*, though powerful and speculatively deep, are, one could say, rather weak on plot. This is not so in the case of the heart of the New Testament, namely the Gospels. They are not all story, but they are predominantly so. So one may look at the Bible as having a strongly mythic motif. It is both mythic and sacramental. The reading of it makes the story of redemption available to us: where the *Upanishads* are static, the Bible is dynamic. So in an important sense, one can follow Aristotle's dictum about a mystery religion – the point of a mystery is not to learn but to experience: *ou mathein all pathein* ('It is a matter of feeling'). With the Reformation and the interiorization of religion through the pietists and others, we arrive at a conception of the Bible as a kind of emotional and moral score. The tune I play is my own life: the notes are feelings and decisions which I experience, as I read the score.

But this experientialization of the Bible – of reading its meaning in terms of feelings – also relates to concrete outer circumstances. It is a common theme in Christianity, especially evangelical, to see events in terms of the biblical types, and the attempt is made to interpret the narrative as relevant in detail to the contemporary and personal condition. Thus the scriptures find their interpretation in changes which occur to a person, and the Bible becomes internalized.

The role of the Bible in emotional causation helps to explain a difference between its use in a liturgical setting and its use by a preacher. In the former, the words of the Bible are integrated into a broader ritual, and what is important is, on the whole, correctness of reading, rather than any rhetoric. On the other hand, the preacher's task is to make the scriptures live, and thus he uses rhetorical means to stir his hearers. Because he has himself internalized the scriptures he can let the Bible, and so let God, speak through him.

But all this is, it seems, predicated upon retaining the integrity of the Bible as 'out there'. This did not necessarily cause too much strain in the days of Wesley or in the early-nineteenth-century revivals; but the beginnings of its seculariza-tion were already apparent, and two developments were to present Christianity with a choice of uncomfortable moves. The two developments were nineteenth-century historical criticism and Darwinism (as representing in a nutshell the possibility of a deep conflict between religion and science). But before we come to this, let us add one extra dimension to what we have just sketched about the role of the Bible in experi-ence. It is not only sacramental as embodying God's word and capable of bringing about spiritual effects, often through the midwifery of the preacher, and mythic in having the capacity to allow men to participate emotionally in the story of God's redemptive dealings with men through Israel and Christ; but it also has, of course, its own special style. Much indeed has been made in recent decades of the special nature of biblical thought, as contrasted for instance with classical Greek thought. The Bible is seen as dynamic rather than static, interested in linear history, anthropomorphic rather than abstract, unphilosophical but strongly historical in basis, materialist almost or at any rate not driving a line between soul and body, emphatic about God's holiness, aware of the gap between Creator and creature, etc. It has thus remained in dialectical tension with other elements in Western culture. And because the myth is stated in terms of Israel's history, with its jagged and (as in all history) untidy contours, there is always something simply *given* in the myth, which cannot be rationalized or allegorized. If often sublime, it is often uncouth. It is, then, a mythic complex, sacramentally embodied in a 'Book out there', capable of moving men's feelings and decisions – a kind of mysterious cassette, which plays the divine voice, with an

233

unmistakable accent. Being both myth and sacrament, it is holy. Tampering with it is therefore likely to arouse strong emotions.

The secular approach to it was therefore bound to be upsetting, for, from the standpoint of piety, any treatment of what is sacred which does not treat it piously is impious. Thus the application of historical methods, in the milieu of the increasingly secularized university, as at Tübingen, for instance, in Germany, not only posed intellectual questions to faith, but seemed almost blasphemous. How did the new scholarship of the early and mid nineteenth century affect the 'Bible out there'? In a number of ways.

First, it began breaking the Bible up. It became a library written by many hands, and showing a historical evolution. This incidentally accounted for many of the inconsistencies without recourse to such older means as the use of allegorical interpretation. The unity of the scriptures was crumbling. Second, it began to blur the face of Christ, as doubt was cast on many of the Gospel incidents, notably those containing a miraculous element. Third, it created a sense of polarity between Paul and Jesus – the Christianity which we know being heavily indebted to Paul; and this thought diminished something of the cohesion of the early faith. Fourth, it made much of the men and their viewpoints who wrote the scriptures, and shifted the gaze from heaven to earth. Fifth, it opened up many questions which could never be definitively settled – it unleashed a maze of probabilities upon the texts. Would faith henceforth for ever be at the mercy of the scholar? These effects upon the Bible (and one could list a number of others) were disturbing, and a threat to the integrity of the Bible out there – first, because of the dislocation of its unity, as we have noted; second, because it lost clarity; third, because it lost its air of certainty; fourth because the new approach shifted authority away from the texts to the scholars; fifth because the detached dissection of the scriptures seemed to rob them of power.

Between the famous *Life of Jesus* of the Tübingen scholar David Strauss, published in 1835, and the magisterial

234

study of the Old Testament by Wellhausen, which was published in 1878, there fell the first main impact of the geological and biological discoveries which changed men's perceptions of their place in nature, and added to the problem of biblical belief. Thus history and science combined to question orthodoxy. There were various directions in which piety could go, as we shall see. Let us note first, though, that the particular kind of challenge presented by Darwin's theory had an emotional as well as an intellectual side to it. Some of the heat generated in debate on the subject of man and the apes came from an unconscious friction. The animal had long been, in Western consciousness, a symbol of ignoble urges – of brutishness. Thus Darwinism could be seen as a nameless ethical threat, as well as a challenge to literal interpretations of Genesis.

One reaction to the challenge has proved its staying power under differing forms – the conservative reaction, at its strongest in fundamentalism. Its basis is the affirmation of the inspiration of the Bible as a whole and the insistence so far as possible on the plainest and most literal interpretation of the text. The psychological logic of this standpoint is in part as follows: Since the Bible can be shown to have emotional and life-changing effects of a dramatic and sustained kind, its status as God's word cannot be shaken; and if it is non-human in essential origin, mediated though it might be through the minds and pens of men, then it cannot be allegorized, selectively interpreted or pruned, since these processes make it subject to human control. Here we meet with an irony which is yet very imperfectly understood by analysts of religion – that the symbolic depth and emotional power of a scripture seem to require, for their operation in certain circumstances at least, their being taken at literal, surface value. Perhaps part of the explanation is as follows.

Consider the teaching of Christ's second coming (often thought to be imminent by evangelicals). Some preachers say it will be a physical return, in a physical body. What does the stress on the literal image do for it? Well, if we say that the doctrine is after all *only* symbolic, not to be taken literally,

235

then people are entitled to ask: Symbolical of what? If not literally, how? We may murmur something about the consummation of history, about eschatological hope (but in what?) and so forth. The image thereby seems to be robbed of all impact. The curious thing is this – that the image is indeed an image, but if it is taken just symbolically it fades away; so you can either have a literal image in lieu of your symbolic image or you do not have any image worth speaking of. The conservative Christian defends the symbolic depth of the Bible therefore by ignoring it, and hammering away for literal interpretation. It is, though, literalism with a strong emotional charge.

Since literalism promises clashes with scientific knowledge, an effect of conservative biblicism is sectarianism; and the price of maintaining the mythic power of the Bible is quite high, although mellower kinds of biblicism can make an accommodation with scientific knowledge, as with Billy Graham, who also maintains strong ecumenical connections. It can be argued that such a mellower religion depends upon a preceding and harsher literalism.

Literalism has to be seen not only in the context of its being one response to new intellectual challenges, but also as having a certain social and psychological background. Allow much in the way of allegorizing or (worse) higher criticism and the route is open to subjectivism. The individual chooses what to believe and what not to believe. In this respect appeal to the literal is a fence against man-made religion. The chief defect of such a man-made faith is that it has no basis for certitude, and true faith is to do with certainties. Thus insecurity, through rapid social change or turmoil, or in the individual for whatever reason, is likely to find its remedy by being projected into a faith which has good certification. The authority of scripture, taken plainly, supplies this.

The 'insecurity' theory of scriptural literalism does not cover all the facts, obviously; and there are many who take the Bible pretty much at face value not because they have thought through things, but essentially for the opposite reason – they have never really met with the challenge of historical and scientific method in any live way. Nevertheless, the insecurity theory helps to explain why often biblical conservatism is tied in with social and patriotic conservatism: for the very forces of instability which may be perceived as threats to social and national life are those which make religious certitude attractive.

What other options, however, are there in the interpretation of the Bible, once the modern trap has been sprung? One possibility – also theologically conservative – was explored by Karl Barth (1886–1968), namely to locate the biblical revelation as 'out there', but beyond the words of scripture. For Barth, the Word of God has three forms. It is seen revealed in Christ; it is proclaimed in preaching and it is written down in the Bible. Of these three forms the first is primary. It is God's revelation of himself in history: it is the event of Christ – of his incarnation and resurrection. That is what preaching and the Bible are *about*. They are the Word of God in so far as they point people to Christ. Consequently, it is wrong to identify revelation with the words of the scripture. Barth (though he was unaware of it) was using a distinction that is made in various places in Eastern religions between the authoritative words of scripture and the whatever-it-is they are about. To concentrate on the words and neglect their reference is like gazing at the finger which is pointing at the moon rather than at the moon itself. The approach here is sometimes called the 'non-propositional view of revelation': non-propositional because what is revealed is not statements or propositions but God (Brahman, the Void) himself (itself).

Barth coupled his non-propositional view with an evangelical one which insisted upon the clause of *sola scriptura* (by scripture alone) even if it was not strictly the words of scripture which form the belief-substance which brings us salvation. In other words, Barth held that only through revelation and not by reasoning or by inspecting nature could one gain any knowledge of God. So, since revelation is mediated by the Bible, though it is not constituted by it, he retained a conservative stance concerning authority. Yet those fundamentalists who, hearing of his influence and of his apparently evangelical rectitude, went to study with him or listen to his teaching, found themselves at odds with his position. For his position clashed inevitably with literalism and inerrancy. The Bible, as congealed preaching, could not be inerrant, as it was shot through not only with God's message, but men's imperfect understanding of it. Still, the Barthian theology was one which helped to make sense of the historical and scientific impact upon scripture without abandoning the essentials of an evangelical theology. Its influence was thus understandable, since it was one of the major moves to be made away from the nineteenth century impasse. It was a new, humanistic Calvinism.

Barth was, as it happens, reacting against another alternative way of coping with the critical problem, and that was to say that the Bible is inspired, in the sense that the men who wrote it were inspired, by God (not in the sense of having the Holy Spirit dictate the words, as seemed to be implied by the fundamentalist belief, but in a general way inspired). If one links this idea to the notion that the New Testament while presupposing yet supersedes the Old, and to the prevalent nineteenth-century idea of cultural evolution according to which men progress on balance as history goes on, then the theory becomes one of progressive revelation. In this form it often accompanied a social optimism. Liberal Christianity, preaching a social Gospel, was attractive, humane, accommodating. But some of its underpinning collapsed in the dreadful days of World War I. It was disillusion with liberal theology of this kind which led Barth to pen his famous commentary on Romans, and later to resist any kind of Christianity which would do a deal with Nazism.

Of course, one might take the inspirational part of the above theory without the optimistic, evolutionary baggage. In essence this seems to be the standpoint of many Christian thinkers, with the addendum that the Bible is also a fairly sober record, in parts, of historical events which are relevant to the unfolding of God's revelation of himself. In short, one could hold that God has an inspiring impact in various ways on the biblical writers. This is compatible with belief that there are confusions and errors in the text and with belief that in its main essentials the Bible conveys what it means to convey, namely the story of our salvation. It is not in principle very far from the stance of Barth, since both approaches are inductive – they use the propositions to get at the reality which they are supposed to stand for.

In all this, the Protestant spirit has an advantage and a disadvantage over the Catholic. Beginning with the latter: the problem is, of course, that a strong doctrine of the Church which in its authoritative capacity deems what the Bible consists of is not so easily available to the Protestant. Indeed the more he is exercised by the status of the Bible the more he will be inclined to treat it as a whole, as having equal authority. Yet it is not easy to avoid the fact that the canon was only gradually formed. On the other hand, it was especially in the milieu of the Protestant theological schools that the whole modern debate on the historical probing of the Bible was generated. Thus Protestantism has, paradoxically, been the source both of the most unswerving biblical literalism and the most radical willingness to examine the scriptures scientifically.

Though Roman Catholic scholarship on the Bible was restrained by the Vatican's attitude to the Modernist movement in the late nineteenth and early twentieth centuries, the 1960s in particular saw a renewed convergence in Christian scholarship. But the inevitable uncertainties which remain along the path of liberal New Testament scholarship, which are made easier to bear within a strongly traditional framework, still leave us with that early question as to how many real happenings (in the life and circumstances of Jesus) have to be provable or at least probable if a person reasonably is to have faith.

Now this is strictly a philosophical and theological question, and not one that needs to be settled within the framework of the history of religions. Except, of course, that the question has generated certain intellectual tensions within modern Christianity. Roughly speaking, one can point to various responses. One is the conservative one: that the Bible is, after all, inerrant, and the modern scholarship is therefore either rejected or rebutted as far as possible in its own terms. Another view, at the other extreme, is that little indeed can be known of the historical Jesus, but that this is not a fatal situation – indeed it fits with theological truth. Why not fatal? Because what is central to the New Testament is the proclamation or *kerygma* which presents Jesus as risen Lord, and this already is an affirmation of faith. The Christian in hearing the kerygma joins with the message of the earliest Church; and in doing so is in the realm of grace rather than nature, and faith rather than (mere) historical knowledge. A major exponent of such a view has been Rudolf Bultmann (b. 1884).

Bultmann wanted to rid the New Testament of its mythic elements and dig down behind them to an original liberating message which he interpreted through an adaptation of the existentialist philosophy shaped by Martin Heidegger (1889–1976). For Bultmann the message of Christianity is obscured by the fact that it is framed in a (for modern man incredible) myth of the fall of man who is however redeemed through a man from heaven who through his death, resurrection and ascension defeats the evil powers controlling the world of men. Rather we should recognize that ever since the Christ-event men have found themselves capable of being liberated from anxiety and given a new freedom to be themselves and to relate authentically to others. Bultmann, together with Bonhoeffer and Barth, is one of the progenitors of modern 'religionless Christianity', which especially in the 1960s attempted to turn Christian faith very radically outwards into social, political and personal concerns, and which expressed a new Christian humanism (though the problem remained: Why be a Christian humanist rather than just a humanist?). Yet always a fragment of the mythic survived, even in Bultmann. The early proclamation, the Christ-event – these were decisive turning-points in human history where God brings something to pass. But much turns on the validity of the philosophical perspective: and Bultmann draws a sharp line between subjective and objective approaches to human, and all, reality; religion belongs to the former – it has to do with the personal dimension of the universe, and the rest is in essence the sphere of scientific enquiry. That is one reason why the New Testament message needs to be purged of extraneous cosmological and other ideas, such as the picture of the three-decker universe (heaven, earth, hell), which cloud the subjective in an outmoded objectivity.

What may be called 'conceptual biblicism' is the thesis,

put briefly, that the categories of biblical thought remain authoritative, even though doubt may be cast on the literal historicity of many of the events recorded in the scriptures. Although one may ask why it is modern men should continue to make use of such ideas as election, chosen people, law, grace, Lord of creation and so on, this approach to the Bible – affirming as it were its style of thinking – does represent a reality. For so long as the Bible is used in Christian worship and devotion the believer remains bound to wrestle with the images and ideas which come through to him as he listens, prays and sings. There must remain then a dialectic, in the nature of things, between the Bible and a person's knowledge and experience. The Bible thus remains given in Christian experience, though quite how it is given or how it should be interpreted will continue to be matters of debate and worry.

And here we circle back to the question posed at the beginning of this chapter. How many biblical happenings, in particular in relation to Jesus, need to be provable or probable as a basis of faith? For Kierkegaard and Bultmann hardly any: just the fact, really, of the intersection of Jesus and the Eternal as a liberating event. For most, however, the myths need to be fleshed out more fully if it is to be credible and illuminating. So we find that the main thrust of so much modern scholarship is to fix upon the earliest message, and behind it there stretches forth the new quest of the historical Jesus.

Also, it is doubtless time for Christian scholars to begin looking again at the material contained in the New Testament from the perspective of the history of religions. Christianity may well thus receive enlightenment from abroad, as to its own origins.

In summary, the Bible has proved a thing of power in the Christian tradition, both for what it reflects in the way of the myth of Christ which is brought to men across time through ritual and preaching, and for its intrinsic style and force. Often the Bible can be seen as a thing which has a semi-autonomous dynamic in men's experience. As a material book, multiplied by printing, it has been the single most important piece of hardware in Christian organization; and as having inward meaning it has proved both a source of authority and a maverick for challenging it. If it reflects something of the true nature of the historical myth it describes, then in a sense it is a printed sacrament, for it makes the saving story real for people today.

It has also been interpreted in a wide and wild number of ways. I once heard a well-known theologian say that one should have the Bible in one hand and the newspaper in the other: such was the dialogue out of which interpretation of scripture springs. But which newspaper? We in his audience were longing to ask.

12

War, Peace and Christian Ethics

Perhaps one of the most extraordinary phenomena in Christian history was the evolution of the fighting monk, in such orders as the Hospitallers of St John, the Templars and the Teutonic Knights. Imagine those dedicated men of God riding toughly into battle, weighed down with mighty armour on huge horses, in Palestine, of course, Holy Land and scene of bloody crusades, and in far north-eastern Europe, along the shores of the Baltic and in the forests and marshes of East Prussia and beyond. Over their armour they, typically, wore a mantle to show their holy calling; beneath the armour, a padded jacket; and on a hot day of battle a monk had to be robust to stand the heat and strain. On his head he wore the conical helmet shaped by the Normans, and he wielded that terrifying Frankish sword which could slice a man through the skull down to the thighs, as is testified by the remains of the unfortunate victims of holy war exhumed in Palestine. As weapons would whistle and bang, the monks would utter prayers to Christ, not the profanities of more worldly knights. But could their avocation have been visualized by early Christians, busy with the kiss of peace and looking to their leader and saviour who had died on the Cross, after signally failing to resist arrest? How can the blood of the martyrs mingle with that of the fallen knight? The knights pose a sharp question in the evaluation of Christian behaviour and the ethical ideals of the faith.

Their story was full of drama and heroism. Both the Hospitallers and the Templars grew out of orders devoted to the care of the sick and of pilgrims. But as the need to protect pilgrims to the Holy Land increased, so did a military function for the monks, and they evolved into fully fledged military groups with the right, moreover, to own land. The Teutonic Knights, when they conquered territories in the north-east, assigned them to the Pope, who then returned them to the

Order to rule as feudal domains. As the military Orders arose from the struggle to capture and defend the Holy Land, let us therefore look briefly at the Crusades and at the psychology which animated them.

In 1096 Pope Urban II preached a sermon which in effect triggered off the First Crusade. How could Christians bear to see the Holy Land under the sway of the hated Muslims, who still threatened Western civilization and against whom some bitter battles had been fought in France and Spain? The call to arms was, moreover, a means of harnessing the turbulent energies of feudal knights, and the Holy Land promised a new and sacred arena for heroic deeds. The First Crusade captured Antioch in 1098 and Jerusalem in 1099. In both cases many of the inhabitants were killed off. The Latin Kingdom of Jerusalem was founded and the Crusaders built mighty castles in what came to be known as *outremer* ('overseas'). As I write this, one of them, by an irony, is being used in southern Lebanon as a base by Muslim guerrillas to attack the Israelis.

The Second Crusade, stimulated by the saintly Bernard of Clairvaux, was a melancholy failure – much of the expedition foundering before it reached the Levant. Later, in 1187, the Kurdish Sultan Saladin, a masterly statesman and general, was sufficiently successful in uniting Muslim forces to be able to take on the Latins, and at the battle of Hattin he largely destroyed the Christian army – a victory culminating in his capture of Jerusalem. This tragedy occasioned the Third Crusade, which took Acre, but not the Holy Places, the main objective.

It was the Holy Places that supplied much of the psychological drive behind the Crusades – for in an age when pilgrimage was burgeoning and indeed had become a vital and integral part of the whole pattern of medieval devotionalism, what greater merit could there be than to tread the ground once trodden by the holy feet of the Son of God himself? The Holy Places and the *outremer* came to be a collective obsession in Christendom, and preachers could get the people wild with exaltation and commitment when they called for a crusade. If the Muslims meant war, the Christian Cross could more than match the Crescent of the infidel. Yet the next expedition, the Fourth, was a disaster – at least for the cause if not for the Venetians. Venice had been growing as a mercantile force, and had thoughts about its opportunities in the Eastern Empire, truncated by Islamic conquest, but still extensive through Greece and parts of Turkey. The expedition sacked Constantinople in 1204, and a Venetian candidate was placed upon the imperial throne. For half a century the Latins ruled the Eastern Empire, unloved. The whole episode scarcely helped the cause of reconciliation between the two great wings of Christianity. Later Crusaders were more successful in re-establishing the Jerusalem kingdom, although it was to fall in 1244 to the dangerous Tartars, while later in the century other centres of the Crusaders' power were successively reduced, the campaign culminating in the bloody fall of mighty Acre in 1291. In most of these battles, including the last, the fighting monks played a prominent and crucial role. Driven from the Holy Land they became a formidable sea power based in Rhodes and then most importantly, Malta. There they learned a new technology of warfare, but in their heyday on land their methods were bound up with the realities and symbolism of the horse.

In the period of the early Middle Ages, the horse was especially important as a weapon, or rather as the major component in a weapons system. The mounted knight was heavily armoured, typically with chain mail, but later with jointed plate armour. Sometimes the horse itself was armoured. The rider would carry a sword, lance or mace – one for slicing people, another for piercing and dismounting them, the third for braining them. The horse, the grooms, the accompanying foot-soldiers and servants, together with the hardware, cost a lot of money – so basically the knight had to be a feudal land-owner. When the Hospitallers and Templars got going as military Orders, they were given land rights and various exemptions from tithing. Generally speaking, though monks, they were of noble birth (the horse itself, of course, became the very symbol of upper class lineage, as is reflected in such words as *caballero* and chivalry). The Orders were convenient for the papacy, growing in power, though they were by the same token suspect to bishops and lords because they became a Christendom within Christendom, an independent force hard to control, and yet loyal to the faith and so to the Pope. But their independence could even upset the papacy – in 1312 for various reasons the Pope was impelled to suppress the Templars and give their property to the Hospitallers, who persisted till as late as 1798 in Malta.

The monks of war, because of their celibacy (though they were accused by some of homosexuality) and brotherly dedication under a rule which impelled them to daily worship and frequent prayer, were a tough and mobile instrument of conquest and defence. Something of their ethos can be gathered from the rite of initiation of one of the Orders where the person who wishes to join is asked by the Master or other person presiding:

> Good friend, you desire the company of the House and you are right in this, for many gentlemen earnestly request the reception of their children or their friends and are most joyful when they can place them in this Order. And if you are willing to be in so excellent and so honourable a company and in so holy an Order as that of the Hospital, you are right in this. But if it is because you see us well clothed, riding on great chargers and having everything for our comfort, then you are misled, for when you would desire to eat, it will be necessary to fast, and when you would wish to fast, you will have to eat. And when you would desire to sleep, it will be necessary for you to keep watch, and when you would like to stand on watch you will have to sleep. And you will be sent this side of the sea and beyond, into places which will not please you, and you will have to go there. It will be necessary for you therefore to abandon all your desires to fulfil those of another and to endure other hardships in the Order, more than I can describe to you. Are you willing to suffer all these things?[1]

Some pride, of course, comes through this allocution. The monks were indeed proud of their toughness. Whether fighting against the Muslims in the gritty heat of Palestine or hunting

[1] Quoted from Jonathan Riley-Smith, *The Knights of St John in Jerusalem and Cyprus, c. 1050–1350*, (London, 1967).

the wily and ferocious inhabitants of Lithuania, they were liable to encounter terrible hardships. In the Mediterranean quite a number were captured and became galley slaves – a condition in which folk were said to envy the dead: they worked naked, scorched, lashed, starved – and if they fainted they could be flogged to death or cast overboard for the fish to contemplate, an ignominious end for a once-proud knight. In the north-east the knights were hammered by redoubtable foes, and if caught could be burnt alive in their armour, like human chestnuts.

Yet whence did such a martial spirit, within Christianity, derive? It was natural, for instance, for the monks' Muslim adversaries in Palestine to fight. Islam proposes a theocracy, and that implies the use of force to maintain and defend the faith. There was no ambiguity about this in Islam, for which the ideal of the holy war or *jihad* was seen as a sixth pillar to set alongside the five essential ones upon which the fabric of Islamic community life was built. But while Islam from its earliest times had been tied in with war (Muhammad's campaign out of Medina against the Meccans), this was scarcely so with Christianity. Christians did not fight from catacombs, and only with some reluctance were soldiers initiated into the faith in early centuries. It was deemed by Leo I, who died in 461, that military service may be blameless, a judgement reflecting a background of opposition to martial vocations. It was customary to bar a soldier who had killed in battle from communion for a period of three years. Yet at the same time, the fact that Christianity had become the official faith of the Empire that of course depended for its existence on military power, implied inevitably that Christianity had to become involved in war. It was then a question of how it should be moderated and conducted. The ideal of the fighting monk was one way of fusing secular and spiritual duties.

A further move along that line was to spiritualize the ideal of the fighting monk – this was the vision of St Ignatius Loyola in creating an order which would have a knightly ethos, but totally dedicated to the service of Christ and the papacy through non-military means. Yet always a question remains: Does something of the spirit of warfare carry over into the preaching of the Gospel when it is carried on under the banner of 'Onward Christian soldiers, marching as to war'?

Side by side with the Christian soldier there stands the figure of George Fox (1624–94), founder of the Society of Friends and a major symbol of the pacifist tradition in Christianity. His peaceableness was part, indeed, of the fabric of his radical faith. He took to a striking conclusion the premise of inner experience of God. He himself, having left home at the age of eighteen to seek spiritual truth, had a number of revelations which he ascribed to the divine inner light. This functioned in two directions, for on the one hand it gave authority to the deliverances of human conscience and insight (it is said that Fox was a very self-confident person: that stemmed from his conviction of inner inspiration); and on the other hand, it implied the equality of human beings. For this reason Fox refused to use honorific forms of address, but used 'thou' and 'thee'. Fox's strictures on the Established Church were severe, and he refused to pay tithes. In these and other ways the peaceable Quakers were perceived as subversive, and Fox himself was imprisoned eight times between 1649, when his main preaching activities began, and 1673. Only a short time before his death did the Act of Toleration of 1689 give the Quakers reasonable security in their life and worship.

But though it may be possible for a group to practise pacificism and non-violence within the broader shelter of a society which itself maintains external and internal order by force, a dilemma awaits the pacifist when he gains power, as happened to the Quakers in early Pennsylvania. The problem had, of course, confronted Christianity after Constantine – and here it was more than the question of soldiers and whether they could be rightly admitted into the Christian community. The question was essentially one of how war could be regulated.

The first major step in this direction was taken by Augustine in his *The City of God*. Here we begin to get the idea of the just war. From one point of view the problem was to give some consistency to Christian teaching in the light of the differing emphases and moods of the New Testament. If Christ had blessed the peacemakers, he had also worked good for the centurion of Caernaum and the centurion at Caesarea. If he had refused to defend himself, he had also said 'Render unto Caesar the things that belong to Caesar'. Though the spirit of early Christianity was seemingly pacifist, it did not discriminate against those who belonged to the official world. And Constantine's conversion was regarded as a blessing, not as the kiss of death. Consequently, some compromise view about the use of force had to be worked out. Augustine was able to work his theory of peace and war into his scheme of history and his doctrine of the two cities. Thus there is the heavenly peace and the earthly peace, the latter the peace of Babylon (*pax Babylonis*). The latter is disfigured by the fact that it is the product ultimately of sin, even where the earthly city or empire appeals to traditional virtues in its struggle to maintain order. But though disfigured, it is good compared with the horrors of war – and war carried out for wrong ends is clearly worse than the earthly peace. However, sometimes evil men seek to overthrow or attack the order which preserves the Church and Christian faith, and it is here that the Christian is justified in the use of force. Augustine thus had a vision of the earthly Empire suffused and influenced by the heavenly city, and thus in some degree sanctified. Out of this approach was born the idea of the two swords, well put in the famous bull *Unam Sanctam* promulgated by Boniface VIII in 1302, in relation to his dispute with the then monarch of France, Philip the Fair:

> And we learn from the words of the Gospel that in this Church and in her power are two swords, the spiritual and the temporal. For when the apostles said 'Behold here' (that is, in the Church, since it was the apostles who spoke) 'are two swords' – the Lord did not reply, 'It is too much', but 'It is enough'. Truly he who denies that the temporal sword is in the power of Peter, misunderstands the words of the Lord, 'Put up thy sword into the sheath'. Both are in the power of the Church, the spiritual swords and the material. But the latter is to be used for the Church, the former by her; the former by the priest, the latter by kings and captains but at the will and by the permission of the

priest. The one sword, then, should be under the other, and temporal authority subject to spiritual. For when the apostle says 'there is no power but of God, and the powers that be are ordained by God' they would not be so ordained were not one sword made subject to the other.[2]

However, such a view could easily lead beyond a doctrine of the just war to the ethic of the Crusade, in which no holds are barred in the combat with the heretic or the infidel (a secular version of this sentiment undoubtedly animated Allied war leaders in World War II, justifying Hamburg and Hiroshima). Against this Wycliffe, among others, protested: war should be undertaken for corrective ends, in a spirit of love and justice, not as a self-righteous attempt to establish holy objectives – especially since the Crusades directed towards Palestine were tied in with the practice of pilgrimage, of which Wycliffe was critical, since it tended to draw men away from service of their fellow men (through the bodily and spiritual works of mercy, which he listed).

In modern times Christian attitudes to warfare and just revolution are a newly burning problem. This is so for two reasons – first, the growth of war technology to the point where, with nuclear weapons, it is virtually bound to have indiscriminate effects. We have added a new dimension to total war. Second, a new awareness of social injustices raises acutely the question of the means for putting these right – very often conceived as guerrilla warfare culminating in a dedicated but possibly tyrannical replacement of the old order. These issues have been debated with particular force in the Catholic Church, partly because nuclear weapons call in question the possibility of a just war, partly because the Church is well represented in the Third World, especially Latin America, where a theology of revolution is relevant. But it is not my aim here to go through the arguments for and against pacifism and the just war. Rather, in counterposing the fighting monk and George Fox, I am drawing attention to the ambiguity which is at the heart of Christian ethics: the Christian is in the world

[2] Henry Bettenson, ed. *Documents of the Christian Church* (London: O.U.P., 1943), p. 162.

but not of it, and yet how can this attitude be translated into concreteness?

In a sense the whole evolution of Christian ethics has to do with the institutional question: is Christianity simply to be sectarian? For the sect which exists somewhat self-contained within society can practise its own ethos, though at variance tolerably with the general values of society: but once a faith has penetrated society sufficiently, to the point of becoming identified with the ruling powers, concrete questions about the relation between the laws of the land and the laws of God emerge. But though there has been a lot of variation regarding Christian attitudes to institutions such as slavery, marriage, the military and so forth, there are also some more constant points. These relate to the religious character of the Christian approaches to moral questions. They can be summarized as follows.

First, the Christian tradition emphasizes in differing ways solidarity with Christ, and hence ethically the imitation of Christ's own life, and by extension the lives of the saints. Thus Christian ethics is informed by divine example, either direct or indirect. Consequently, though thinkers such as Aquinas have made use of the idea of natural law – what is required in the way of conduct on the basis of nature and the exercise of reason – even the fulfilment of ordinary duties is seen in a special light by the Christian. Thus giving up that which is evil is seen as a form of sacrifice which by analogy mirrors Christ's taking up his Cross. If therefore there have been ambiguities in the ethical dimension of Christianity this is a fact arising from the mysteriousness of the Gospel pictures of Christ – his many faces, as we have called them. But Christians, in reflecting upon this imitation of Christ, have had to proceed by analogy (the fact that Christ was unmarried need not imply that all true Christians should be unmarried, though some have made this heroic inference), and so there have been interpretations in differing ages of the manner of the imitation.

Second, not only can ethical values be seen in the light of the religious ideal, but also they can be subsumed, in a sense, under the ritual dimension of the faith. Indeed, ritual and ethical requirements are mingled in the Ten Commandments which Christianity inherited from Judaism. But more particularly, daily life can be seen as prayer or worship, as in the tag *laborare est orare*, and Christian social action is often perceived as *service*, and therefore of a piece with worship. Again, marriage has been seen as a sacrament, and so analogous to baptism or the Eucharist: inward grace is conveyed through external means. The ritual overlay of ethics reflects itself too in the way right and wrong are perceived. The latter is sin, the former holiness. So, to look upon the matter for a moment from the Eastern Orthodox perspective, the process of deification is both spiritual and ethical: it involves regular attendance at the sacrament, prayer, reading the Gospel and following the Ten Commandments. The fusion between the moral life and the spiritual life has not gone without tensions – for instance, the dispute between Augustine and Pelagius reflects the see-saw between the ideas of grace and responsibility in moral-spiritual action. Such tensions have sometimes swung people into one extreme or another – to antinomian satisfaction with one's spiritual state at one end, and into a simple identification between Christianity and the Christian ethic on the other hand.

A further question in Christian ethics has been the problem of the relation between the new Christian order and the Jewish law. The tension is already deeply embedded in the writings of Paul, and it is implicit in the Gospels. On the one hand, the early Church perceived that Jesus' particular stress on inwardness related to the gracious initiative of God in his work of redemption. But on the other hand, Christianity was also a form of Jewish faith, so that it was not surprising that a number of Christians, led by James the brother of the Lord, could be very close adherents of the Torah in its strict form. What emerged was an adapted acceptance of the ethical dimension of the old law – adapted in that the total context of the law was changed. Indeed, if the Torah functioned for the Jewish tradition as a symbolic concretion of God's will its function was taken over by Christ himself. Still, the Ten Commandments and moral lessons drawn from the Old Testament continued to have a rich effect in shaping the Christian ethos. By releasing Jewish history from the confines of Judaism itself, Christianity gave its themes universal application, for good or ill: it was easy for embattled nationalism to look back to God's help to the ancient men of Israel.

Thus Christian ethics has been complexly influenced by the motifs of the imitation of Christ and deification, the perception of the moral life as the extension of the sacramental life and of worship, and the acceptance of morality as God's law. Hopefully these motifs could be bound together through the two great commandments, to love God and to love one's neighbour as oneself. But they also existed within the fabric of the total Christian world-view, a cosmology with a historical dynamic, in which the struggle between good and evil culminates in the victory of Christ and the judgement of the living and the dead. Thus the Christian saw himself as caught up in the workings of a dramatic universe, and so as part of the warfare against the Devil. And as an individual his life was lived between hope and sin: he recognized the future hope because of his faith, but the demands of love continuously reminded him of his shortfall. As the Jesus prayer puts it (at least in one form): 'Lord Jesus Christ have mercy on me *a sinner*'. From one point of view, Christ's internalization of the Law (the man who lusts after a woman already commits adultery) could have a similar effect to the various dietary and other rules governing holiness – a constant reminder of the divine relationship.

But an even stronger reminder of the ethical demands of the faith is to be found in the eschatology, and in the whole conception of the relationship between the living and the dead. The latter was a continuity, and is and was seen to be so most clearly where the Christian cosmology stressed the hierarchy of beings, from inanimate things, through animals and men to angels and God. The unseen departed were part of the great cloud of witnesses and angels and part too still of the Church. Prayers for the dead are thus a means of expressing help for fellow beings in the faith. Indeed some of the Eastern Fathers have looked to the possibility – it can for various reasons be no more than that – that all in the end will be saved, even perchance demons. However, typically, Christianity has posed as very real the alternatives of heaven and hell – of the ultimate destinations of men after the final judgement. In some phases of Christian history the torments of hell have been vivid in the imagination of people. And since God's judgement has to do with the quality and intent of a person's actions in this life, it has deeply affected ethical attitudes: for morality has been seen as a crucial ingredient of the pilgrimage of man.

The doctrine of the last things not only helps to give a sense of the culmination of history, but imparts a strongly dramatic quality to the decisions of individuals. In effect, by sacramental and other means the Christian faith has tended not only to bring a past event such as Christ's resurrection into the present, but it has also involved time travel in the other direction: the last judgement is made real here and now, just as also heaven is brought to earth by the sacrament and preaching. Classically, in both East and West, part of the foretaste of judgement is found in the sacrament of penance. Though in the early Church and in some forms of modern Protestantism such confession is a communal affair, in that man sins both against God and his neighbour (here identified with a fellow Christian), for the most part it has been a private matter between the penitent, the priest and God. In the Eastern Church the confession is not only the occasion for absolution and where relevant the imposition of some penance, but it is also an opportunity for the lay person to receive spiritual advice from the confessor. Thus a certain psychotherapy has been implicit in the custom, but the primary way in which the individual is helped is through the absolution; the priest in effect channels God's forgiveness, and tells the penitent 'Have no further anxiety; go in peace.'

The dramatization of the last things has also taken a more directly millennial form in revivalist preaching, but here the assurance to be gained by faith is more psychological than sacramental in character. Yet the typical puritanism of much evangelical Christianity also has an outer-inner structure: the fruits of conversion are to be seen in the outer behaviour of the Christian. Such puritanism perhaps has its clearest expression in conditions where the order of society is seen under some threat

– the underlying anarchic elements are seen in sexual laxity, drink, scepticism and so forth; in the formative days of modern America, for instance, undergoing both nation-building and the creative storms of the industrial and agricultural revolutions, the revivalist ethic was something which could be perceived as a means of creating social stability. But apart from this, there is a question of the role of puritanism in the whole Christian ethical tradition. If the faith could display ambiguities with regard to war and peace, so it could also, for instance, in relation to sex.

The tension was already apparent in the very earliest Church. From one point of view the evaluation of marriage was high in the new Christian community. For one thing Jesus frequently used the idea of the wedding or marriage in his symbolic teaching: his first miracle was at a wedding feast, the parables looked on married love as an illustration of the Kingdom of God, the Messianic meal is a wedding feast (and thus the *agape* had echoes of this image), and marriage is like the relation between Christ and the Church. Moreover Jesus' apparent banning of divorce can be seen as preserving the dignity of the woman. Also, women's position was enhanced by the special role which women played around Jesus himself, but perhaps more importantly too by the pouring out of the Spirit upon the women in the congregation – so that pagan critics of Christianity would complain that it was ruled by women. (Still, Paul ruled that women should stay silent in the churches, and in this extended the rule of the synagogue to Christian practice: Paul's decision being a primary text for modern resistance to the ordination of women.) On the other hand, marriage as an institution had the disadvantage that its goal is rather long term; and it is after all an integral factor in the continuance of society. But the early Church expected a pretty imminent *parousia* or the second coming of the Lord. Thus ethics and institutions were at first seen as interim. It is true that in the marvellous transformations which the Coming would bring and in the resurrection of the dead there would be new shining personalities and a whole new order of things, but it was not relevant to marriage: the risen ones neither marry nor are given in marriage, but are like the angels in heaven. Paul, deeply struck by the urgency of the interim, considered that it was better not to be troubled with the duties, cares and joys of marriage. If a person is burning with desire and cannot restrain himself, then it is better to marry, rather than to commit fornication or whatever (incidentally, one sees in this the notion that irregular sex is defiling: the body is like the Temple – the spirit of Jewish ritual purity continues in Pauline and Christian thought).

From the point of the general principles of Christianity and its Jewish heritage, monogamy is, then, stressed as a high ideal and marriage is given a sublime status; but the expectation of the Coming tends to negate this evaluation. The Coming, however, was a long time in arriving, and other factors began to influence the Christian estimate of marriage.

One was the growth of the monastic ideal. The life of virtually uninterrupted prayer and contemplation was thought, as it was also in a number of other cultures, best conducted in isolation or in at least isolated communities. This was in practice incompatible with marriage, but more importantly the renouncing of sex was often thought highly important for the achievement of the mystical life: sex was the most powerful distraction of the senses, and if one were to turn one's eye inwards and towards the invisible God it was best to conquer sex. It was indeed a stern battle. St Anthony goes into some detail about the fleshy wiles of the great Adversary. Furthermore, asceticism was encouraged by the spread of Gnostic ideas, which saw the world as evil and the procreation of children therefore as to be discouraged. Marcion, deemed a heretic, condemned marriage; while though Augustine was a great champion and shaper of Christian orthodoxy, his attitude to sex was coloured somewhat by his contact with Manichaeanism. Partly because of his interpretation of original sin, and for other reasons, sex acquired something of a sinful flavour in the West, which it retains, in a secularized form, today. Origen (c. 185–c. 254), great Christian though he was, controversially castrated himself so that he could without danger teach female catechumens and in accordance with that strange and dangerous text in Matthew about 'eunuchs who have made themselves eunuchs for the sake of the kingdom of heaven' – as did the Russian sect of Skoptsy in the eighteenth century. Whether Origen actually did it or not is open to a little doubt, but the story testifies to the currency of the idea. For those who considered the world evil and sexuality dangerous, it was one solution to the burning problem posed by St Paul.

However, pressures to make all the clergy celibate were resisted in the East. Indeed the Council of Nicaea decided on a compromise, in that bishops were to be celibate, but the lower clergy could marry. In the West, of course, the forces of celibacy won. Both systems represent a kind of division of labour, but there was some implication still as to the connection between the holy and the renunciation of sex. That implication, however, was repudiated by the Reformers in the general attack upon works as a means of salvation and upon certain aspects of Catholic sacrality. By preaching a return to what were perceived to be the attitudes of the early Church the Reformers encouraged an ideal of this-worldly asceticism, in which chaste marriage functioned as a midpoint between the rejection of sex and the acceptance of false worldly values. Generally speaking Christianity has been conservative in its response to social change in these matters in the present century, so that though the freer use of contraception and abortion (for instance) have attracted support from a percentage of Christian leaders, the average attitudes are most cautious. Yet there can be little doubt that Protestant individualism has notably contributed to modern romantic ideas of love, which tend to fit a highly personalistic approach to sexual relations.

This Western personalism is not paralleled in other cultures, so that another way of looking at Christianity's dynamic ambiguity is this – the faith in its major historic manifestations has favoured a sacramental, monogamous idea of marriage and thus has presented one of the traditional motifs of marriage as integral to society; and yet it uniquely has fathered an atomistic and personalist extrapolation from the prizing of the individual. Perhaps this is because the central pivot of Christian ethics, *agape* in Greek, sometimes tilts one way, and sometimes another.

To put matters another way: the central problem in diagnosing the style of Christian ethics is the relationship between love and obedience to divine commands. It is typically in the realm of obedience that lie the structures of law, punishment and the curbing of sin. However, since love is the dominant value of Christianity, in that God is described – in a certain sense defined – as Love, it may be useful to see how it differs from certain other conceptions.

Influentially Anders Nygren (b. 1890), for instance, Swedish bishop and scholar, in a book entitled *Agape and Eros*, contrasted the Christian idea of love with Eros, love as understood by much of Greek philosophy (it figures in Plato, Aristotle, Neoplatonism and the mystery religions). The contrasts that he drew were perhaps too sharp, but they give something, nevertheless, of Christian Agape. Thus he saw Agape as sacrificial giving (for it was incarnated in Christ). It comes down from on high for it is God's nature, while Eros passionately reaches upwards: there is even a certain eroticism in the striving beyond the erotic to the purity and sublimity of what is divine. Agape is unselfish and gives freely, because it has the richness and security of the divine, while Eros even at its noblest is self-regarding (the lover loves the lover, to boost his own joy). Agape, moreover, is directed towards both friend and enemy – Christ was insistent upon the command to love our enemies. But Nygren's chief point is put thus:

> Agape is precisely God's love, God's Agape, that is both the criterion and source of all that can be called Christian love. This Divine love, of which the distinctive feature is freedom in giving, has its direct continuation in Christian neighbourly love, which having received everything freely from God is prepared also to give freely. Here, therefore, we have no need to make room for neighbourly love, nor to find any external motivation for it.[3]

Certainly Nygren is correct to see in agape something which is distinctively bound up with faith about the nature of God,

[3] *Agape and Eros*, rev. ed. (London, 1953), tr. Philip S. Watson, p. 218.

and one justification for asceticism, whether it be this-worldly as in much of Protestantism, or more other-worldly, as in the case of the Orthodox holy man and the Catholic monk, is that it involves a training in self-giving. Still, a paradox remains – one which runs through the Christian life – namely that there is training for something which should be spontaneous, or to put it theologically, it seems to be necessary to work at achieving that which comes through grace. One is reminded at one level of the Zen notion of hitting the target without aiming, and Zen's whole system of rigorous training to achieve a creative effortlessness.

At another level, however, the comparison with Zen is misleading, for finally Buddhist compassion and benevolence are different from Christian love. The Buddhist abolition in theory and practice of the ego also involves concern for the welfare of others, but it is based upon emptiness and insubstantiality. This is not to say that the Buddhist ethic is worse or better, but to point out that it is predicated on a very different, indeed opposite, view of the goal and nature of living beings. Thus in so far as Christianity centres on love, it does so with the sensation that love is full to overflowing; it is dynamic, and it transfigures the individual and washes away the evil substance, sin. On the other hand, Buddhism looks to (not fullness but) the emptiness of serenity, and sees compassion as at the service of wisdom which will overcome the (not sin but) ignorance of living beings, benighted in the world, waiting for illumination. These points have been made in a more militant manner by Hendrik Kraemer, a noted applier of the theology of the Word (in the style of Brunner and Barth), to the question of mission and the encounter with other religions. He writes:

> It is useful perhaps by way of summary to say that when we particularize about the 'error' in terms of self-deliverance and so forth, this is an insight which can only be brought to birth in the light of Jesus Christ. What it brings us to see is that the great religions, at their most profound and in the very fundamentals of their message, fail to give any adequate account of the sheer contrariety, the utter mysteriousness, of man, his greatness and his wretchedness, his

259

reaching out towards the highest and his satanic devilishness, his place half-way between angel and ape; and they fail because they never give any real weight to the one basic fact which the Bible calls sin.[4]

In brief, he sees the Buddhist quest for liberation as based upon a misperception of the realities of human nature. Whether he is right or not, it does bring out the centrality of the idea of loving one's enemies: for the Christian these are God's enemies, in other words sinners (but of course each individual sees himself, in the Christian perspective, as a sinner: hence he has to love himself too, a point where critics consider Nygren exaggerates the gap between Agape and Eros).

Christianity's central value confers on it a different style not only from Buddhism, but also from other religions. It came to abandon the Jewish Torah because this great holy and disciplinary projection out of God could not be central when a new norm and pattern had been revealed in the shape of Christ. It differed from Islam clearly over the latter's interpretation of Jesus; but for all the Caesaropapist elements and the synthesis between classical culture, secular power and the Gospel tradition, it did not have the directly theocratic impulse, like Islam. It retained an ambiguity towards civil power and social institutions. As for Hinduism, its plurality of duties, its detailed hierarchy, its whole perspective of reincarnation and karma provided a very different scene from the dramatic choices and fiery climaxes of human life and history as seen in the greater stretches of Christian faith. The naturalism of the Chinese Tao and the poise of Confucianism again are far from the supernatural placing of Christian love. Agape is unique, but its diagnosis of the human condition is open to question. Certainly, since the idea of sin is not just a moral one but involves God, for it involves estrangement from God, Christianity is bound to claim that its ethical posture is not based just on an examination of men's constitution, but must include the light which God in Christ sheds upon that constitution.

But Christian love has also been charity. The organization of help for the needy was characteristic of the early Church.

[4] *Why Christianity of All Religions?* (Philadelphia, 1962), p. 98f.

By the late fourth century we discover the following passage written by St Basil of Caesarea:

> Whom have we injured in any way by building these places of refuge to shelter strangers who come to this country, or those who need some special treatment because of their health? It is for them that we have arranged in our house the means to provide them with the necessary aid, with nurses, doctors, porters, guides. It has been indispensable to add to it the industries necessary for life, and the arts designed to adorn it. For this reason it has been necessary to construct buildings where these various kinds of work could be carried out.[5]

Some of the sick were separated from the rest, notably the lepers, so that what St Basil had caused to exist was a primordial version of a number of later Christian charitable institutions: the leper-house, the hospital, the hospitality centre or hospice, the training school and the alms-house. The connection with healing was a very central problem in the early Church, since not only was it a Christian duty to care for the sick, but charismatic healing was prominent as one of the effects of the new faith. Christ was often referred to as the physician, with power over sickness and demons. Characteristically, such good works came to be centred on the monasteries or undertaken by specialized orders. The monks of war after all started as hospitallers, dedicated to the service of the sick and the welfare of pilgrims. Something of the same general spirit is found in the thinking of Wycliffe, who both echoed medieval attitudes and looked forward to Reform. He listed seven bodily and seven spiritual works of mercy. The latter were teaching, counselling, reproving, comforting, forgiving, suffering and praying. The former were: feeding the hungry, giving drink to the thirsty, showing hospitality, clothing the naked, visiting prisoners, visiting the sick and burying the dead.

St Basil's vision was in various ways repeated and varied in later ages – as, for instance, with the paternalistic California missions of the Franciscans, where a holistic attempt to look after both the bodily and spiritual welfare of the Indian popula-

[5] *Patrologia Graeca*, 32: 485, quoted in Micael Riquet, *Christian Charity in Action*, tr. P. J. Hepburne-Scott (New York, 1961), p. 62.

tion was undertaken. But more typically the functions became more differentiated, and then taken over by the State (the rapid social change of the Industrial Revolution in any case injected new dimensions of poverty and suffering which the Church organizationally was scarcely able to cope with or prepared mentally to face realistically). Nevertheless, it remains an important aspect of the Christian ethic that it is oriented towards the sick, the needy and the prisoner. Charity as institutionalized may be cold, but it is a logical consequence of Agape and of Christ's style.

I have here merely sampled the ethical dimension of Christianity. In practice Christian ethics are embedded in the circumstances of differing societies. If one were to generalize about the Christian ethos, the first thing to say is that the application of the tag 'By their fruits ye shall know them' is hard in general, though clear enough perhaps in particular. For the ambiguities of the Christian tradition mean that there is much variation as to which fruits are to be prized. And this arises not just from the fact that the faith in permeating a society comes to accept values which are in some measure external to it. It is also because of the inner dialectic of the religion itself. Looked at from one side God is numinous, powerful, authoritative, judgemental. The Christian in identifying with the divine imperatives looks to the commandments, hierarchy, authority in this world, punishment and penance. The Old Testament, seen of course from an entirely different perspective from that where Judaism's angle of vision is, sets the scene for the normative, power-oriented motif in Christian ethics – doubtless a necessary motif if Christianity is not to be just sectarian. The Constantinian turn was momentous, but perhaps inevitable.

But the graciousness of the numinous God gives another view of the Christian ethos, and this is reinforced by not only the example of Christ but also by the mystical and ascetic motifs: the Christian does not only identify with order and command, with virtue and success, but also with the poor, the sick, the unfortunate. The ideal of holy poverty is a means of gaining greater insight and control, no doubt, but more importantly it is also a way of affirming solidarity with mankind's lower human depths.

Yet, paradoxically, the Son of Man is represented as coming earthily, eating and drinking: the incarnational motif in Christianity tugs against the forces of asceticism that are also vital in the tradition. The differing ways in which Christianity has been embodied have been so many experiments in living. The triangle of forces represented by the numinous, mystical and incarnational strands woven into the fabric of Christianity has been in interplay with the common moral sense of men, the diversity of societies, and of course with the various anti-spiritual impulses, whether called ignorance or sin, which entangle human judgement. All this has given Christian ethics an uncertainty and dynamism scarcely matched in other faiths.

13
Christianity, Doctrine, Philosophy

As I have remarked in Chapter 10, Jesus' teachings, so far as we have them in the New Testament, were hardly analytic: they did not itemize reality in a system or analyse meticulously the human condition. Jesus was not the Buddha. His teachings were parables, images, injunctions, sermons, prophecies of the kingdom, calls to a new life. They interpreted the onset of the kingdom and obliquely pointed to Jesus' own place in the Jewish (and perhaps world) scene of myth and history. Jesus transcended the categories of his time, for good or ill; but he also depended upon them. And likewise with his most notable proclaimer in the early Church – Paul. Consider the following passage from Paul (Romans, xi.1):

> I ask, then, has God rejected his people? By no means! I myself am a descendant of Abraham, a member of the tribe of Benjamin. God has not rejected his people whom he foreknew. Do you not know what the scripture says of Elijah, how he pleads with God against Israel? 'Lord, they have killed thy prophets, they have demolished thy altars, and I alone am left, and they seek my life.' But what is God's reply to him? 'I have kept for myself seven thousand men, who have not bowed the knee to Baal.' So too at the present time there is a remnant, chosen by grace. But if it is by grace, it is no longer on the basis of works. Otherwise grace would no longer be grace . . .

This is, of course, a radical new look at Israel's history, but it is not metaphysics: it is sacred story-telling, and the drawing out of its practical implications (hence the remark about grace and works). But there are hints already of a transition towards a more systematic, philosophical presentation of the proclamation. The Christian community is already on the road towards Christian doctrine.

It is not simple to draw a clear distinction between myth and doctrine or between myth and dogma (dogma being those doctrines which have been accorded community consensus one way or another). Nevertheless, one can see doctrine as, typically, more philosophical, or abstract, or analytic than a sacred story. The doctrine of the Trinity for instance – three Persons in one substance – employs relatively technical terms to analyse the inner nature of God, given that God is revealed in sacred story as Creator, incarnate Lord and Spirit.

But Christianity has, of course, produced an impressive complex of doctrines – too many some would say. And often Christianity has been much committed to philosophical and other learning. This leaves us with some ambiguities, maybe. It has been vital to the faith's adaptability that it should be active along the interface between myth and learning. On the other hand intellectual constructions have a habit of leading a life of their own, cut off from the context which nourished them in the first place. Christian theology can thus become theoretical, isolated from practice. Besides this, the interface I referred to has been crossed in both directions, and some who wish to preserve the mythic side of Christianity from what they consider to be corruption by learned (or pagan or whatever) ideas may resist too intellectual an emphasis. The Latin Father of the Church, Tertullian, could ask about what connection there is between Athens and Jerusalem, or as we might say in more modern times, between Cambridge and Jerusalem. Does the faith which originated in a manger peter out in a library? There has, then, been a tension between the mythic and philosophic aspects of the religion; but there has also, especially in the writings of some of the Greek Fathers and of Aquinas and others, been a remarkable fusion. Let us then explore the reasons behind the development of the doctrinal dimension in Christianity, and some of the drives which have animated it.

A first reason is already apparent in the passage which was quoted from St Paul. Reflection on the scriptures and on the Christian proclamation of the early Church induces a need to interpret them consistently. The impulse to schematize has begun, and it is given edge by the practical exigencies of Christian life as it began to establish itself into a pattern in the diverse communities springing up through the Eastern Mediterranean, Greece and Rome.

A second reason related to the interface between the sacred story and learning, notably Greek learning. Though Christianity to many had the appearance of a mystery religion, it had a universal dynamic. It was not in principle just for (largely self-selected) initiates. It was in principle open to all men. It was, moreover, making headway in the Graeco-Roman world, and so needed to say something to that world. Thus the first main epoch in which the interface became vital was one in which that interface was also a cultural one – between the hard mythic world of Jewish monotheism as reinterpreted in the light of the life of Christ and the splendid world of Greek philosophy and science. Along the mental interface (as I shall call it), various moves are possible – one (like Tertullian) to try to shut out alien premises; another is to accept alien learning and attempt a fusion; another is to shut out the mythic aspect, or at least to subordinate it. That is why so often the mental interface is both perceived as a threat and as a challenge, as in modern times, as we see from reactions across the frontier between biblical religion and the biological sciences. Built into Christianity is this tension. If we imagine the way transactions have occurred across the frontier as a series of pendulum swings, with the pendulum vertical at the frontier, then we have: first a highly biblical mythic faith, then a swing towards the metaphysical, then a swing back and so on. After liberal theology of the nineteenth century, there was Barth, after Barth Tillich and a more inclusive theology. Where the biblical swing is very hard, as in modern fundamentalism, it also provokes and is provoked by a hard swing in the opposite direction, into the rejection of Christianity on scientific, or supposedly scientific, grounds.

Another potent reason for the definition of doctrine has been the question of the unity of the Church. It is sometimes thought that Christianity caught creeds as a kind of disease, and so attracted the unpleasantnesses of Councils, definitions, excommunications, hairsplitting – as though the voyage of the faith into the Hellenistic and Roman world meant picking up the vice of identifying spiritual truth with intellectual formulae. But what is not appreciated enough is that beliefs, whether more mythically or more doctrinally expressed, were the charter of the new Israel. With the old Israel there was hardly a problem, or at least not a very serious one: descent and initiation made a person a Jew. After that he might quarrel with other Jews as to what true Jewishness amounted to, and he could take his choice among the interpretations and movements on offer. But the Christian was initiated into a people of the mind. They belonged not by circumcision but by baptism into a community defined by faith. It was implicit in this that sooner or later definition of what had to be in the mind would occur. If it turned out that such definition took place in the language of Greek philosophy, Roman law and so forth – this was a result of cultural fusion, but it was not the cause of doctrinal credalism. The difference between Jewish attitudes and Greek ones have been exaggerated in this regard.

This definitional reason for doctrine was reinforced by the new position in which Christianity found itself as a state religion, for definitions became legal entities as well as expressions of commitment and credal rectitude. Roman imperial Christian doctrine became systematized myth multiplied by Hellenistic philosophy multiplied by mental initiation multiplied by law. This set up multiple tensions within the fabric of faith. Myth tugged against metaphysics; commitment against speculation; inner feelings against the requirements of law. In the period of classical Christendom some of these tensions were resolved: by the scholastic synthesis and above all in the work of St Thomas Aquinas; by the association of learning with the monastic orders; with a multiple framework of piety.

Certain motifs have run through Christian doctrine which have set limits to what is generally acceptable as Christian belief. One such motif is the gulf between God and man and between God and the world. No fusion of God with the human soul so that the two are seen as identical can be other than heretical. Pantheism has been the object of suspicion. Thus Christians have often criticized what they perceive to be (not altogether correctly) essence of Hinduism as being pantheistic and monistic – as obliterating the distinction between God and creatures. What lies behind this fear of pantheism? Partly what animates such fear is the structure of the biblical myth; but one may look upon the matter in another way, from the standpoint of religious experience.

Gods are numinous, and the Jewish God was supergod. He transcended all other gods, which were things of nought; and he outstripped his non-existent rivals in power and awesomeness. The story of the Fall testifies to the gap which separates God from man, and is reminiscent of other myths in which God prevents the first man from being like himself. The suggestion made by the serpent represents this fear: 'You will not die. For God knows that when you eat of it your eyes will be opened, and you will be like God, knowing good and evil.' And so Adam and Eve were banished, lest they should become like God through eating of the tree of life. There are of course some problems about what the two trees represent. But the story underlines the gulf which God must maintain between himself and his creatures. Indeed one could put the question of the jealousy which God has towards other gods as a rejection of any being as object of worship who is lower than himself; and this itself means putting an unbridgeable distance between himself and men who have such gods. It is true that the Old Testament often depicts men as on rather intimate terms with the Creator. Partly this is in the context of a God who also makes a covenant or deal with his people – it is not that men can insist upon such a relationship. But by the time we come to early Christianity the picture is paradoxically sharpened up. Paradoxically, because the very idea of the Incarnation is one in which God and man fuse together: but yet the distance between man and God is exaggerated if anything by the very dark interpretation placed upon the notion of the Fall and of original sin. The dialectical structure of Christianity makes for a greater fearfulness in God, precisely to account for and act as contrast to the total redemption effected in Christ. For this reason, there was always a danger of Marcion's heresy – the fearful God of wrath could easily seem a symbol of evil. In the numinous the line between good and evil is hard to draw.

This gulf between God and man and more generally between God and the world was given doctrinal expression in the notion of causal dependence of the cosmos upon God as First Cause. Here, in its fusion with Greek thought, Christianity had to adapt and alter the idea of the conception of the Demiurgos, God, that is, as Craftsman or Shaper of the world, for such an idea presupposed a certain material with which God had to work, a somewhat difficult something which is not fully in the control of the Creator. It was for religious rather than metaphysical ones that Christian theology took the path of *creatio ex nihilo* ('creation out of nothing'). So we have the conception of the world and God as two things, with the former absolutely dependent on the latter. Furthermore, because the world is made by God it is in essence good. It is often said by Christians that Hinduism and Buddhism are world-negating, and this is at variance with the positive valuation of Christian faith. The judgement is at best a half-truth, but it echoes early battles against forms of Gnosticism and Manichaeanism (not to mention the Albigensians, victims of a powerful crusade) which affirmed the evil nature of the material world, ruled as it was by evil powers.

The Platonic conception of the creation gave a sort of explanation for the presence of evil in the world. Moreover, especially in the writings of Plotinus, Neoplatonism was far from pessimistic about the darker side of the world – on the contrary Plotinus was very sensible of the beauties of the cosmos. The problem of how evil and suffering come to exist in the world has remained to plague Christian theology and philosophy, since the exaltation of God to sole creator seemed, unless one posits a diabolical antigod, to thrust responsibility upon the Creator. At least the Fall of Satan, mysterious precursor of the Fall of Man, supplied for most of Christianity, until the modern period, a living myth which not only accounted for the perversion of God's good world but also gave the Christian a sense of participating in a cosmic battle. Zoroaster after all had left his imprint upon European civilization.

The doctrine of duality between creature and Creator was threatened at least partially by the Incarnation and by mysticism. The latter's tendency towards a sense of union in inner experience could easily pass over into an interpretation which seemed to imply identity. But this would be blasphemous, namely it would infringe the sense of the holy otherness of God. As for the Incarnation, a complex set of tensions had to be expressed. On the one hand Christ had to be in some sense identical with God; on the other, his humanity was necessary as an ingredient in the drama of redemption. That tension could be resolved, it was hoped, by saying that Christ has two natures, one divine and one human. But this in turn caused a problem of how those two natures were fused in a single person. The instability of the Chalcedonian definition was such as to show how well-meaning Christians could on this issue be technically heterodox by espousing Nestorianism and the Monophysite formulation. Nestorius had been perhaps too frightened by the title *Theotokos* or mother of God as applied to the Virgin Mary. He feared she thereby became a goddess, and maybe in some respects he had good cause in that the cult of Mary owed something to ancient sentiments regarding a mother goddess. Isis perchance was reflected in Mary. The matter was perplexing: Mary was mother of Jesus; Jesus was Lord, God incarnate: it seemed to follow that she was mother of God, and the Church in both Catholic West and Orthodox East for the most part accepted the conclusion. The Reformation, however, revived Nestorius' fears.

Since the doctrine of the God-man could be thought to infringe the principle of duality, it was important at least to stress its uniqueness. Indeed, though Christ through his human nature could be seen as being in a state of solidarity with men, he stood to other supposed incarnations as God to the supposed gods. This doctrinal insistence upon the uniqueness of Christ served to reinforce a sense of history, in that Christ was anchored in particular events in a way in which no other man could be.

The duality principle raised some severe problems about the nature of man. It implied that God was the only holy being and that man could only participate in holiness and thus salvation if that was freely given by God; on the other hand, it seemed to imply a certain independence and goodness in man as a being other from God and created in his own right. Since Christianity furthered the moralization of the idea of holiness – saw holiness as comprising moral goodness – a tension was created between the holiness of God and the idea of man as moral agent. If men can be good of their own accord, surely this means that they can contribute to their own salvation? And is it reasonable to think that when a man does wrong it is his own fault, but if he does good this is due to God's grace?

This problem became a key one in Western doctrine, and it is useful to see it in its first main phase – as expressed in the controversy between Augustine and the Celtic theologian Pelagius. The latter did not intend heresy: indeed his concern was with the decline in Christian moral standards as a consequence of the success of the faith. He argued that a man has freedom to pursue the good or to perform what is wrong, and it is no good pleading human weakness to excuse wrongdoing. There could be no justice in God's rewards and punishments if this freedom of the will did not exist. To Augustine this commonsense approach was dangerous, from various points of view. It made nonsense of infant baptism, which he himself had vigorously defended, for baptism washes away sin, and what sin (on Pelagius' account) could an infant have committed? Again, the belief that men could attain righteousness through their own efforts contradicted the principle that God is source of all holiness. Finally, Augustine had, even independently of his theology, experience which seemed to demonstrate the fallen nature of man. His nature is sinful because of his self-will, shown in Adam's transgression which was in essence a refusal to accept his place in the divinely appointed order. Having sinned, Adam's vitiated nature was incapable of reversing the situation: and it is this nature which is handed on to us all. Only the magnetism of the good can draw men to itself, and the good is God. Hence human goodness is a result of God's magnetic grace.

Augustine was to go further in drawing out the logic of the numinous all-holiness of God. If God has foreknowledge, and he does, then he knows already who will be drawn to the good (himself) and who will not. He will thus know who is to be saved and who is to be damned. Thus was born the doctrine of predestination in Western Christianity. Scripturally it had its chief text in Romans ix–xi. The doctrine, then, runs from Paul, through Augustine and Aquinas, to Calvin.

It is characteristic that Augustine balanced this somewhat severe teaching with a general theory of ethics which overlapped greatly with the tradition of Plato. His picture of reality was ordered in a hierarchy, at the summit of which was of course God. Men should know and conform to their proper place in the order, and that is one where they serve God. It was Adam's sin to look to his own interest before that obedience – to substitute self-love for the love of the Divine Love. By injecting Adam into his structure, Augustine caused a sea-change, and it was the fusion of the biblical myth with an ordered ethics which confronted Pelagius. Augustine's system was rich, logical, faithful to at least one major motif on sin in the Bible, and integrated into an intelligible cosmology and theory of history. It dealt relevantly too with practical issues about baptism and the question of rigorism – whether those who had lapsed during persecution should be readmitted to the Church. It thus fulfilled the various roles of doctrine. It is no wonder that it proved so potent an influence upon Christian theology of later ages. But it cannot conceal its tensions, or rather the tensions which existed in Christian faith as received biblically and later interpreted. On both freedom of the will and on the question of the depravity of human nature profound divisions have occurred in the course of Christian history. These reflect the root tension behind the doctrinal dispute – between a myth expressing the duality principle, and hence the religious experience of the Other, and moral experience, which can occur independently of the religious experience.

It may, incidentally, be noted that Augustine's powerful defence of the doctrine of original sin helped to reinforce it as the prevailing teaching of Catholic and (less enthusiastically) Orthodox Christianity. It distinguishes the Christian doctrine of man from that of other faiths. Despite Augustine's Platonic heritage, the teaching shifted the essential problem of mankind from the area of knowledge and ignorance to the area of good and evil will. As with Platonism, so with Eastern religions – there knowledge or insight is liberating, and men's woes are due to ignorance.

If the doctrine of Christ in part constituted a rationale for his uniqueness, and the doctrine of creation asserted God's sole supremacy, the Trinity doctrine was a way of trying to preserve the unity of God, even though he had a threefold aspect. Of all the doctrines which were hammered out in the early centuries of the Christian community this was the most difficult and subtle – and at first sight far removed from the style of thinking found in the New Testament. It is a good case of how the sacred story by itself was not enough. Christian monotheism had to be explained. Moreover, if it were in fact true that God has operated (and eternally operates) in three guises, as Father, Son and Holy Spirit, then sensitive exploration of his nature should yield insight. As West and East drifted apart the dispute about the *Filioque* clause became a symbol of the divide, and indeed a number of differing problems of the relationship were bound up in this controversy. But it was also a deeper matter than formulae or questions of authority.

How did it matter if the Western Church wanted to say in the Creed that the Holy Spirit proceeds not only from the Father, but also from the Son? Was it not Christ who promised the Spirit and indeed in some sense sent him, at Pentecost? But this second question, which was part of what was in the mind of Westerners in adding the *Filioque*, rests upon a confusion, for it fails to make the distinction between what goes on inside the Trinity and what goes on outside. What goes on inside has to do with the divine structure: what goes on outside has to do with God's governance or economy of the world. Basically, it is the distinction between what occurs timelessly, and what occurs in time. It is in the outside, temporal, economic sense that Christ sends the Spirit.

The idea of a timeless structure of God, for the idea of procession – the way one Person in the Trinity proceeds from another – refers to a timeless relationship, might at first sight seem to be speculative. Even if there were such a structure, what could we know about it? There are those who have wanted to confine talk and thought about God's nature to what is revealed of it in the scriptures. However, the non-mythic doctrinal account of what lies on the further side of revelation has a religious function – to indicate that God transcends his self-revelation. Indeed without the universe there could be no revelation, so the latter idea presupposes God's existence independently of the universe and so independently of time.

For Eastern theologians the major problem was the unity of God, precisely because they inferred an inner theological Trinity beyond its practical 'economic' manifestation. The thought that both Son and Holy Spirit proceed eternally from the Father pointed to the fact of a single source or cause within the Trinity. It was thus felt that the *Filioque* clause introduced a loosening of the Trinity and so threatened a lapse into polytheism. By contrast Western theologians tended to look on the Spirit as the bond within the Trinity, so that saying that it proceeds both from the Father and from the Son served to emphasize unity. Even so, this seemed to the Orthodox to imply that there are two primary principles in the Trinity, and this was to split it up.

It may be noted that the Trinity doctrine, especially in its Eastern form, differs rather profoundly from the Three-Aspect (or Three-Body) doctrine of the Buddha, with which it has sometimes been compared – namely the doctrine that the Buddha can be conceived as the transformation aspect (earthly Buddha), bliss aspect (celestial Buddha, analogous to God as personal being) and truth aspect (identical with the ineffable Suchness which is what basically the world 'really' is). It differs in various ways, but most deeply in that the Trinity describes an inner relationship, not a series of modes in which the Divine Being manifests himself.

Apart from the theological issues which the *Filioque* stimulated, there were of course some practical divisions which it reflected – most notably the question of the authority of the Pope. It is ironic that a dispute in which both sides thought they were using a formula which would preserve the idea of the essential unity of the Divine Being should have come to be a symbol of the largest division in the Church.

We have seen earlier that Tertullian was among those who posed a special question about the role of doctrine in Christian history. For not only did Christianity make use of Greek and Roman concepts in fashioning its own *Weltanschauung*, but it also had a problem of how religious and secular (or pagan, as some saw it) notions were to be brought together in a total world-view. To put it another way: How was biblical faith to be related to human learning? One solution was to arrive at a normative outlook based upon the relatively early solutions to the problem, and to stay rather conservatively within this framework. Such a solution long governed Eastern Christianity. A similar normative outlook took longer to fashion in the West, and even then was destined to achieve official status only somewhat patchily. I refer of course to the amazing synthesis achieved by St Thomas Aquinas. One aspect of his philosophy is worth examining here, for it set the agenda for much later debate relevant to the status and influence of Christian doctrine: namely, his conception of natural theology. Let us try and set this in the context of his century – the thirteenth, being one of the most productive and revolutionary in the history of Western culture.

It was revolutionary in at least two relevant respects. First, it was at an economic turning point. Increase in commerce, the growth of towns, the establishment of guilds, the use of new technologies, contact between Christian Europe and the Jewish and Islamic culture of Spain, the greater understanding of the classical tradition, the revived learning and new monasticism – all these gave Christian civilization a new confidence and excitement. Admittedly there were threatening questions. Albigensians and others, together with Islam, represented a challenge to mainstream Christian belief, and the new reverence for the writings of Aristotle did not seem altogether easily to blend with faith. The second respect, then, in which the century was revolutionary was in its tendencies to rationalism. Ibn Rushd (1126–98), better known by his Latinized name Averroes, the influential Islamic philosopher of Cordoba in Spain, was something of a symbol and source of such a dangerous prizing of reason. Thus he held that there can be

275

conflicts between faith and reason. Now in one way this idea need not be too serious from the point of view of Christian truth – what cannot be believed on the basis of reason can be believed on the basis of faith, can it not? Yet if reason and faith are both authoritative, some means must be found of reconciling them when in conflict. Since Averroes was a major figure in the mediating of Aristotle to the medieval Christian world, it was not surprising that Aristotelian doctrines, especially popular in the University of Paris, should have brought alarm to some influential ecclesiastics. Moreover, followers of Averroes denied the immortality of the individual soul and considered that the universe was infinite in time (that is it has no beginning or end): here were two major conflicts with the doctrines of Christianity as derived from the Bible.

Aquinas' position was a moderate one, for he was necessarily influenced by the tradition of Augustine, which had proved so powerful a factor in the thinking and faith of the intervening centuries. On the other hand, he was deeply impressed by the subtlety, power and structure of Aristotle's thought, which came to him and many of his contemporaries as a strangely ancient and modern discovery – ancient, for that was where Aristotle was placed in time, modern, because he represented a forward-looking systematic attempt to understand the fabric of the universe.

The way forward was to see the world under a fourfold guise: as belonging to the realms of nature and grace and as accessible to reason and faith. The created order – the natural world – had its own inner logic, and this could be figured out by human reason. It was also knowable as created, again by the use of reason. At the same time, it bears not just the imprint of God as creator but that of him as redeemer – through the operation of his grace our natural powers are open to perfection. God as source of grace is accessible to human faith, through the scriptures.

The synthesis was a moderate one. Thus for Aquinas, rational arguments were such as to leave it open as to whether the universe is everlasting. Without revelation, this is where reason would tend to take us. But revelation as found in

Genesis teaches the finitude of the universe, so this is the conclusion which must be accepted. Again, though reason can establish that God exists – and Aquinas systematized the arguments into the Five Ways or Proofs – it cannot tell us about salvation. So though all men by the light of reason can have some knowledge of God, this knowledge is by itself insufficient. The synthesis, as well as helping to illuminate Christian belief by the light of new knowledge, and to reshape the latter through the moulds of the faith tradition, gave relative independence to scientific enquiry – after all if things in the world have, in view of their particular natures, an inner logic open to exploration by the human mind, large scope is given to the exercise of reason in secular matters.

But the synthesis could, and did, crack in various places. It extended reason from earth to heaven, for by taking thought, men could come to see God's existence and in doing so see something of his nature, his creative goodness, for example. Reason thus could come to stand for a source of divine knowledge from outside of the Bible. It, moreover, seemed to make of God something akin to a scientific theory. In connection with the latter, however, later kinds of scientific picture of the world, not using the framework of Aristotle's thought, could arise, having no place for a First Cause or Creator. In Aristotle, metaphysics and physics were intertwined. But science, as it became more empirical and at the same time more mathematical, found itself increasingly self-sufficient in its explanations of how the universe functions. Thus the arguments for God's existence, which were a crucial part of Aquinas' system, became more and more open to question, for if science was increasingly self-sufficient, it was also increasingly functional – seeing one aspect of the universe as a function of another. In this way, it became implausible to go on a scientific basis from what lay inside the cosmos to what lay outside (God). Not only this: the development of science saw the crumbling of many particular tenets of Artistotle's science. The problem of motion was in Newton if anything the opposite – things move unless they are stopped, and they are not static unless pushed, as Aristotle saw it; the moon was no longer smooth, but cratery

277

and untidy; the earth moved round the sun. If Aristotle was to survive it was only as a philosopher not as a scientist, and yet this for him would have been a kind of death. When Leo XIII in his encyclical of 1879 commended Aquinas as theologian and philosopher, giving him semi-official status as the normative interpretation of Catholic truth in a general way, Aquinas was no longer the Thomas of the thirteenth century, but a rather conservative style of approaching philosophical problems in the field of theology and religion. It was a mite over six centuries since some of his propositions had been condemned by a timid Church. It was five and a half centuries or so since he had been canonized. Now in the late nineteenth century he was revived, but he could scarcely any more be universal: he was a pattern of (in effect) denominational Christian belief.

Denominational, because in the meantime certain strands in Protestantism had cut at the fourfold root of Aquinas' philosophy of the world. There were those, in other words, who thought that not only might there be problems about science and Aristotelianism, but also the complementarity of reason and faith and of nature and grace was radically vitiated. Reason might stay at the service of faith – it had a function to play in deducing the right conclusions from the revealed truths of the Bible (and nobody could be more systematically reasonable in such a context than Calvin). But Thomas' idea that there were Ways by which reason could climb from the facts of this world to the existence and nature of God was profoundly mistaken. What is the point of the knowledge of God? Salvation. But it is God alone who brings salvation, so it is only through God's activity, namely the operation of grace, that knowledge of God is given to men. The idea of natural theology therefore was impious, and unscriptural.

In the increasingly revolutionary ambience of the centuries since Calvin, Christian doctrine has found itself undergoing fragmentation and obsolescence. Fragmentation, because the denominationalization of the Protestant Reformation has naturally called forth a variety of doctrinal divergences; and obsolescence (and retooling) because changed contexts have called forth changed responses, which themselves easily get

278

overtaken by further changes. It may here be useful to go on a short excursus about meaning and adaptation in religious belief.

If we go back for a moment to Augustine, we can there see what a highly educated person of the fourth to fifth centuries made of Christian belief. Quite clearly he was influenced by Neoplatonism, for example. What he in effect did in his writings was to take Christian faith as articulated in the scriptures and Church tradition and give it a doctrinal shape which connected with the thinking of his time. In doing this he was consciously and unconsciously following a principle: If first-century Christian teachings are T_1, then fourth-century teachings should be T_4. Reinterpretation of the Bible can thus become a method of recovering its impact by interpreting it in terms of its new milieu. Another way to look at the matter is this: Christianity travels not just in space, from one kind of culture to another; but also in time, and thus from one milieu to another. The problems of travel are the same. There is therefore an important sense in which a rigidly unchanging set of teachings actually undergoes a change of meaning as it travels, as missionaries often learn too late. Conscious sameness becomes unperceived transmutation. This represents a perpetual problem in religion, and in particular in the case of Christianity. For the proclaiming and enactment of the faith in teaching and liturgy have necessarily a traditional nature: men have through such a means an access to Christ, as they perceive it, but Christ, though present thereby, is rooted in the historical past. In addition to the immediate historical past of Christ's life, death and resurrection and the events of the early Church, Christian groups and movements also look to the secondary canon of various credal affirmations. All this places a heavy burden of interpretation upon theologians as the faith travels through space and time.

Given also that the theologian has the task of remaining loyal to the particular doctrines he inherits within his denomination, since they help to define his identity, he has an expressive as well as an intellectual role to play. And indeed this leads on to a more general problem of how one relates issues concerning metaphysics and human knowledge on the one hand to the problem of maintaining the expressive power of faith as formulated. The special character of religious language (more generally any language which functions to express a world-view) is that it both states the way things are and will be and calls forth an emotional and practical response. It reflects in its doctrinal expression, or at least to do its job it ought to reflect, the power and ambivalence of myth. This is perhaps a major reason why Existentialism has had such a powerful grip upon the imagination of so many modern theologians – Bultmann, Tillich, Buber, Rahner, for instance.

The attraction of this approach to theology lies partly in the very fact that the demarcation of the personal and subjective aspect of existence from the objective and measurable is seen also as a way of drawing the boundary between religion and science. It is interesting that in recent times philosophers who have defended Christian belief as meaningful in the face of empiricist and positivist accounts of language have tended to look upon the empirical world as ambiguous – as being capable of interpretation as divine handiwork, but not demanding the conclusion. Far from it, for since the time of Kant in particular, received opinion is that traditional arguments for God's existence – such as those ways or *viae* that were the very corner-stone of the edifice of Thomistic natural theology – are invalid, or at the very best merely suggestive. So God is scarcely to be 'read off' the environment, but if anything to be 'read in' to it. The world can be *seen as* God's creation; but neither reason, experience nor science is compelling.

Indeed, on the contrary, there are many manifestations of evil and disorder which could impel in the other direction. The history, moreover, of tension across the border between religion and science and the confusion of voices within Christian theology mean that increasingly in the period since the Enlightenment in the West the Christian reading of the universe has become a minority choice among intellectuals.

Christianity has also experienced a triple crisis with regard to perspectives which, one way or another, challenge the classical and modern European tradition. First, the great voyages to the

East in the fifteenth and sixteenth centuries helped to start a deep, sometimes stormy relationship between Christianity and the major Eastern religions. The earlier confrontation with Islam did not, potentially, represent such a challenge, in that for all the differences between Islam and Christianity, certain basic ideas were held in common between the two faiths – belief in a personal omnipotent God, distrust of idolatry, the prophetic heritage of Judaism and (in large measure) Greek philosophy. The dialogue with Islam at its more favourable moments was fructifying for Christendom, partly because of the affinity of the cultures. But with the great Eastern faiths, matters are altogether different. Buddhism did not share the monotheistic imperative, and Hinduism looked on the unity of the Divine in quite a different manner from the Semitic faiths. Confucianism and Taoism – indeed the whole temper and complexity of Chinese culture – started from very different axioms. So, first, the new voyages prepared for a modern situation in which, resurgent, the old cultures of the East posed the question of the basic pluralism of religious experience to a West easily accustomed to simple assumptions about the sense of God.

Second, the modern period saw the death of the colonial epoch and the demands from within Christianity itself, among the 'younger Churches' of the Third World, for styles of belief that did not depend so heavily upon the European inheritance. Christian doctrine, moreover, should speak to the condition of the poor. But now the poor were divided not only within societies but globally in the distinction between the richer nations of the northern hemisphere and many of the peoples of the tropics and the south. Sometimes this has called forth a new radicalism, expressing the search for a different shape to Christian political attitudes, so frequently identified with the more conservative establishments. This challenge connects up with the third, and illustrates a certain ambiguity about Christianity's relationship to Marxism.

For the third aspect of Christianity's modern crisis lies in the emergence of secular ideologies, which have a powerful intellectual and emotional dynamic. They function as quasi-religions, to adopt an expression used by Paul Tillich. Christianity's increasingly pluralistic and individualistic emphasis in the West left it with uncertainties as to how far Christian doctrine can be reinterpreted in the light of such ideologies.

Thus in the latter half of the twentieth century ecumenical Christianity is involved in a search and a multiple dialogue – on the one hand there is a search for a new means of formulating a distinctive schema of Christian belief which is sensitive to the challenges and offerings of other traditions and modern quasi-religions; and on the other hand there is a continued tendency to try to enter into constructive conversation with them. The achievement of a new synthesis, analogous to that which Aquinas put together, is as yet far off. Perhaps such a synthesis must now, in view of the changes which have come over human knowledge since the Renaissance, forever be abandoned. But of all modern attempts at such a task, the nearest to an all-embracing system was the theology of Paul Tillich (1886–1965), especially as expressed in his *Systematic Theology*, published between 1951 and 1963. It is useful to look briefly at his ideas, in that (for all the criticisms which have been directed at his work) they exhibit some of the practical relationships which the doctrinal dimension of Christianity reflects. Thus his system can be seen not just as an intellectual endeavour, but also as an ideological and spiritual one. In one direction he was influenced by socialism, and the need to reinterpret the Christian ethic in social ways; from another he was influenced by the mysticism of Boehme.

Perhaps the most original part of Tillich's thought is his so-called 'method of correlation', in which he sees Christian theology as providing answers to questions which are posed by human reason and reflection. Thus firstly, in contemplating the question of the existence of things, we see that they are contingent and that they could not exist without the ground of being. Theology presents that ground of being in the form of God, though Tillich is much concerned to rid that of the anthropomorphism which pictures ultimate reality in a human and virtually finite manner; instead, we should take the language of the Bible as depicting and expressing truths about ultimate

282

reality in symbolic form. Second, when we look at human life we see it alienated, in that there is a gap between human nature as it exists and as it expresses itself ideally. This gap of finitude and death is overcome through Christ, who is the New Being, unique in human history, who combines the power of being with human nature, and who as the Christ who is God for us undergoes death and overcomes it. Third, the quest for the sense of purpose and meaning in life is met by the theological virtues of faith and love: love being realized in the new community created by and through Christ and informed by the Holy Spirit. Finally, the contemplation of human history leaves us with the problem of the ultimate meaning of its processes; and for Tillich this is found in the Kingdom towards which history tends, but which is also present now in the new life of the Christian.

One may point also to another correlation. Tillich in his writings made much of what he called the Protestant principle, that is to say the doctrine of justification by faith but given by Tillich a much wider scope. It implies that no finite thing can exist without the ground of being: all idolatry is absolutizing what is finite, and the attempt on the part of a man to achieve his own salvation is a denial of his dependence on ultimate reality. So the Protestant principle itself involves a correlation between the Lutheran teaching about justification, which is theological and scripturally derived, and the wider philosophical recognition that no finite thing is self-existent or self-explanatory. The Protestant principle is a continuing basis of criticism of ecclesiastical claims, for Protestantism itself keeps throwing up absolutes – biblical inerrancy, for instance.

Though the language Tillich used is very abstract, in fact he did not mean by ground of being (for instance) some flat reality, but rather that which is mediated to us through symbols, which in turn grasp us. Thus religious symbols function in two directions, one by pointing to the mysterious ground of being – towards the transcendent, as we might say to use different language; and the other by engaging the involvement of the individuals or groups for whom they are symbols. Sometimes indeed symbols die – the gods of ancient Greece are largely dead. And this is where we come to an interesting paradox about the modern situation which is exemplified by Tillich's own language. It is this: that the abstract itself has acquired a potent symbolic force today – consider the way in which the abstractions of Marxist analysis function to rouse men to passionate action (revolution, workers, class-struggle, alienation, exploitation, and so on). Thus there is a tendency, which I shall discuss further in the final chapter, to revitalize symbolism by pushing to a more abstract language to describe what it is thought that the more mythic symbols point to. Consider, in the realm of a Christian attempt to come to terms with an evolutionary view of human history, Teilhard de Chardin's use of such terms as 'noosphere' and 'Omega point', where in earlier times eschatology would be more anthropomorphically and pictorially expressed. In the case of Tillich we note too a mystical motif, and mysticim has characteristically been inclined towards more impersonal language. Tillich is reminiscent of the Neoplatonists. It was partly because of this that in the last years of his life he found a new world in Eastern religions, with which he felt some affinity and some promise of a fruitful encounter.

It turns out too that Tillich's language of being and ultimate reality is shot through with the affective – for being, the question of being, is seen not as a speculative matter, but as posing a threat and a promise. In this Tillich was part of the Existentialist movement, in which reality is seen in the light of human responses to it, and what lies out there is seen through the lens of the human psyche and its structures. In some ways therefore Tillich, despite the impressiveness of the system which he built, is parochial, for the language which he used was not widely shared. The system illuminates the Gospel, but it itself becomes a matter of commitment. This is a bit like the situation of Aquinas in the modern era: a system based on reason is yet sanctioned by authority, itself a matter of faith. It may be that Christian theology exists in too plural a world to rediscover a universal basis.

But Tillich does point unmistakably, via his Protestant principle, to a major function of doctrine in Christianity, as

284

other faiths, and that is to serve as a constant reminder of the transcendent aspect of myth. For myth by itself can easily slide either towards the fanciful, when taken merely as story, or towards the literal, when taken as authoritative. But it has to exist between: and doctrine, for all its abstractions, indeed in a sense because of them, helps to point to the hidden depth of the myth. It attempts thereby to reinforce its truth as against its fancifulness, and its depth, as against its literalness. We might call this the 'transcendental' aspect of doctrine. This is one function among others to which I have drawn attention in this discussion of Christianity's doctrinal dimension. The others are as follows.

There is the credal function – doctrine as defining beliefs which themselves help to define the true community, since the new Israel is not based upon descent but on a different charter which includes belief. Second, there is the synthetic function–attempting to bring together knowledge from outside direct revelation with the deliverances of the faith tradition. Third, there is the interpretive or hermeneutic function, for as knowledge and society change so too does the impact and significance of the scriptural revelation. Fourth, running through all the others there is the function of making faith coherent – dealing with the tensions which may exist between differing parts of the collage of teaching and experience.

All of this perhaps could be reduced to one thing – doctrine is the way Christian identity has been formulated and understood. Naturally it has existed in close interaction with both the mythic and ethical dimensions of the faith.

14

Christianity in Comparison
and Retrospect

Though Christianity is, of course, unique, plurally so in its diverse manifestations, it is also a religion among religions and a tradition among traditions. It also incorporates a world-view which may here and there overlap with secular ideologies, but yet stands as an alternative (or a series of alternatives) to them. Thus it is useful to delineate some of the features of Christianity by contemplating it in comparison with other great faiths. In doing this I shall be taking in some of the brief comparisons which I have fragmentarily made along the way.

If one looks first to Christianity in practice, there can be little doubt that a major and a minor motif have existed in Christian worship. The major motif is the Eucharistic sacrament, the minor one the emphasis upon preaching the Word. In saying 'minor' I mean merely that for a very large part of Christianity and over a long time, it has not held the same central place in the practical expression of Christianity as the Eucharist. If for some Protestant denominations, the preaching is central, that has to be set against the experience of other great branches of the tradition. Of course, both the Eucharist and preaching are in their differing ways sacraments, so that one could make the general observation: Christianity is predominantly a sacramental religion. But they are of such differing kinds, that perhaps it is better to take them separately. Let us begin, then, with the Eucharist.

The way in which Christ's body and blood is present to the believer, the whole notion, that is, of a real presence, is in general reminiscent of a great range of phenomena in religion, in which divine power is somehow conveyed or communicated through external means. Thus the consecrated statue of the God in a Hindu context likewise has within it, so to speak, the real presence of the God symbolized. The power *brahman* operates in and through the Vedic sacrifice. Leaving aside some phases of Mahayana and Tantric Buddhism, the general principle of the sacramental mediation of divine power is most clearly discoverable within the Hindu tradition. But it operates, of course, in such a radically differing context that it has sometimes been difficult to see the sacramental aspect of Hinduism (because of preoccupation with the problem of idolatry). One major strand of Hindu religious thinking has been to perceive the divine power as permeating the whole world, yet also concentrating its power in certain places and actions – in, for instance, the sacrificial rites whose inner meaning forms such a central question in the *Upanishads*. In devotional Hinduism, the sacramental power becomes more personalized and fragmented into the many names and shapes of God – Vishnu, Shiva, Rama, Ganesh and the rest. Both in the religion of the Brahmin priesthood and in popular *bhakti* cults, however, we can see a sacramental universe. But it is one of a remarkably different content from that of Christianity, and it is this difference of content that has often blinded us to the comparison.

The difference is partly that which one might have expected given that Christianity inherited Judaic theism: 'Thou shalt have no other gods but Me.' On the face of it the Hindu is multiple in his practical divinities – a polytheist in action even if often a monotheist at heart. That monolithic jealousy whereby the God of Israel cut a swathe through the gods of his Near Eastern environment has imparted to Christianity a horror of idolatry. Perhaps the Christian recognizes in his bones that but for this severity the faith would have been just another mystery religion (it was in a sense a mystery religion, but not just another one, because of its jealous and so universalistic edge). Thus Christian theism looks with some suspicion upon the syncretic vagaries of the Hindu pantheon, or rather panenhentheon (all gods in one God). If Hinduism has always tended towards a unitary conception of one divine Reality, it has scarcely ever felt any urge to cut back the prolix growth of the many gods who are the various names and shapes of that Unity.

But there is another way too in which the sacramentalism of Christianity contrasts with that of the Hindu traditions. For in the latter, there has existed a very different cosmology, in part derived from and shared with that of Buddhism. Christianity, inheriting the Hebrew scriptures, and interpreting them according to its own rather restricted cosmological viewpoint, saw the world as really rather small. It did not take so many steps to trace Christ's ancestry back to Adam, and for early Christians it would not be long before the whole process of human history would, in effect, be wound up. The Hindu and the Buddhist on the other hand saw the cosmos as wheeling onwards in immense cyclical ages: the macrocosm was so to speak reborn, just as individual living beings kept repeating themselves through virtually endless ages. The past was huge, but somehow rather dim and confused, full of legendary figures and mythic events. By contrast the Christian past was, if narrow, clearly defined: it was the history of Israel through to the coming of the Lord. Consequently, the sacramental emphasis in Christianity is much more restricted and focussed. If the Christian cosmology was rather unimaginative, compared with the florid mathematics of the Hindu and Buddhist *kalpas* (culpas), it was adapted to a concentration upon the importance of historical time, and within it a particular strand – the Christ line which is drawn like a golden thread through the chaotic fabric of human civilizations.

It is characteristic of sacramental religion that the outer form of the divine-human communication expresses the kind of power which is conveyed. In the case of the Eucharist what is communicated is the power inherent in the redemptive life of Jesus: what is made manifest most centrally at Easter, but whenever the Eucharist is celebrated, so is a piece of history – a piece of divine-human mythic history, but events all the same. This gives Christianity a distinct taste as compared with the flavour of less historically-oriented religious traditions and as compared with the flavour of Islam and Judaism which, though historical in ideology, are scarcely sacramental.

The sacramental emphasis in Christianity has given an extra strength to its sense of being a congregational, gathered, religion. For it is of the essence of the Eucharist not merely that Christ is really present in it, but that he is wholly and equally so wherever the Eucharist is performed. Likewise there has been a tradition that the Church is the individual community.

The Hindu approach to the sacramental has had a less personal and a more personal side to it. The great *bhakti* or devotional strand in the Indian tradition is parallel to the personalism of Christian worship. One can see something of the personal-impersonal contrast at work in differing phases of Christian practice in relation to the Eucharist: for example, the development of the medieval mass, the use of monstrances, the system of indulgences – such phenomena tended to make Christ's power independent of his personal presence. On the other hand, the reaffirmation of Christian personalism through the Reformation teaching about grace could easily tend towards the weakening of sacramentalism, and the substitution of an immediate *bhakti*-type faith impatient of ritual externals (as happened in the Indian tradition in the teaching of Guru Nanak among others).

Even here, however, a certain kind of sacramental religion existed in Christianity even where the opposition was strongest to the Lord's Supper as in itself a channel of divine power (rather than seen as a memorial to past significant events – somewhat, incidentally, in the style of the Jewish Passover, but without its being embedded in family life). That sacramentalism took the form of preaching the Word. Insofar as anything took the place of bread and wine, it was the Bible, considered as having special power to alter the hearts and minds of people, especially if properly interpreted: hence the centrality of the sermon, as a kind of conduit through which the biblical message, itself replete with divine and saving power, flows. In modern times, as we have seen, this has given a special character to Christian evangelism.

Here there is an interesting contrast to Islam. For Islam the Koran too is replete with holy power, but of an altogether different order or circumstance. In Christianity, when over a long period in the West the Bible was essentially the Vulgate, it had its due liturgical place and it was the object of often profound study; but something of its power to change men was lost. The dynamism of the Bible was seen in its clear new form after the advent of Gutenberg: a Bible translated into tongues which men could understand without too much education and which could be miraculously multiplied by the printing presses – a Bible which could be carried around by the travelling preacher and which was not carefully administered by priests – this Bible showed its power. On the contrary, the Koran loses its substance when translated out of Arabic. It is no longer the Koran, but just an interpretation, subject to human vagaries. But Christianity requires the interpreter, the Holy Spirit. So for Christianity, translation releases power, for the Koran it destroys it. The Arabic is the unreplaceable incarnation of Allah's word. (For which reason, the Koran approximates in a sense to the Incarnation in Christianity, rather than to the Bible: hence it does not really make sense to look on orthodox Muslims as fundamentalists.)

The power which the Christian sacraments mediate has a certain dialectical and paradoxical character. For undoubtedly the God of Christianity is replete with a majestic dynamism and terrifying splendour enough to daunt the boldest: even Christ appears in numinous majesty as Pantocrator and Judge. The numinous aspect of Christianity is, traditionally, well-developed, and indeed is reinforced by the dread doctrine of original sin, which adds alienation to the yawning distance between Creator and creature. Yet this great and exalted power of God is in a sense negated. The idea of *kenosis*, of Christ's self-emptying, expresses in another way the desolation of the Cross and the rejection of Satan's temptations to power and glory. The Christian, in identifying with Christ, glories in humility. This paradox suggests that the power conferred on the Christian by Christ is the power to do without power.

This is where there is a certain parallelism with Buddhism, though Buddhism approaches the matter from the opposite point of view. But let us consider the likeness first. In Mahayana Buddhism, the figure of the Bodhisattva is of central ethical importance. He is the Buddha-to-be, the person destined for enlightenment and so for ultimate release, but he puts off his salvation for the sake of other living beings. How can liberation be acceptable when there are others who still suffer in the toils of this unsatisfactory world? Through heroic self-sacrifices over many lives the Bodhisattva acquires so much merit that he has a virtually inexhaustible supply which he can confer on the otherwise unworthy faithful, if indeed they but call on him in their need. There are echoes of Christ's self-sacrifice and his redemptive capacity. The Buddhist idea of the transfer of merit has analogies to Christian notions of justification and grace. Yet what is liberation at the end of the day, from the Mahayana Buddhist point of view? It is the realization of the Void, of the emptiness and insubstantiality of everything. The logic of Buddhism is that at the deeper level there is no power. There is no God as understood in the Christian tradition. Mahayana sacraments are in the end devices to change attitudes, so that ultimate knowledge of the true and empty nature of things can be had, and with it release from the world. The Buddhist way is a more radically negative one than the Christian *via negativa*. One might look upon Buddhism as solving the problems of men by dissolving them, for not merely is the world empty of substance but also the individual.

Christianity has not of course lacked – as the reference to the *via negativa* reminds us – a tradition of severely qualifying its personalistic (not to say anthropomorphic) descriptions of God. This is detectable already in the opening to St John's Gospel: talk of Logos differs in style from talk of persons. The upward movement beyond a God personally described, the living Being who enters into so many transactions with man and with Israel, had at least two impulses behind it: one was the desire not blasphemously to assimilate God to men, and the other was the thrust of mystical religion. The contemplative style, however, has not had unqualified acceptance in the Christian tradition. As we have observed, it is weak in Protestantism, especially modern Protestantism, and it has often flourished best in an ambience of monasticism. Nevertheless, mystical theology has been a vital strand in the experience of the faith, though it tends ultimately to be subordinated to the religion of worship and sacrament. Thus Christian mysticism retains typically some sense of the otherness of the Being who is encountered in the interior castle of the soul or in the cloud of unknowing. This implies something for those who have tried to assimilate Christianity to the theory of the perennial philosophy, that is to the theory of the essential oneness of all religions as leading men to an experience of unity with the Divine. Such a view, espoused by Aldous Huxley and a number of distinguished Hindu teachers, among others, does not fit very well with classical Christianity, whether in its Catholic, Orthodox or Protestant form. For Christian mysticism, vital as it has often been, is interpreted in the light of a particular and somewhat jealous myth of history, to be realized in sacramental or personal experience. This does not, of course, mean that one cannot validly say that there are strong analogies between the contemplative life in Christianity and that in other religions, even in such an 'opposite' faith as Buddhism: the Void and the Cloud of Unknowing may in a sense be the same place (though unlocateable). It seems, moreover, to be a feature of all great religions that at some time, whether from the beginnings or from a later time, they develop a mystical strand. Christianity thus is no exception. Moreover, though I have drawn somewhat heavily upon the contrast between numinous and mystical religion in my treatment of Christian mysticism it is worth saying that there were ways in which the contemplative accent and the devotionalism supervening from within the numinous motif were in harmony, and indeed reinforced one another. This is evident, for instance, in the influence of mysticism upon Martin Luther. Let me expand a little upon this harmony (a harmony, incidentally which finds expression both in Sufi Islam and in Hindu *bhakti* schools).

It arises as follows, and let us look at it first from the side of the numinous. The terrifying awe which the majesty of God inspires also, as Rudolf Otto said, fascinates: the God who inspires terror also attracts the gaze, and the mingled reaction is expressed in worship, the abasement of the person confronted by God. The rituals through which the relationship to God are more elaborately expressed – the sacrificial cult of the Temple for instance – help in a sense to channel the divine power, and to open up acceptable communication between God and man. This is expressed in the Jewish-Christian tradition in terms of the covenant relationship which controls man's religious response to God and so makes God accessible. But note that in accordance with the severe logic of belief in one and only one God there is no question of this arrangement in any way being a human invention: only God is holy and so only he can be author of those cults which express and shape human holiness and righteousness. As author therefore of man's ultimate welfare, both earthly as creator and spiritually as saviour (and such a sentiment is of course much reinforced in early Christianity by the intensity of Christian awareness of the saving work of God in Christ), God is object not just of external cult and fear – that fear which is the beginning of widsom, as it is said – but also of loving adoration. The numinous Otherness of God harbours within itself the motifs of grace and love. As in the *Gītā* so too in Revelation the divine Being is an explosion of power with a loving face. In line with this, Christianity tries, in its renewals especially, to stress the feeling, the interiority, lying within and behind the sacramental rites. Often such rites steer towards a magical objectivity; sometimes they disappear into a pure subjectivity; but the trend in the latter direction is often a means of reaffirming something of vital importance in the spiritual dimension of the faith.

Thus there are two characteristics of this experiential expression of the religion of the numinous: one is a renewed emphasis upon the *interior*, the inner experience; another is on the loving nature of the divine power. Such motifs can be seen dramatized, for instance, in the biography of Luther, so that for all the idiosyncrasies to which he was prone as a man of his time, for example his anti-Semitism and incipient German nationalism, he did importantly express something profound in the historical experience of the faith – a rediscovery of the interior life in relation to sacramental religion. Now let us turn to look at the matter from the side of the mystical quest.

Though the latter classically expressed itself through the monastic life it also for the most part latched on to the symbolism of love, and so by implication was not cut off from the whole ethic of love of one's neighbour. The most powerful Christian mystics, even the suspect Eckhart, saw service in the world to be a vital ingredient of the contemplative life, which could so easily, if not checked, disappear into a self-satisfied rapture and isolation. Moreover, this ideology of love fitted well with the contemplative experience. From one side the whole inner quest was predicated on the premise that the vision of God is to be prized for its own sake – it depends upon pure attraction: the love of God for his own sake. From another side in that intimate and dazzling obscurity of the mystical experience it is hard to disentangle the lover from the Beloved. The numinous Otherness seems to fade and disappear, and yet it also was somehow incorporated into the fabric of the quest and so existed so to speak at the back of the mystic's mind as he entered into the depths of his soul where the Maker who sustains the world without is to be encountered within. Not surprisingly, as we have noted in the earlier discussion of Christian mysticism, the imagery of human love is often used, for there we have that sense of two-in-one. Earthly love mirrors heavenly conjunction.

Thus both as God appears as it were from without and as he appears from within the figure of love becomes increasingly apt, and it is this essential harmony, reinforced of course by the very nature of Christ himself, which helped to give energy to the element of devotionalism in much of modern Protestantism.

However, though there are strong and legitimate comparisons which can be drawn between the devotional emphasis of Christianity and Hindu *bhakti*, a profound difference also exists with regard to its content. For especially where the central concern in mediating God's power is laid upon preaching the Word, Christian piety takes the shape of a dramatization in individual experience of the work of redemption. The Christian who is twice born relives somehow in his own soul the death and resurrection of Christ. Through the shift from priest to preacher, Christianity moves from sacramental power to psychological dynamism. Thus a large question is posed in modern Protestant Christianity in particular as to the relevance of this psychological replay of the Fall of man and his redemption to the psychological and spiritual needs of the individual. Thus, for instance, the doctrine of original sin is seen in part at least as pointing to a detectable state of the individual soul. Here there is another contrast in content between Christianity and other faiths.

Thus though there are elements of the idea of man's primordial sin in the Bible the whole emphasis upon the doctrine is strong in Christianity, but weak in Judaism, which takes a much less stark view of men's condition than does classical Christianity. This prompts us to note a special feature which Christianity and Islam both possess – namely commitment to a heritage also possessed by men of what has come to be seen as a separate faith. Thus the Christian message requires as an intrinsic element the faith which is expressed in the first part of the Bible. But it undergoes a sea-change of interpretation, being transformed into something that looks the same and yet has subtly been transubstantiated by the Christian glosses: the Hebrew Bible become the Old Testament, and the story of Israel points throughout to Jesus Christ. Thus for example the whole idea of the Suffering Servant in Isaiah now has a reference point in Jesus' passion and paradoxical Messiahhood, and the Son of Man of apocalyptic literature is mysteriously fleshed out in the historical Jesus. The Old Testament is so changed that one is reminded of the wry joke that the plays of Shakespeare were not written by William Shakespeare but by another guy named Shakespeare: the first great part of the Bible is not written by Yahweh but by another God called the Father. Similarly one can point to the way in which Islam has transubstantiated the tradition both of Judaism and of Christianity. In a sense, what Christianity has done to the Old Testament Islam has done to the New: the central drama of redemption is profoundly altered in that mysterious passage in the Koran which seems to say that it is a simulacrum of Christ that was upon the Cross – a prophet could not die so ignominiously as Christians thought, and of course the very idea of the Divinity of Christ is seen as a blasphemy, a setting up of a god beside

God, the ultimately most profound error of men's religions, which have to be opposed in this spiritedly and if necessary with violence. The icons of the Christian face are to be smashed, as the blasphemous-seeming statues of the Buddha in north India. By a strange irony Christianity thinks it appropriate in a way (though deeply and shatteringly surprising) that the God-man should die in disastrous and humbling circumstances, while Islam rules that this is not good enough for one who is seen as manifestly a Prophet of Allah, though not of course ultimately the supreme Prophet – a role assigned to Muhammad. Just as Christianity says to the Jew: 'Our faith is the crown of Judaism', so Islam says to the Christian: 'Our message is the crown of Christianity'.

Such theories of course, though understandable as spiritual reinterpretations of the mythic history of God and man, were also elements which could be woven into ideologies of hostility. If the Jews failed to perceive the truth, they could be seen as perverse and egregiously sinful: it is worse for the Chosen People to miss the truth than for other more benighted folk. The unhappy history of anti-Semitism owed a lot to the logical relationship between the Jewish and Christian myths, and likewise, though often Islam's relations towards Jew and Christian were excellent – there was after all a positive evaluation of the two religions in the Koran itself, and in the terms under which the Peoples of the Book were to be held in modern subjection within an Islamic theocracy – it was easy for the Muslim myth too to be a handle of hatred in the sadly bitter conflicts between Christendom and Islam. Although in recent times a renewed dialogue between the three faiths of Abraham's heirs is in process, yet the fundamental fact remains that the very overlap between the three historic myths is a root of dispute rather than of harmony.

The alienation between man and God expressed through the idea of original sin is overcome through the atoning work of Christ, and here we note a contrast between the Christian diagnosis of the human condition and that found typically in Indian religions, and most notably in Buddhism. For the Fall is the consequence of a mysterious act, whose nature and implications lend themselves to a number of interpretations; it is implied therefore both that the Fall has to do with the human will and that it has to be cured through an act. Hence Christianity turns upon not so much the teaching as the work of Christ. This is not to say that Jesus' teachings are unimportant, especially as they display a peculiar intensity, originality and a strange transcendence of ordinary categories of understanding God's relationship to man: still, as we have noted earlier, they are secondary to the passion and resurrection.

It is that drama of redemption which subjectively is re-created in the Christian's individual experience and which is, in its triumphant power, made available exteriorly to the Christian through the sacraments. Now though certain parallels to the idea of intervention in history are not absent from the Buddhist corpus, the main emphasis is the other way round – it is the teaching of the Buddha, the *dharma*, which is primary. The function of the Sangha is not just to cultivate the good interior life but to mediate the teaching to mankind at large. If the cure is through teaching, it is not surprising that the primordial cause of humanity's unsatisfactory condition (indeed that of all living beings) is not so much an act but a defect – ignorance. Spiritual knowledge is what cures this deep and pervasive ignorance. In Western terms, the cure is a kind of *gnosis*. To some extent this idea of existential knowledge is reflected in Christianity through the Neoplatonism which was incorporated into her early medieval fabric, but yet it remains subsidiary as a motif. The assumption is that we may know the Good but are hindered by sin from properly realizing it in our lives: the Buddhist assumption is rather the opposite – we do not realize the Good in our lives because we are hindered from knowing it. Here is another way in which Buddhism is Christianity upside down, or if you prefer to put it the other way round, Christianity is the Buddhist *dharma* upside down. (For which reason I feel that the fundamental issue in the dialogue of religions is whether these two great faiths can be seen as complementary, or whether they are destined to remain in a kind of contradiction and so ultimate rivalry.)

The Greek motto, beloved of Socrates, *Gnothi seauton* or

Know Yourself has in modern times found its chief application through that kind of existential self-knowledge which psychoanalysis both theorizes about and claims to bring about. The therapeutic character of such knowledge is reminiscent up to a point of the Buddhist conception of knowledge – and not surprisingly some modern Buddhist scholars such as K. N. Jayatilleke and Padmasiri de Silva, both teaching in Sri Lanka, have emphasized. Yet it is interesting that at least for Freud the theory had a strong mythic aspect: his whole account of the genesis of religion and the Father figure is an alternative account of men's troubles – alternative, that is to say, to the myth of Adam. It is again not surprising, though from a different angle, that psychoanalysis should have a strong vogue in America above all, among a people whose being and whose religion tend to emphasize the need for interior conversion, for the new *Gnothi seauton* is a different, perhaps more scientific, dramatization in inner experience of saving renewal.

The Buddhist account of knowledge, or *gnosis*, has another consequence. Not only is the historical Buddha seen primarily as a teacher, but also his sermons are full of analysis and philosophy. When the Buddhist scriptures came to be compiled the last of the three baskets or sections, namely that which is known as the *Abhidhamma*, was virtually all analysis, with much of the discursive and mythological elements which enliven the dialogues of the Buddha and other sections of the Canon. But it stands as a symbol that Buddhism can from one point of view be presented as a system of philosophical psychology and analysis of reality, without having to rely much upon the mythic and poetical elements which contribute so largely to the central scriptures of (say) Christianity. The somewhat cerebral style of Buddhism compared with the pungent and flashing parables and visionary utterances of Jesus can be a little misleading, for after all Buddhism remains a practical and not a theoretical quest, and in its incarnate reality the teaching is shot through with myth and ritual, while on the other hand Christianity soon found itself giving a philosophical slant to the doctrinal distillations from its mythic substance. Still, the initial contrast is a strong one. If myth be defined as sacred story, then Christianity is just about the most mythic of all the great religions.

Part of the reason for this might be put by saying that Christianity is the most incarnational of religions. It is true that in Hinduism there is the conception of the *avatar*, the descent of the God into human or other form, while there is a sense in which the Buddha can be seen as incorporating the transcendent Dharma in his own person; yet for various reasons they are less dramatic instances of divine identification with the historical process. This is partly because the logic of monotheism follows into the logic of incarnation. As there is but one Father so there is but one Son, and as there is but one Old Testament so there is but one New. The incarnational intensity of the Christian faith is one source of its sacramentalism, of course; and it is also a factor in Christian hope, namely the belief that the world itself will be transformed. In Eastern Orthodox terms, this points to the deification of man. In modern ideology it is partially expressed in the idea of progress, or, if we are to go to Marxism, in the historical dialectic with its upward rhythm and hints both of catastrophe and Utopia.

The acceptance, within a monotheistic framework, that Jesus is Lord was remarkable in itself, and makes the Christian faith hinge upon the experience of the risen Christ. Leaving aside for the moment the question of the historical trust-worthiness of the narrative (and what in any case is one to make of such mysterious reports, hovering on the edge of the miraculous?), the experiential dimension of the Resurrection is important for its numinous quality, especially if we can see the Transfiguration as a displaced resurrection event. The dramatic manifestation of Jesus to Paul had an evidently shatter-ing quality, while the way in which the disciples perceived Jesus both as bodily and yet somehow as not bound by the ordinary earthly rules, suggests a strange combination of intimacy and otherness, also expressed through the fact that (for instance on the road to Emmaus) Jesus was not at first recognized. Many writers have, moreover, remarked on the power of the experiences, since so many of the apostles were to voyage far, sometimes to martyrdom, and to be transformed from a rather narrow despondency into evangelistic energy. The resurrection experiences also, of course, stand as prototypes of later Christians' inner encounter with the risen Christ. From the point of view of the historian, at any rate, the experience of the earliest Church, whatever it was, proved to have transforming power, analogous to the revelatory experiences of the Prophet Muhammad.

Partly because of its incarnational intensity, partly because of the general stress upon human history, and partly because of the teaching that man is made in the image of God, Christianity has classically made a rather sharp divide between men and other living beings. Partly because of rebirth, this was not characteristic of Indian religions, while Taoism in China and the mainstream of African religious consciousness have for other reasons seen a much closer relationship between man and the rest of nature. The fusion between the idea of individual resurrection on the one hand and the Greek conception of the soul has produced a strong personalism, though perhaps at the cost of abstracting man unduly from his environment. Moreover Christianity has been resistant to anything which it could characterize as 'pantheism'. Even now it is a frequent comment in Christian theological writings that such-and-such a position is pantheistic, and so to be resisted. The principal objection arises from the thought that in blurring the distinction between this world and the divine Being or the divine Principle, such as the Tao, monistic viewpoints also merge the individual human soul in the divine Soul. Though this might be a possibility were the main emphasis in the Jewish-Christian tradition mystical, the strict and numinous monotheism of the tradition implies an ineluctable gap between a creature and his Creator.

It is true of course that Christianity follows One who is both God and man, and who could say 'I and the Father are one', but monistic interpretations of this claim, though common among those who espouse the perennial philosophy (see p. 292), have been at variance with the mainstream Christian understanding of Christ. It is not that Christ is a luminous soul who has realized his identity with the Divine and can show others the way. Rather his identity with God is

300

the consequence of a gracious divine initiative seen from the beginning as a response to the problem brought about by man's fall. Even in the traditional way in which the relation between Father and Son (and Holy Spirit) was expressed, Christianity shows a difference from the monism of, for example, Hindu Advaita Vedanta. For the Trinity consists of three Persons in One. The mysterious identities here suggest interpersonal relationships within the fused unity of the Trinity, and this is a different situation from that indicated in the famous 'That art thou' of the *Upanishads*, which points, at least on the Advaitin interpretation, to the numerical identity of *ātman* and *brahman* – of self and divine Being.

Thus a polarity between God and man persists in Christian feeling, and though God became man it is not strictly possible for a man to become God. Yet on the other hand, man is made in the image of God, and so he stands at an uneasy midpoint between the rest of creation and his transcendent Maker. There is here a three-level universe (with two more levels if one adds angels and devils), consisting of God, man and world. This discontinuous picture of reality is modified in that God penetrates by incarnation and grace downwards into the human world, and by his immanent power upwards through nature. Even so, this model is far removed from the monism of the Tao. It has also been an occasion for conflict with science, in that the latter treats discontinuities as special cases of continuities.

The strongly mythic character of Christianity as a religion, in the sense that the faith depends centrally upon a story which bears special meaning in reflecting divine activity, gives it, clearly enough, an unavoidable historical givenness. Indeed, the very doctrine of God is unintelligible save in terms of the story. Thus no special logic drove religious people to postulate the existence of the Holy Spirit as the third Person of the Trinity. The latter doctrine itself is a means of making sense of certain historical events, above all Pentecost. This givenness of Christianity is continuous with that of Judaism and Islam. Thus in saying that Christianity is a *revealed* religion something more is being said than that it possesses a traditional authoritative deposit of faith, that it accepts certain scriptures as true. It is notable for instance that in much modern theology of a 'liberal' kind, the scriptures are only in a rather weak sense said to be true. The statements of the New Testament are admitted by many Christians to be open to error or to be dated in that they are expressed in thought-forms no longer fully or at all applicable in modern times. Rather Christianity's givenness is of the following form: that God has acted in history and in particular through Christ. But this implies that the givenness lies essentially in the particular character of God's actions in relation to the world and men: and this is a whole dimension of reality that can be reflected upon and probed for its significances, but in its particularity has to be accepted. It is something to which religious experience is relevant, in so far as such experience accompanies God's self-revelation, but it transcends it in its concreteness. It is not that God's actions cannot be explained – for they can up to a point – but that God might have acted otherwise. This is what constitutes the givenness of revelation in the Christian tradition. And this imposes a limitation upon the degree to which mainstream Christianity can reach a full agreement with religions which do not recognize this particular pattern of divine self-revelation. There is necessarily a certain arbitrariness about Christian faith.

Indeed a sense of this is apparent in the Christian conception of the creation of the world, which distinguishes it both from the main pattern of the Hindu idea of creation and from those views which see the coming into existence of the world as a kind of emanation from a first Principle. God creates out of nothing by divine *fiat*: it is a decisive act, and purposive, differing in atmosphere from the dance of Shiva in which the God dances out the cosmos out of sheer exuberance, as an expression of his feelings. The world, therefore, and its history is seen as radically dependent upon God's will; and this constituted both a problem and an advantage – an advantage because God's goodness could be seen as reflected through the natural world, but a problem because of the sharpness *ex nihilo* gave to the conflict between this idea of creation and the existence of evil and suffering in the world.

For Jesus himself, so far as we can judge from the Gospel narratives, Satan was real enough; and his wiles were evident enough to the Desert Fathers and to the early mystical tradition. Moreover, over a great period of Christian history the figure of the Devil was a very real one to the masses. Classical Christendom can, indeed, scarcely be understood without reference to the immense power of Satan, even if ultimately he was destined to be defeated. By comparison in most of modern Christianity the Devil is a very pale figure indeed. This is one of the major changes of substance which has occurred to Christianity in the period since the Reformation. Looked at from this perspective, Christianity's analogy to and historical indebtedness to Zoroastrianism would be much more evident. For classically Christian worship was seen in the context of angelic life – man is co-liturgist with the angels in offering up glory to God, as in the chant of the Trisagion, 'Holy, Holy, Holy'. It was a rebellion from within this upper realm that prefigured man's rebelliousness. Since it is pride, not any lesser or fleshly sin – for the Devil was thought of as without true body of his own, since to operate in the world he needed to possess someone and so to take over a counterfeit body – that drives Satan to his conflict with the Creator it is the desire to usurp the place of God which ultimately concerns him. Thus Satan came to be seen in the Christian tradition as an antigod; and the struggle between God and the Devil reached epic proportions. Yet also he was a kind of co-operator of God's (this harking back to an early function of Satan, for instance in Job), and had his own reward, the administration of hell and the tortures of the damned. Though the Devil's (and hell's) power may have faded in the modern imagination, there is no doubt of the grip once held by it: the strongly mythic character of the Christian religion was highlighted in the murky struggle between the radiant prince of light and the old lightbearer, Lucifer, now the prince of darkness.

The thunderous quality of the historical and other-worldly drama expresses itself in more recent times through millennial movements, but these have tended to exist in a sectarian and relatively peripheral form. The fact is that since the Reformation Christianity in the West has undergone such great transformations that it leads us to ask whether change itself is not something which gives it a character setting it apart from most others of the great religions. By change I mean more than external fortunes and disasters. Thus Buddhism has undergone some catastrophes in the last fifty years – constrained to the point of disappearance in China, wiped out seemingly in Cambodia, in captivity in Vietnam, repressed in Mongolia, gored in Tibet. But basically, with the exception of some new movements in industrialized Japan, Buddhism remains, where it does remain, very much confident of its past teachings and able to continue them without great alteration. The same cannot be said of Christianity, and it is useful to list some of them. First, there is the gradual fading, as we have just noted, of the Christian mythology of evil, though a faddish rebirth of interest in Satanism has made itself felt in the 1970s. Second, there has been a partial reinterpretation of Christian eschatology in terms of a philosophy of progress – though such optimistic millennialism has been criticized from within Christianity and has faltered somewhat in the face of mankind's aggressive disasters. Third, Christian scholars have opened up the whole question of the historicity of the scriptures, and in so doing have created a new dimension of religious self-criticism (which also of course has generated somewhat bitter resistance). Fourth, Christianity has gradually abandoned its Constantinian posture. The Reformation cracked the Empire, but left the notion of official religion still strong, challenged albeit by the radical Reformation. Gradually the growth of toleration, and the creation of a new style of state after the French Revolution, brought much of the old Christendom effectively to a condition where Christianity became a set of denominations and sects. Thus even the Catholic Church in Italy accepted implicitly its place within the structure of a plural society when it sponsored the Christian Democratic movement after World War II. Fifth, partly in line with the fading of triumphal Christianity, there has persisted a remarkable process of fragmentation and the generation of new churches and movements. This serves as a counterpoise to the growth of the movement towards Christian unity: ecumenism is a sixth major change, partly attributable to the recognition that internal divisions further weaken Christianity with regard to the great outside forces challenging it in modern times. Seventh, the faith has, in the eighteenth through to the first part of the twentieth century, achieved great expansion through what was the colonial world, most markedly in Africa, and newly independent Churches have begun rather radically to challenge the relationship of the older established Churches to European and American power structures. Eighth, one can point to a whole variety of attempts at *aggiornamento* – Vatican II itself, liberation theology, black theology, red theology, the women's movement within the Christian Churches, Christian yoga, evolutionism in the style of Teilhard de Chardin, the theology of the death of God, demythologization and so on. It has also been a period of practical experimentation, in reordering Christian worship (though the Orthodox in this as in most else have remained gloriously conservative), in ethical attitudes in relation to birth control, abortion and so on, in architecture and music.

Such change and experimentation is in part caused by outside forces and to this extent is a sign of the weakening of Christianity in the last few centuries; but it is also a sign of some vigour, in that it develops the power of self-appraisal within the religion in a way which perhaps itself is a sign of confidence. At any rate, Christianity's changeable forms demarcate it from most other religions, and are in part the result of its living in close proximity to its unruly offspring, such as humanism. However, many of the phenomena of change which I have listed have been tied in with a diminished authority of Christianity and in a number of countries a decline in adherence as measured by participation in Christian rituals, etc. Thus it has been natural to look upon the present age as being one of progressive and perhaps irreversible secularization. Certainly in the 1960s and early 1970s the Christian Churches of the West were eager to translate their concerns into secular terms, and to revive in a new form the social Gospel. The results were sometimes problematic, in that without a fairly strong and clear basic theology such secular orientations themselves may be sucked into the very process of secularization to which they are shaped as a response. Moreover, in the social democracies of Europe and to some extent in America and other English-speaking societies, the new postwar prosperity, distributed not of course with anything like utter fairness but sufficiently spread around, had brought a situation where many of the grossest problems of hunger, shelter, poverty and worklessness had been very largely alleviated. In principle (it was often felt) the various social agencies should be able to mop up residual problems, and it was easy for the Christian Churches to see themselves as playing something of this supplementary role. It was traditional enough for it to be concerned for the poor. But of course, important often as such a social task is in mending lives and helping those who are in despair, it does not represent an adequate destiny for a movement of such richness and power manifested so diversely over two thousand years. Moreover the thesis of irreversible secularization does not chime in with various facts – the rebirth of interest in the spiritual life, albeit often in non-Christian forms, the continued strength of evangelical Christianity, the remarkable vivacity of Orthodox spirituality in strained circumstances, etc. This leads us to see the present time in a longer perspective, for it is important to remember that we exist only at a certain point in the development of mankind, and if Christianity has transformed itself in the past it still doubtless will find new forms in the future. Maybe we are only in early days of the religion, and that present confusions are the prelude to a further growth of the Christian organism.

The demise of effective establishmentarian Christianity – the end of the age ushered in by the Emperor Constantine – has meant that Christianity finds itself in three major situations. One is that typified by America: where Christianity is tolerated and indeed in many ways favourably treated, though the State itself remains above religious engagement. The favourable treatment itself owes something to the fact that certain kinds of Christianity, notably elements stemming from the radical Reformation, have contributed to the theory of democracy and toleration; it also owes something to the generally Christian ambience of Western culture (despite some anti-clericalism and militant atheism). The second situation is where Christianity exists in a holistic, typically Marxist-dominated, society, where the official ideology plays the role which Christianity itself did in some societies in times gone past. This new captivity has by no means issued in the demise of the faith, as we have seen, even if it has often brought considerable suffering to Christians. The third main situation is the former colonial one, where Christianity, identified rather with the European powers in the past, has been implanted and is involved in building new societies where its European aspect has necessarily to be diminished. The thesis of secularization only makes much sense in the first of these three ambiences; for in the second of them Marxism itself functions in a manner close to that in which establishment Christianity functioned in earlier days. It is too artificial to treat religion and ideology as differing in substance, rather than content. Where they are rivals they are in a struggle over men's deepest concerns.

For this reason, it is worth looking at Christianity not just from the perspective of other religions, but also from that of other world-views, such as humanism and Marxism. With regard to the former, it so happens that Western humanism in the modern sense owes much to the values of Christianity: it involves a kind of reformed Christian personalism centring upon the Commandment of love. If it remains rather a weak force, this is probably because it has no great scheme of things, no great cosmology and view of history, no great hierarchy of beings, no penetrating and mysterious symbolism. It appeals to the cool and worthy, liberal-minded, educated person. It is not unimportant for that reason: it has proved vitally influential in the formation of modern social democracy, which is itself a powerful new turn in human politics. But it does not have the evangelical power of Marxism, which now for better or worse shapes the milieu of half of mankind, and strongly affects the thinking of so many of those who grapple with the mighty cultural and social problems of the Third World.

The spread of Marxism is reminiscent of the way Christianity spread in its expansion into Northern and Eastern Europe. Often there the rulers were in search of a powerful ideology which would help to reshape and to consolidate power. The Christian faith appealed partly for its spiritual power (as Marxism now in part because of its intellectual power), but substantially also because it provided a system of belief and values which would make a country or group essentially more prosperous. In the Reformation also we have seen like forces at work. If Marxism finds itself, on the whole, save in some kinds of liberation theology among the more radical Christians, antithetical to Christian faith in its classical forms, part of the reason lies in the way in which Marx's atheism is crucial to the system. But also, the promises of Marxism have an analogy to the Christian promise, but translated from imagery into an abstract but this-worldly concreteness. Let me explain this last point.

Modern times have seen the power of ideas which resist anthropomorphism – which move through purity and objectivity to an understanding of nature. The temper of science has proved in some respects antithetical to that of older religion – the dogma tested in personal and community life is replaced by the theory tested within the ethic and methods of the scientific profession; the symbol reverberating through ritual into the heart is replaced by the model manifested in experiment; the psychic power of the sacrament is replaced by the applied powers of technology. Yet at the same time, science has remained ambiguous and aloof. It may change the world, but through the mediation of the passions of men. Marxism deals with how to change man, and how thereby to change the world. And instead of myth in the old style it gives us a means of schematizing the unseen, inner forces of history, and so placing men in a history-conscious cosmos. Moreover, it wears the habit of science, and so brings the symbolic power of science to bear on human commitment. It also promises, through its abstractions, a new world, a new order of things in relation to which personal and group destiny can be measured. But in all this we have something intermediate between the pure science and the old mythic personalism: there is now an abstract symbolism ready to harness passion and action, a scientific world-view in which the cosmos has, if not a human face, a human hand through which our planetary destiny is fashioned. It is as if a myth, to have its power now, must hide itself in the flesh of science and sociological analysis. Moreover, Marxism offers one method of national reconstruction among those societies whose fabric has been eroded and torn by the rapid changes of the industrial and imperial era, for it is both revolutionary and comforting, and it is both modern and hostile to those forces in modernity seen as destructive. In short it has become a vital engine of new-style nationalism. Christianity in modern times has not functioned with the same directness in creating hope, and for this and other reasons has not displayed great political and social dynamism save among some of the new religious movements in Africa (but even here it has had an uneasy relationship to the new nationalism). This is not, however, to deny the importance of some Christian persons and Churches in the liberation and social struggles of the Third World.

From the standpoint of Marxism, Christianity involves a projection of human feeling on to the figure of God, and fails to see the ideal as a byproduct of material factors. But though some Christian thinkers have gone far in trying to assimilate much of Marxist social theory into the fabric of a Christianity anew concerned with the solution of the problems of economic deprivation, the question remains as to whether the central shape of Christianity retains its independent dynamic. That shape has been, as we have seen, determined by the nature of numinous experience and the Jewish tradition, the given history of Jesus interpreted in mythic relationship to the problem of human alienation from the source of the world, and the sacramental dramatization, whether externally or in inner experience, of that redemptive story. Judging from the continuance of so much Christian observance in Eastern Europe and the Soviet Union, the central myth and the values of faith, hope and love which spring from it still retain a mysterious magnetism. The recurring question is how they can be integrated into the wide concerns of a strange age. Part of the problem here relates to the whole question of the institutionalization of Christianity.

As we have seen, there are many faces of Christ, and the Christian story has been open to wide varieties of interpretation, while the sacraments are embedded in differing ways in society. The fluidity of the centre of Christianity, despite the imposition of creeds and definitions, accounts for the way in which it adapts to many cultures, but also for the way it retains the power to flow over boundaries that may be set.

It may be that the whole history of Christianity can be seen as a continuation of the problems confronting Jesus' own contemporaries. If it be the case that he used existing categories, only to transcend them, and thereby failed to fit many of the questions brought to bear in trying to establish his significance and identity, so the very mysteriousness and ambiguity of the redemption which he brought about is reflected in the diversity of inferences drawn from faith.

The different ingredients of the Christian experience have thus lent themselves diversely to institutionalization. In a sense the whole religion centres on power – the power of God, yet paradoxically too the powerlessness of Christ as man. That power has reinforced or combated the powers of this world, and has been mediated by different styles implicit within the sacred story itself. Thus the hierarchical universe of the classical period of Christianity which culminated in the medieval synthesis provided the pattern through which sacred power permeated the ordered structure of feudal society. The ideology of the Third Rome was part consequence of the way the Messianic dream of Christianity infused the national consciousness of Russia and the structures of the Tsarist polity. Ritual religion helped in such processes, for it was dependent upon the priesthood and this contributed to forming a sacred counterpart to the secular administration. The radical Reformation, on the other hand, moved away from the more

310

complex sacramental religion of the past towards a simplicity which echoed another side of the basic story – the self-emptying side of Jesus' career. Identification with Christ here could infuse vitality into groups, such as the Anabaptists, who formed patterns of loose sectarianism and who fathered, through the power of purity, the ideal of inward-looking groups, such as the Amish, who expressed one extreme in the way in which holy power becomes congealed in communities. The incessant divisions of Christianity, most marked of course in the period of the Reformation, also often coincided with national and cultural groups. Sacred power in this way could reinforce social divisions, as in Northern Ireland, where Presbyterianism (and other forms of Protestantism) and Catholicism form, in their differing styles, integral elements of two cultures living so uneasily together. Christianity thus has multiplied and sustained diverse identities – Ethiopians, Copts, Romanians, Zulus, American Lutherans and so on – and in doing so has helped to create a mosaic of values in which sacramental and evangelical power fuse with other forces in shaping and reflecting communal life. So there is, really, no sociology of Christianity, but only sociologies of the various Christianities. Diffracted through them is to be seen the outline of the living story which mediates to Christians the experience of the divine phenomenon.

This phenomenon will remain one of the ingredients of the life of our planet. Through the religious structures of Christianity there play the forces of the numinous and the mystical; but the tradition has its own style, the style of the strange historical myth through which God's saving power is understood, retold and appropriated. The power of the story flows down the conduits of ritual and uttered words, and pulses, sometimes vigorously and sometimes uncertainly, in myriads of hearts. It flows sometimes into strange receptacles, and causes sometimes the engines of torture and war to throb as well as powers of mercy and hope.

For so large a dynamo of history Christianity remains little understood. Its full meaning, moreover, lies in the future, for we have experienced less than two thousand years of this tumultuous faith. It may be that the best is yet to come. However, here I have tried only to draw a collage together, and some analysis, and not to pass judgement either on Christianity's past or future.

The beginning of understanding it is noticing its strangeness.

Further Reading

A good brief introduction is:
Stephen Reynolds *The Christian Tradition* (Encino,
California: Dickenson, 1977); note that this has a reason-
able bibliography at the back.

A lively history is:
Paul Johnson *A History of Christianity* (London:
Weidenfeld & Nicolson, 1977; New York: Athenaeum,
1977).

For a quarry of historical information:
K. S. Latourette *History of the Expansion of Christianity*, 7
vols. (Exeter: Paternoster Press, 1971; New York: Harper
& Row, 1937–45) and his *Christianity in a Revolutionary Age*
(Exeter: Paternoster Press, 1971; New York: Harper &
Row, 1958–62).

Index

Filioque clause, 20, 21, 23, 27, 110, 273, 274
Fogazzaro, A., 42
Fox, George, 145, 248, 250
Franciscan Order, 32, 46, 159, 162, 171, 261–2
Free Church of Scotland, 111
free will, 271, 272
fundamentalism, 99, 103, 235, 237–8

George, St, 55, 60, 64, 188
Gnosticism, 151, 223, 256, 269
God; Creator, 269, 302; judge, 212–13; numinousness, 68–9, 70, 217, 262, 267–8, 292–3
good works, 109, 132, 168
grace, 108, 132, 149, 151, 179, 259, 271
Graham, Billy, 95, 103, 236

Harnack, A. von, 77
Hegelianism, 76, 81, 82, 143–4
Heidegger, M., 240
hermits, 60, 61, 148
Hesychasm, 18, 163–4
Hinduism, 200, 260, 267–8, 269, 281, 287
history, 143–4, 155, 190–1, 220–1
Hoen, Cornelius, 88
Holy Spirit, 27, 273, 274, 301
Hospitallers, 159, 243, 245–6
humanism, 139, 144, 169, 240, 305, 307
Hus, John, 79, 195
hymns, 130, 131, 134, 192–8, 221

Iconoclastic Controversy, 17–18, 184, 185
Ignatius Loyola, St, 46, 247
ikons, 17, 18, 19, 22, 25, 28–9, 184, 185
Incarnation, 269–70
indulgences, 69–70
Industrial Revolution, 73, 74, 94, 111, 262
ineffability, 157–8

Isis, 36
Islam, 25, 45, 108, 185, 209, 281, 295–6; clarity of origins, 203; and Ethiopia, 50, 51, 53, 55; expansion, 58–9; and holy war, 247; and Orthodoxy, 16–17, 129; Sufi, 149, 292; of Wahhabis, 133

Jehovah's Witnesses, 140–1, 142
Jerome, St, 225, 227
Jerusalem, fall of, 32, 59
Jesuits, *see* Society of Jesus
Jesus Christ; category-transcendence, 205–10, 216, 224, 264, 310; of experience, 201–2, 206, 216–17; faces of, 145, 166, 206, 211, 216, 251; as focus of faith, 202, 216–17; as healer, 119, 141, 142, 215; the historical, 202, 203, 204–5, 239, 241, 295; imitation, 90–2, 132, 251; messianic role, 206, 208, 210; Resurrection, 25–6, 201–2, 299–300; as Suffering Servant, 210, 212, 295
Jesus prayer, 163, 176, 253
Jews, 15, 32, 45, 46, 47
John the Baptist, St, 206, 208, 209, 213
John Chrysostom, St, 183
John of the Cross, St, 46, 149, 169, 188
John XXIII, Pope, 37, 43, 79
Judaism, 178, 184, 185, 186, 187, 191, 198, 252, 281, 295, 296
Judas, 208, 218
justification, 69, 70, 283

kenosis, 215, 290
kerygma, 239–40
Kierkegaard, S., 80–2, 83, 85, 241
Kimbangu, S., 122, 123–4, 125
King, Martin Luther, 103
Knox, John, 106, 107–8, 109, 111, 192
Koran, 134, 203, 289–90, 295–6
Kraemer, Hendrik, 259

318

secularization, 305–6, 307; of Bible, 233–4
Servetus, M., 110
Shankara, 165
Shembe, Isaiah, 118–19, 120, 123, 125
Simons, Menno, 87–8, 89–90
sin, 133, 260, 263
Smith, Joseph, 140, 142
social gospel, 101, 103, 238, 306
Society of Jesus, 46, 53–5, 61, 171–3
Söderblom, N., 80–4
Solzhenitsyn, A., 16, 28
speaking with tongues, 136–7
Spener, P. J., 78–9, 195
Stanley, H. M., 106, 115–16, 126
Straton, J. R., 100–2, 218
Strauss, D. F., 234
Sunday, 187
symbolism, religious, 283–4
Syntaxis, 178, 180

Taizé Community, 174
Taoism, 161, 174, 260, 281, 300
Teilhard de Chardin, P., 156, 284, 305
Templars, 159, 243, 245–6
Tertullian, 154, 265, 266, 275
Teutonic Knights, 243–4, 247
theology, 11, 28, 128, 129, 164, 265; and Existentialism, 280; liberal, 77, 302; natural, 275, 276–8, 280
Theresa of Avila, St, 46, 149, 168
Thirty-Nine Articles, 20, 229
Thirty Years' War, 67, 78, 195
Thomas Aquinas, St, 40–1, 145, 212, 251, 265, 267, 282. See natural theology
Tillich, P., 171, 266, 280, 282–5
Torquemada, J. de, 45–6
transubstantiation, 43, 72, 88
Trent, Council of, 43, 181

Trinity, doctrine of, 20, 21, 25, 27–8, 110, 265, 273–4, 301
Tübingen School, 76, 234
Tyndale, W., 71, 228

Unam Sanctam, bull, 249–50
Uniates, 15, 55, 129
Unitarianism, 94, 132, 138; in America, 101–2, 142–3
Upanishads, 163–4, 232, 287

Vatican Council II, 42–5, 48, 129, 138, 179, 185, 305
Virgin Mary, 28, 36–7; Ethiopian reverence, 55, 60, 64; as Theotokos, 56, 58, 270
Vulgate, 43, 225

Walther, F. W., 84
war, 247–50
Watts, Isaac, 193, 195
Wellhausen, J., 235
Wesley, Charles, 195, 197
Wesley, John, 80, 145, 195, 233
Westminster Confession, 20
Williams, Roger, 96
Word, preaching of, 109, 179, 186–7, 192, 197–8, 286, 288, 294
World Council of Churches, 62, 82, 138
World War I, 81–2, 238
worship, Christian, 184–7, 189, 192, 198–200
Wycliffe, J., 226, 250, 261

Yoga, 149, 174

Zealots, 208, 209
Zen Buddhism, 174, 259
Zinzendorf, Count N. von, 79, 195
Zoroastrianism, 215, 269, 303
Zulus, 11, 117, 118, 120, 143, 311
Zwingli, U., 90